The
Sponsorship
Seeker's
Toolkit

Third edition

The
Sponsorship
Seeker's
Toolkit

Kim Skildum-Reid & Anne-Marie Grey

Third edition

First published 1999
Reprinted 1999, 2002
Second edition 2003
Reprinted 2003, 2006
Third edition 2008
Reprinted 2010, 2011 (twice), 2012, 2013.

National Library of Australia Cataloguing-in-Publication data:

Skildum-Reid, Kim.
The sponsorship seeker's toolkit.

3rd ed.
Includes index.
ISBN 9780070138605

1. Corporate sponsorship – Australia.
2. Special events – Australia – Marketing.
3. Fundraising – Australia.
I. Grey, Anne-Marie. II. Title.

658.152240994

Published in Australia by
McGraw-Hill Education (Australia) Pty Ltd
Level 2, 82 Waterloo Road, North Ryde NSW 2113
Acquisitions Editor: Michael Buhagiar
Production Editor: Jane Riley
Editor: Janice Keyton
Cover Design: Luke Causby
Illustrator: Shane Nagel
Typesetter and Illustrator: Anne McLean, Jobs On Mac
Indexer: Russell Brooks
Printed in Australia by Griffin Digital

Forewords

On a recent trip to a bookstore I was flipping through the pages of a historical perspective of the 20th century and all of the highlight events that have changed the world and, in fact, our lives, during that time frame. It was quite an eye-opener as I stood among the endless shelves of titles and recalled events, both big and small, that had happened within my own relatively short lifetime. Events that covered almost every imaginable arena—from wars and politics to space travel and moon landings, deep sea discoveries to miracles of modern medicine, civil rights to musical genres, spectacular sporting moments to life-altering technology, Post-it® Notes and Wite-Out® to the World Wide Web—and the list went on and on.

I thought about the generational differences that my grandparents and parents must have experienced and how the events of their lifetimes would have affected them in their decisions, lifestyles, education, professional lives and more. And I thought about how fast things are moving and changing around us today and wondered what life will be like for my son as he grows up. The computer games and communication tools that he has known since reaching adolescence make me feel old beyond my years.

In my position as the President and CEO of the International Festivals & Events Association (IFEA), I have witnessed from a unique perspective the amazing pace and impact of change on our own industry. In truth, it hasn't been all that long since we even recognised ourselves as an industry, going from the days of 'spare-time event management' to new professional expectations in a field where more than 300 worldwide institutions now offer degree programs and certification in event management. For events, the world today is closer together than ever before; ideas and partnerships flow freely across global networks; new resources have changed how we design, market, operate, manage and sell our events; and our biggest challenge is simply keeping up with the marketplace around us.

The one thing that hasn't changed throughout all of this is our need for funding—to support our programs, our events and our causes. But the challenge of securing that funding, especially sponsorship, has changed dramatically. Over the years sponsorship itself has gone through its own growth phases of infancy, adolescence, maturity and now wisdom. Fortunately for all of us, Kim Skildum-Reid and Anne-Marie Grey have kept up for us and share their expertise in this newest edition of the top-selling resource, *The Sponsorship Seeker's Toolkit*.

Whether you are an experienced sponsorship professional or new to the game and looking for those all important insights that can save you years of hands-on catching up, these two industry-leading authors offer a complete and easy-to-understand guide to planning, targeting, sales, measurement and follow-up, all updated to today's new world and expectations, with new case studies, new chapters focusing on changes in cause sponsorship and cause-related marketing, new insights into emerging benefits and techniques, and a fully updated section on the critical and constantly changing area of sponsorship measurement.

If you thought you knew the rules, throw them away and let Skildum-Reid and Grey introduce you to the world of best-practice sponsorship, a consumer-centric, experiential, added value, highly integrated, holistic, accountable and creative world, where sponsorship adds value to the audience's event experience as opposed to intruding upon it, resulting in positive evolution that we will all be able to look back upon with pride.

Steven Wood Schmader, CFEE

President & CEO

International Festivals & Events Association (IFEA)

Idaho, USA

When Kim Skildum-Reid asked me to write the foreword for the first edition of *The Sponsorship Seeker's Toolkit*, the 'how to' workbook for understanding and leveraging sponsorship, co-written with her colleague Anne-Marie Grey, I jumped at the chance. I had known Kim for nearly two decades and respected her knowledge of the global sponsorship industry and her ability to teach the discipline to both the sponsorship expert and novice alike.

Kim and I had gotten to know each other through our joint participation at the annual IEG Conference on Sponsorship in Chicago. After working in sponsorship in the United States, we both soon moved abroad; I to England and Kim to Australia, where I followed her career and growing reputation from afar.

The first edition of *The Sponsorship Seeker's Toolkit* proved to be an outstanding piece of work. I have worked on all sides of the sponsorship model—as a corporate sponsor, agency head, property sales agent and property owner. I found Kim and Anne-Marie's book to be useful, thorough and appropriate for all facets of the sponsorship industry.

But, this third edition is even better. More stories, more examples, more knowledge, more wisdom!

Sponsorship, as a medium, has emerged as the single best form of marketing communication, not only because of what it can and will do to build and enhance brands, but because of what it does to boost the effectiveness of other forms of marketing communications like advertising, public relations and promotion. And sponsorship's effectiveness can be measured!

This book shows you how to maximise your sponsorship endeavours and to activate to achive maximum results. I hope you will find it as useful to your endeavours as I have to mine.

Rick Jones
Captain, FishBait Marketing
Wadmalaw Island, South Carolina USA
15 July 2007

Contents

About the authors

Kim Skildum-Reid

Kim Skildum Reid is widely recognised as one of the top corporate sponsorship consultants, trainers, and speakers in the Asia-Pacific area, with 22 years' experience across the US, Europe, Asia, the Middle East and Australia/New Zealand through her companies, Power Sponsorship and Skildum-Reid Consulting.

Over the better part of a decade, she worked for numerous Fortune 500 companies in the US on their sponsorships of blue chip properties as diverse as the Superbowl, US Open Golf and the International Chili Society Cook Offs, as well as dozens of major professional sporting organisations and national concert tours.

Kim moved to Australia in September 1992, and in January 1994 she started her own consultancy, Skildum Reid Consulting, specialising in corporate side sponsorship strategy. Her clients are some of the top sponsors in the region and beyond, and have included Lion Nathan Australia, Telstra, Qantas, ANZ Bank, the Dubai government, Australia Post, Yellow Pages, Optus, Weet-Bix, Dunlop Tyres, Volvo, NEC, Lion Breweries, ABN AMRO, Peters Ice Cream, Canberra Milk, AAPT, Vic Roads, George Weston Foods and Daewoo.

In addition to consulting, Kim now travels the world offering workshops and in-house training to corporate sponsors and sponsorship seekers, and has recently added sponsorship coaching, webinars, and e-books to her repertoire.

In August 1997, Kim retired after four years as President of the Australasian Sponsorship Marketing Association, Inc., an organisation of which she was a founder. During her presidency, Kim led the growth of the organisation from 30 members to one of the strongest and most active sponsorship associations in the world.

Kim is recognised around the world as a dynamic and insightful speaker. She also writes, with many dozens of articles and columns to her credit, and provides expert commentary on sponsorship to organisations such as *Harvard Business Review*, CNN, CNBC Asia, *Marketing News*, Brand Republic, *Sponsor Magazine*, *Marketing Magazine*, ABC and the Canadian Broadcast Corporation, among others.

Anne-Marie Grey

Anne-Marie Grey is Chief, International & Corporate Alliances for UNICEF, with responsibility for leading the development of global partnerships with corporations, including Unilever, Procter & Gamble, IKEA, ING, FTSE, Amway Europe, DPWN, Futball Club Barcelona, The Body Shop, Volvic, KPMG and Disney.

Prior to joining UNICEF, she was the Vice-President of Marketing and Strategic Alliances for the United States Fund for UNICEF, where she oversaw the US fund's corporate partnerships & alliances and marketing activities. Anne-Marie held the position of Director, Creative Enterprises and Marketing at Share Our Strength, one of the United States of America's leading anti-hunger and anti-poverty organizations, working with partners that include Evian, American Express, Tyson Foods, Williams-Sonoma and Coors. Before joining Share Our Strength, Anne-Marie established Grey O'Keefe and Associates, an Australian-based consulting firm specializing in developing strategic alliances between cultural, sporting, non-profit organizations and the private sector. Anne-Marie has led the development of public/private partnerships for cultural and non-profit organisations including the National Museum of Australia, the Australian National Gallery, the Australian Sports Commission and the Australian Healthcare Association.

Anne-Marie studied at Colby College, the Australian National University, the Graduate School of Management at the University of New South Wales, and Monash Mt Eliza.

Preface

Sponsorship is an investment in sport, the arts, a community event, individual, venue, broadcast, institution, program or cause which yields a commercial return for the sponsor.

Sponsorship has existed in one form or another for centuries. Ancient athletes competed not only for the love of their homeland but for the glory of the wealthy sponsors who fed and housed them while they trained. For hundreds of years, artists endeavoured to attract wealthy patrons, allowing them to live comfortably while the patrons used the relationships to bolster their standing among their peers. And intrepid explorers circled the globe in great sailing ships sponsored by royalty who wanted theirs to be the flag flown by the heroes of the day.

Modern sponsorship, however, is a relatively recent occurrence. In the early 1980s, only a handful of corporations were using event marketing, as it was called then. The majority of sponsorship dollars were spent on advertising spot buys during televised sporting events, and event signage gained popularity. Sports attracted almost all the money, with corporate expenditure in the arts or on causes still treated as philanthropy. Back then, sponsorship was measured in terms of impressions—one person seeing a logo one time is one impression—without much concern as to whether those people were in the sponsor's target market. Actually measuring shifts in customer behaviour or perceptions was extremely rare.

With the massive price rises in advertising rates throughout the 1980s, the advent of new delivery media, including cable television, as well as an increased consumer awareness and appreciation of sponsors, sponsorship became accepted as a new alternative marketing medium.

According to IEG, Inc. (see Appendix 2), by 1988 sponsorship was the fastest-growing form of media in North America, and by all accounts, has yet to slow down. Sponsors were moving beyond seeing sponsorships as simply an opportunity for corporate entertainment and enhanced profile. Companies were using sponsorship as an interactive participatory platform for involving customers and building sales. Corporations' belief in sponsorship grew. They knew that it was contributing to their overall marketing success, but the true impact and potential of the medium remained a mystery.

Since then, sponsorship has grown increasingly sophisticated, objective-based and integrated with overall marketing programs. The results have been huge, with sponsors around the world finding that sponsorship, when done well, has a higher and more lasting impact on the perceptions and buying behaviour of their customers than any other marketing option. This is because sponsorship is a two-way medium. It creates a *relationship* between sponsors and their target markets. Sponsorship says to consumers that the sponsor understands them—that the sponsor cares about what they care about. Sponsorship has now finally come into its own as the most powerful of all marketing media.

According to IEG, Inc., in 2007, almost US$15 billion will be spent on sponsorship in North America. Worldwide spending is estimated to be US$37.7 billion. Sponsorship is growing, and has grown faster every year since the recession in 2003.

And it's not just elite sports any more. Sponsorship properties now range from the Olympic Games to local public schools, arts festivals to federal government conferences, sports stadiums to the Internet. Elite athletes wear golden Nikes. The local milk authority sponsors a rugby team of nine-year-olds. The privileges of American Express membership include free entry to art museums. And for every can you buy, Pal dog food will make a donation to the Guide Dogs Australia.

Because sponsorship has moved out of the realm of managing directors supporting their favourite football teams or museums and into the realm of achieving very real marketing objectives, your job as the sponsee has become even harder. You need to accept that sponsorship isn't about you any more. It's about what your sponsor needs, and they will sponsor whoever will provide them with the most cost-effective way to achieve their objectives. That means that you are not only competing with other organisations of the same type for sponsorship dollars, but are on an even footing with all sponsorship seekers, including sporting organisations, the arts, community events, celebrity endorsements, entertainment and sporting venues, and causes.

Sponsorship is about how much value you can provide to a corporate sponsor, and how they can turn what they provide into a real connection with their target markets. It is important that both parties achieve their objectives and recognise that they have achieved something of value. That is the magic word that separates sponsorship from philanthropy—value. This book has been written to provide you with the expertise and tools you need to shift your focus and create that value for a potential sponsor.

We cannot guarantee that every proposal you present to a sponsor will be successful. Nor can we promise that all your sponsorship programs will be flawlessly executed. We can, however, assure you that the techniques, tools and templates included in this book will assist you in creating and maintaining strong, objective-oriented sponsorships. By following our step-by-step program, you will have a solid foundation on which to build highly innovative win–win–win partnerships (more on this later!).

Acknowledgments

This is the third edition of *The Sponsorship Seeker's Toolkit*, and so many people have helped us to make the original book a success that we hardly know where to start.

First and foremost, we need to thank all of our readers around the world. Your support and enthusiasm has been tremendous. We have lost count of all the emails and calls we've received from readers who love the book and have recommended it to others. We are eternally grateful for your support and wish you all the best in your sponsorship pursuits.

We would also like to thank all of the people who have attended our workshops all over the world. We appreciate your openness about the challenges you face, and we appreciate all of your input, allowing us to continually improve our skills. Without you, this book would not have been possible.

We would also like to acknowledge the following people and organisations for their assistance in the original development and production of this book: Joy Window, Alison Kahler and Peter Hansen for getting us in front of the right people; Steven Schmader and Rick Jones for gracing us with your wonderful forewords; Lionel Hogg for going above and beyond the call of duty with the agreement pro forma; and Anne Bicknell and Donald McBain for all your fantastic media advice. We would also like to thank all of our colleagues and clients who have allowed us to share their experiences with our readers, as well as all of the sponsorship and marketing associations and media who have supported our books.

Thanks to the team at McGraw-Hill Australia, especially Murray St Leger, Bob McLeod, Michael Buhagiar and Kim Seibokas for supporting our vision and making us look so good.

And finally, a special thanks to Edward for continually motivating us to achieve more than we ever thought possible.

How to use this book

There are a lot of people who think creating sponsorship requires some kind of mystical, magic power. We're here to tell you that as surely as the beautiful assistant doesn't really get sawn in half, there is no magic behind developing strong, lasting and mutually beneficial partnerships with sponsors.

We fully believe that building and maintaining these partnerships can be achieved by people with little or no sponsorship experience, so long as they have two things: enthusiasm and a roadmap. The enthusiasm you will have to supply yourself but this book is your roadmap.

We suggest using the book as follows:

➤ Read through the book once first, taking notes as you go. This will help you to understand the desired outcome when you start to implement the strategies that we have outlined.

➤ Ensure that key stakeholders within your organisation know what you are doing (reading the book themselves may help). The system we advocate is a big departure from the approach many organisations are currently taking to sponsorship—you need to ensure you have support for the change.

➤ Check out the resources we have outlined in Appendix 2. Start increasing your knowledge level right away.

➤ Go through the book, doing the exercises outlined along the way. Don't get hung up on the formats. The ones we have used are those that work for us, but feel free to alter them so that they work for you.

➤ Use the exercises collaboratively whenever possible. There are a number of places where two or more heads are definitely better than one.

➤ Be proactive with potential sponsors. The assumption is often that, because they have the money, they know what they are doing. This is often not the case at all. Once you have completed this book, you may very well know more about doing sponsorship right than they do, and it may be an educational process for them too.

➤ Have fun with it. Good sponsorship is a highly creative process. If you don't allow yourself to have big, creative, sometimes silly ideas, you'll never hit upon the really great ones.

Special notes

Throughout this book, we will often generically use the word 'event' to describe the property for which you are seeking sponsorship, whether that is an event, venue, cause, organisation, program, individual or team. Also, if you don't understand a term, be sure to check out the glossary of terms in Appendix 1.

If you don't understand a term, check the glossary on page 194.

Overview of sections

The book is broken into four general sections. Below is an overview of what is included in each of them.

Part 1—Planning

In this section, you will look closely at both your event and your organisation to determine what you need to plan and implement a sponsorship program effectively. Long before the selling process begins, you need to determine whether you and your organisation are prepared to engage in long-term relationships with the corporate sector. We will guide you through creating internal policies, undertaking market and corporate research, creating a marketing plan and negotiating promotional media.

Part 2—Sales

In this section, you will learn about preparation and persistence. Both are required to guide your proposals successfully through to the negotiation stage. This section shows you how to identify potential sponsors, research them, create a customised proposal for every potential sponsor and negotiate a mutually beneficial deal. Included to assist you are a number of detailed checklists and forms, as well as a sponsorship proposal template.

Part 3—Servicing

This section outlines how to create and implement innovative sponsorship servicing programs that ensure your partnerships are win—win for all parties concerned. Covered are steps that will get your relationship off on the right foot, quantification and reporting mechanisms, and a wide range of maximisation options, which will assist your sponsors in achieving all they can from their investments.

Part 4—Appendices

It is essential that you continue to develop your sponsorship and marketing skills and build up your resources. To this end, we have included a listing of resources, including associations, Internet sites and publications that will assist you in creating and developing a sponsorship portfolio that will bring your organisation and your sponsors the results you desire. Also included is a comprehensive glossary of terms and an outstanding Sponsorship Agreement Pro Forma template, provided by one of Australia's foremost experts on sponsorship law.

Part 1

planning

Chapter 1

Internal planning

Before your organisation begins the sponsorship acquisition process, it is essential to consider your organisation's ability to enter wholeheartedly into a marketing partnership with a corporation. Too many organisations turn to sponsorship as a last minute resort for raising much-needed funds. Sponsorship, however, is no longer a fundraising activity but, rather, a joint marketing activity involving both your organisation and a corporate partner. If you are not prepared to be part of a win–win partnership and share the 'ownership' and glory of your programs, your sponsorship efforts will fail. You may be successful in raising sponsorship, but retaining your sponsors will be very difficult.

Understanding your new role

Your job as a sponsee has changed dramatically over the past few years, driven primarily by sponsors' increasingly sophisticated expectations. They want to achieve multiple objectives, integrate sponsorships across a myriad of marketing activities and, more than anything elese, truly connect with their target markets. That last one is often a hard pill to swallow for sponsorship seekers, but it is true. Sponsors are no longer interested in being 'associated with' your event. They don't want to connect their brand with football or the arts or whatever. They want to connect with the target markets on a personal level, fostering relationships and creating a degree of relevance that a less passionate marketing media, like television, could never equal.

Historically, sponsorship has been all about connecting a brand with your event, and the very clear focus of negotiations and sponsorship leverage have been about enhancing that connection—bigger logos, more signage, players using the brand on TV commercials, event logos on product packaging, on and on and on. The assumption that went along with all of this was that if the two organisations were connected in a highly visible, thorough way, then the target market would just get it—that the guy in the pub watching football would say to himself, 'That's my favourite team, and they're sponsored by XYZ Beer, so I should drink XYZ Beer'.

> Sponsors don't want to connect with your event. They want to connect with your target market.

That delusion was nice while it lasted, but a lot of research has shown that this approach is only minimally effective.

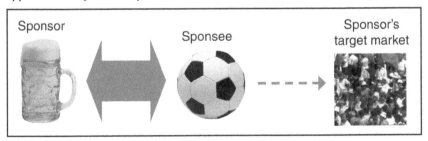

Figure 1.1
Traditional sponsorship model diagram

Don't believe us? Ask yourself, or better yet, a friend, the following questions:

➤ What was the last major sporting event you attended in person (with which you weren't professionally associated)?

➤ How many logos do you think you saw that day?

➤ Just give me a number—how many do you think you could name right now?

➤ Okay, name them…

➤ Of the sponsors you've named, have any of them changed your perception of their brands? Have any of them made you behave any differently with their brands—trying the brand, becoming more loyal, telling other people about it, or whatever?

We've asked these questions hundreds of times, and the answers are virtually always the same: people claim to have seen somewhere between 15 and 100 logos, think they can name 8–10, can actually name two or three, and none of the sponsorships by those brands have affected their brand perceptions or behaviours in any way. That's traditional sponsorship thinking at work, and it's not very effective.

Modern, best-practice sponsorship turns this thinking on its head. Best-practice sponsorship starts from the premise that a sponsor doesn't want to connect with you, they want to connect with your audience, and they want to use their sponsorship of your event to deepen their connection with their audience. Given that, the new model of sponsorship looks like this:

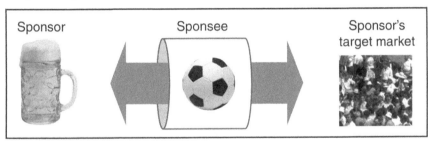

Figure 1.2
Best-practice sponsorship model

Best-practice sponsorship makes the relationship between the sponsor and whoever they are targeting the primary connection, and changes the sponsor's goal from getting 'in front of' an audience to adding value to the target market's experiences with the event and the brand, to demonstrating their understanding of and alignment with their target market's passions, and deepening their relevance and relationships with key markets.

Your role as a sponsee has changed from being a flag-waver to being a conduit, providing a variety of benefits and opportunities that will help your sponsors achieve that level of connection. They now also count on you to help them understand your audience in a much deeper way than before. They don't just want to know age and gender any more, they want to know why people attend your event, what are the drawcards and downsides, and how they, as sponsors, can improve or enhance that experience.

This does mean more work for your organisation, but this is not such a bad thing. Back when sponsorships were selected based on the amount of exposure they could deliver or the 'poshness' of the hospitality program, there was always another event that could deliver more. Events were interchangeable commodities, making your sponsorship income very unreliable. The new model of sponsorship is based on partnership and produces strong, multifaceted results that any sponsor will find difficult to leave.

Creating a sponsorship-friendly organisation

If you want to succeed in modern-day sponsorship, it is important that everyone within your organisation understands that sponsorship is about creating a win–win–win partnership. It used to be just win–win—both parties achieve their objectives without undue strife. Best-practice sponsorship has introduced the third 'win'—the target market. They must get a meaningful benefit, however small, from the sponsorship if it is going to really work for anyone.

Your goal should be to create a win–win–win partnership.

This shift from the neediness of a fundraising mindset (just one 'win') or the objective orientation of a traditional sponsorship ('win–win') and into a holistic, market-driven approach is the major point of difference from sponsorship programs in the '70s, '80s and '90s, to best practice in the new millennium.

Throughout this book, there will be ample case studies that showcase this thinking, and it will be critical for you to engender this mindset within your organisation if you want to position your organisation to take advantage of the vast opportunities that best practice can present.

The majority of organisations that seek sponsorship do so from a position of need —the need for funds is continual and ever pressing. Many organisations are concerned that corporate partnerships and sponsorship will threaten their credibility and integrity. And this is just the tip of the iceberg. In fact, there are often several hurdles that you will need to overcome in order to gain the support of your staff and board.

Some typical areas of concern with sponsorship include:

- being seen as 'going commercial'
- perceived ownership of an organisation or event
- selling out to the corporate sector
- compromising the integrity of programs and services
- placing financial objectives before programming objectives
- allocation of much-needed resources to marketing activities
- placing consumer needs ahead of staff needs
- lack of recognition as to the value of sponsorship to the organisation
- refusal to deal with particular industries or specific companies
- 'Government should fund this program and we should not be seen to be absolving them from their responsibility.'
- 'We tried it before and it didn't work.'

As a sponsorship manager, you will need to determine what the critical issues of concern are within your organisation and devise strategies to deal with them. Interviews with staff throughout your organisation, as well as interviews and surveys with board members, clients and customers, are efficient methods for determining the critical issues of concern. Many of these issues may not appear to be legitimate to you. However, perceptions and issues are always real, even if they are not accurate. You will need to address these perceptions nonetheless.

Often you will need to lead your questioning in order to pull out the specific area of concern or the exact nature of the issue. Reluctance to engage or support sponsorship activities is often highly emotive. Exercise great care, compassion and consideration in your interviews. As a start, you may want to consider asking the following questions:

- How do you feel about corporate sponsorship, generally? Is it a good or bad thing?
- Do you think it is appropriate for our organisation to be working with corporate sponsors?
- How is sponsorship currently affecting what you do? How involved are you in sponsorship? How much do you know about what we do in sponsorship?
- Are you having any sponsorship-related challenges? Have you in the past?
- Which of our sponsors is the best partnership? Why?
- Describe the ideal sponsorship for our organisation.

There are often several hurdles to overcome in order to gain staff support.

Sporting organisations are not immune to staff dissension on sponsorship.

➤ Sponsors provide funds, but can provide a lot of other things, as well. Is there anything besides money that a sponsor could provide that would make your job easier, cheaper or more effective?

➤ Is there anything else I should know?

We should acknowledge that most sporting organisations have long held a commercial outlook on sponsorship. If you are in the sporting area, you will probably have a much easier time garnering internal support for your activities. This does not make you immune from internal dissension and questioning, particularly if you are expanding your sponsorship program to include grassroots or community service activities.

Once you have determined what issues are relevant to your planned sponsorship programs, you are better able to develop and implement strategies to confront them or to take corrective action.

In order to develop a sponsorship-friendly organisation, we recommend a multipronged approach:

➤ stay in contact with your staff and board

➤ educate all internal stakeholders

➤ provide reports, case studies and so on to all staff

➤ create a sponsorship team

➤ ask better questions.

Stay in contact

Just as you need to keep in close and constant contact with your sponsors, you also need to communicate continually with your staff, members and board. You want to cultivate an appreciation of sponsorship marketing principles and create an organisation that will fully maximise every partnership.

Educate staff

We have found that conducting staff workshops, explaining sponsorship marketing principles and organisational approaches to sponsorship, is an effective strategy for engaging staff in a sponsorship program. Regular presentations to the board outlining policies, strategies and results are not only effective but also politically wise.

Report results to all staff

Regular case studies, progress reports and interviews with sponsors should be included in all staff communications. Remember to involve all staff, not just marketing and public relations people, in your communications program.

Create a team

Creating a sponsorship team of decisionmakers from across departments and outside resources is a great step in creating a shared sense of responsibility for sponsorship across your organisation.

Monthly meetings with your sponsorship team are almost guaranteed to provide you with additional opportunities for building a commitment to sponsorship within your organisation, while maximising your sponsorships and minimising your costs. For the investment of a couple of hours and a tray full of sandwiches, you will gain insight into many untapped resources and unearth potential trouble spots that could cause problems further down the track. Most importantly, though, you will gain the support, cooperation and understanding that it takes to create a fantastic sponsorship program.

When putting together your team, remember not to overwhelm the group with 'marketing people'. The point is to create a multifaceted think tank. Consider including representatives from the following areas:

- advertising agency
- media partners
- corporate communications
- information technology
- customer service
- human resources
- market research
- merchandising
- tourism
- packaging/production
- product management
- public relations
- membership
- ticket and group sales
- concession sales
- sales promotion
- sponsorship consultants.

Remember to keep the team up-to-date on all developments throughout the process—a one- or two-page update a couple of weeks after each meeting should be adequate.

Ask better questions

Our guess is that you will have a lot to say to your colleagues about sponsorship as you go through this book, and by all means, share. Just as important, however, is using every appropriate opportunity to ask a few key questions. For instance:

➤ 'Great idea! Now, how can we turn that into a win for our sponsors?'

➤ 'How can we make this a 'win' for the fans?'

➤ 'How does that get Sponsor X closer to their target market? Is there some way we can tweak this so it's more about that relationship?'

These aren't difficult questions, they are just *different*, and if you ask them enough, your colleagues will start asking them, too.

Planning your sponsorship programs

As is the case with any successful program, outstanding sponsorship programs require thorough research, careful planning and flawless execution. There are two critical strategic planning documents that should be the linchpin of your sponsorship activities: a sponsorship policy and a sponsorship strategy. Both documents dovetail with your organisation's mission statement and business plan. See Figure 1.3.

Sponsorship policy

Find out if your organisation has a sponsorship policy in place. If it has, ensure it is updated to reflect your current situation. If not, start developing one as a matter of urgency.

A sponsorship policy is a necessity for every organisation seeking sponsorship, even traditional sponsorship seekers such as sporting groups. It is one of the most often overlooked components of a sponsorship program despite compelling reasons for having one. For example:

➤ Any program generating or distributing substantial funds should define the principal objectives and administrative processes of the sponsorship program.

➤ A sponsorship policy will ensure that your organisation has a uniform approach to sponsorship.

➤ A policy outlines accountability and responsibility. This point is particularly important if your organisation is in receipt of government funds or enjoys non-profit status.

➤ A policy outlines specific issues that are relevant to your organisation's approach to sponsorship and will detail exclusions and limitations.

Components of a sponsorship policy

A sponsorship policy should contain certain information. This is outlined below.

Background

The background outlines the history of sponsorship within your organisation, as well as your organisation's approach to sponsorship.

Definitions

The definitions state what does and does not constitute sponsorship (this is particularly important if you receive government funding and/or philanthropic donations). They also define the internal stakeholders in the sponsorship program.

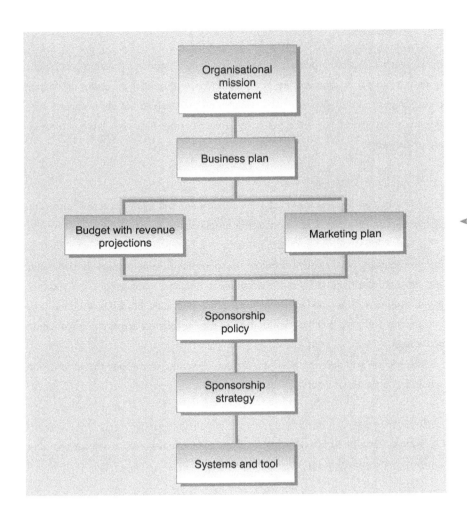

Figure 1.3
Internal planning process

Situational analysis

The situational analysis identifies all current issues that may impact on your sponsorship program.

Exclusions

The exclusions section clarifies and describes fully what companies and industry sectors you will not engage with in a partnership arrangement.

EXAMPLE

In Australia, Commonwealth government legislation prohibits tobacco companies from engaging in sponsorship marketing partnerships. Also, many organisations that work with children will not enter partnership agreements with companies producing alcoholic beverages.

For each exclusion, provide a rationale as to why a partnership with this company or industry sector is unacceptable. You may find over time that the issues prohibiting partnerships are no longer valid. You will also be prepared to answer questions from the board and members of the public as to why partnerships with these companies are unacceptable.

Processes and procedures

The processes and procedures that your department will use to secure sponsorship agreements and manage your sponsorship programs are specified here.

If your sponsorship acquisition process is to be centralised, explain why. Outline the processes by which you will follow up sponsorship leads or provide comments and progress reports to the senior management, financial management and auditors. If you are an organisation with a national office and state branches, describe how information and leads will be shared and benefits negotiated across the organisation as a whole.

This section will describe how you are actually going to manage the sponsorship acquisition program and service your sponsors.

Delegations

Delegations describe who within your organisation is delegated to sell, receive and approve sponsorships, and to what dollar level.

Many organisations are required to have board approvals on delegations related to the distribution of organisational information and financial transactions. Preapproved delegations can certainly make the audit process smoother for everyone involved.

Approvals and contracts

This section explains who can approve a sponsorship and clarifies when a contract is required.

Accountability and responsibility

Accountability and responsibility describes who within your organisation is responsible for your sponsorship programs. Responsibilities will include seeking and reporting sponsorship funds, processing, banking and investing funds and servicing sponsorship relationships.

Review and evaluation

Review and evaluation defines when the policy will be reviewed and evaluated. Review your policy at least every six months. Publicise the results of the review process and encourage input from staff and members.

Frequently asked questions about sponsorship policy

Who should create the sponsorship policy?

If your aim is to create a policy that your staff and members feel they own, involve as many of the staff and members as possible.

Some smart sponsorship managers create a draft policy after discussions with staff, sponsors and members and then present the draft policy to staff for comment. Other managers form a working party to thrash out the draft document. Whatever method you choose, ensure that you involve your chief executive officer, as well as your financial and human resources managers. Without their backing, your policy is not going anywhere. Finally, you will want to have your policy formally accepted by your board.

Alternatively, secure the services of a sponsorship consultant to guide your organisation through this process. Sometimes, it can be easier and far more effective to have a consultant do the work for you. Ensure that the consultant works closely with your organisational stakeholders or the organisation will have no sense of ownership for the policy.

How long should the policy be?

Your sponsorship policy should be as long as is required to outline your organisation's sponsorship principles, processes and accountability procedures. Some sponsorship policies are as short as two pages, while others are closer to ten pages.

Is a sponsorship policy necessary? Shouldn't I be concentrating on getting the money in and not worrying about documenting processes and systems?

Non-profit organisations, in particular, are under increasing scrutiny from their boards, their members, the media, auditors and government departments as to their source of funds. The time you invest in creating and documenting your guidelines, systems and processes is never wasted. A policy, endorsed by your board, ensures that your organisation is credible, legitimate and strategic. You have a responsibility to your stakeholders to ensure that your processes and accounting procedures are as transparent as possible. Taking the time to plan and document today may save you a lot of time and heartache in the future.

How do you motivate staff to create a policy?

Staff in your organisation may have been through many of these exercises previously. How do you motivate them to go through one more of these planning sessions?

If the issue is important to them, they will participate. You need to listen carefully to what issues are of concern and be prepared to engage in a relevant discussion of their issues. The bottom line is increased revenue and marketing muscle for your organisation. Staff might not be particularly interested in how you get it but they are bound to have ideas on how to distribute the funds. Find the nerve point and work from there.

Sponsorship policy questionnaire

Go through the sponsorship policy questionnaire below to ensure you have covered all issues. At the end of this process you should be ready to draft your sponsorship policy. Take the time to consult as widely as possible before drafting your policy.

List the key stakeholders that will be affected by this policy and then ensure you speak with a representative from each stakeholder group. Include staff and union representatives, marketing and public relations staff, front of house staff, sales staff, finance and resource officers, auditors, board members and senior staff. Also include program staff and recipients of sponsorship funds, along with members of your organisation if appropriate.

Background

➤ Why does our organisation want to engage in sponsorship?

➤ Do we see sponsorship as a fundraising exercise or a marketing activity?

➤ Do we want to develop long-term win–win–win partnerships?

➤ What are the overall principles of our approach to sponsorship?

Definitions

➤ How does our organisation define sponsorship?

➤ How does this differ from philanthropy and/or government support?

➤ Who are the internal stakeholders? (Board, sponsorship department, marketing department, etc.)

Situational analysis

➤ How many people are currently engaged in seeking sponsorship for the organisation?

➤ Is this our only responsibility or are we responsible for several other major activities?

➤ Where does the sponsorship office fit into the organisational structure?

➤ To whom do we report and how frequently?

➤ What resources are presently allocated to the sponsorship department? Are the funds sufficient?

➤ What training and professional development are available to the sponsorship department?

➤ Have there been any changes to the organisational structure or staff changes that impact on the department?

➤ Are there any political issues that affect our programs?

➤ How does our business strategy or organisational plan affect the sponsorship?

➤ Does our organisational culture embrace sponsorship and win–win–win partnerships or does work need to be done in this area?

➤ What issues will affect our sponsorship program?

➤ What issues do staff and our board need to be aware of?

Exclusions

➤ What companies and industries do we refuse to work with in a partnership? List each company or industry sector and provide a detailed rationale as to why they appear on the exclusion list. Indicate when you will review or repeal this decision.

If corporate responsibility is important to your organisation (e.g. you run an environmental education program), consult ethical investment firms and the investment area of your bank to get up-to-date information on companies with socially and environmentally responsible values.

Processes and procedures

➤ What are our organisation's principles guiding the selling of sponsorships?

➤ How will we ensure that sponsorship does not influence tendering processes (in the case of government and non-profit organisations)?

➤ How will we manage sales rights within our purchasing processes?

➤ How will we ensure that a sponsor does not exert control over our organisation or sponsored event?

➤ How will we protect and maintain our organisation's integrity and credibility?

➤ How will we value in-kind or contra sponsorships?

➤ How will we keep staff and other departments or sponsors informed?

➤ How will we train staff?

➤ How often will we report to the board and to staff?

➤ How will we evaluate sponsorships for our organisation and for our sponsors?

➤ What procedures are in place for:
  • selling sponsorship?
  • maintaining and servicing sponsors?
  • determining what projects will attract sponsorship?
  • ensuring all funds are accounted for?
  • distributing funds?
  • ensuring that the public interest is best served?
  • reporting on the program to the board, members and staff?
  • handling inquiries from auditors, accountants, taxation officials, media and the general public?

➤ How will we handle a controversial sponsorship?

Delegations

➤ Has our resource management section ensured that the relevant financial delegations are in place for receiving, selling and approving sponsorships? State the specific delegations and approvals within the policy.

Accountability and responsibility

Who is responsible for:

- selling sponsorship?
- maintaining and servicing sponsors?
- determining what projects will attract sponsorship?
- ensuring all funds are accounted for?
- distributing funds?
- ensuring that the public interest is best served?
- acquitting sponsorship funds?
- reporting on the program to the board, members and staff?
- handling inquiries from auditors, accountants, media and the general public?

Approvals and contracts

- Who determines what benefits are available to potential sponsors?
- How is this determined?
- How often do we review our benefits list?
- Who can negotiate a sponsorship deal?
- Who can approve a sponsorship?
- What is the process for approving sponsorships?
- Who can sign final contracts?
- Will we use a letter of agreement or a contract?
- When will we consult a lawyer?

Review and evaluation

- When and how often will this policy be reviewed?
- Who will be involved in the review process?
- How will we review this policy?
- How will we communicate the policy amendments to our stakeholders?

Sponsorship strategy

Your sponsorship strategy is, very simply, the process that you will take to gain and retain sponsorship, and the attitude you take with every aspect of your sponsorship program.

The bulk of this book is about sponsorship strategy. When you finish the book and all of the exercises in it, you will have developed an approach—a personalised system that works for you. Document it—this is your sponsorship strategy.

Chapter 2

Marketing plan

If you want to succeed in your quest for sponsorship funds and strong sponsor relationships, you must ensure that you have access to people with the relevant marketing skills, sufficient resources, a good strategic plan, a marketing plan, market research information and a commitment to applying that market research.

Your organisation must be able to demonstrate to potential sponsors that it can capture and retain its audiences. Your products and services must be based on genuine market needs and values as opposed to what your staff think your clients want or what your organisation thinks its clients need.

As part of your organisation's strategic planning process, you will need to create a marketing plan. This is not a plan for marketing the sponsorships but rather is a plan for marketing your organisation and its events or products. In the case of an event or a property, every marketing plan must have a media plan, a publicity plan and an evaluation plan to measure performance. Every marketing plan must be based on audience market research as it needs to reflect your audience profile, the number of people who will attend your event and your ability to reach out and speak with your audiences. Developing your marketing plan will help you to determine what makes your organisation valuable to sponsors.

This chapter will take you through a series of worksheets, many in a question and answer format, that will assist you in completing the marketing plan template found at the end of the chapter. Tip sheets and checklists are scattered throughout the worksheets to assist you in your planning. The result will be that you will be better placed to get more from your audience (more money, more participation, more heartshare) and create a far more valuable proposition for sponsors.

> Every marketing plan will have its base in market research.

> Realistically, no event will appeal to everyone.

Defining your brand

In previous editions, we started this chapter with developing your target market profile. While that is still an absolutely essential part of getting your marketing plan right, we have realised that many of the difficulties organisations have with getting their marketing plans right—including their target market definitions—go straight back to how they define their brand.

Companies have brand managers, there are brand marketing agencies, and many a magazine and website are dedicated to the cult of 'the brand'. All of that makes it seem like brand development is terribly complicated and only for big corporations with a lot of money. Not so! Brand development isn't complicated at all, is within reach of even the smallest organisations, and can be the difference between financial success and failure.

Going through this process will benefit your organisation in many ways:

➤ You will differentiate yourself from your competition on every level.

➤ Your marketing messages will be more specific and compelling.

➤ Your sponsor hit list will be more concise and effective.

Unfortunately, most sponsorship seekers tend to define who they are and what they do in very general terms, creating virtually no differentiation in how they present themselves, even when there may be some very important differences. What strong brand development boils down to is understanding, in very specific terms, what constitutes the personalities of your organisation and your events. The easiest way we've found to do this is to create brand bullseyes for each of your 'brands'. There are a number of ways to to this, but we've developed a method that is effective and doesn't over-complicate the process.

Creating a brand bullseye

Your organisation is a brand, and so are each of your events. This process will need to be replicated for each of them, but for your first go at this, just pick one reasonably uncomplicated event to practice the skills. This is a directed brainstorming exercise, so it is much more effective if you do it in a group. Invite people from across your organisation and, ideally, interested parties from outside, like your sponsors.

Before you start, rather than putting a lot of pressure on yourself, try to imagine this as a very straightforward process of describing the personality of your event or organisation. It's that simple. In fact, if you find yourself struggling with this process, try practising all of the steps below using your best friend or spouse as the subject first, and then move on to your event.

The first step
in defining your
brand is realising
that *you* don't
define it.

Step 1: Get over yourself

Accept that, as much as you'd like to think you do, you don't control your brand definition. Your audience does. Yes, we know, that's a bit of a hit to the ego, but it's true. Think about it this way . . . when the biggest bank in your country or region runs advertising that says they care about you, that they're with you in good times and bad, and that they want to make your life better, do you believe them? If you're like most people, the answer is probably 'no'. So, what do you believe about that bank, and which is a more powerful brand definition, the one you've built based on your experience or the one they talk about in their advertising?

We hope there isn't that much of a disconnect between your brand as you see it and your brand as your audience sees it, but there are probably some aspects that you haven't really thought about that could create opportunities or obstacles for you and your marketing program.

Step 2: Create a benchmark

Imagine someone has just left your event or otherwise finished an experience with your organisation (such as making a donation, volunteering, becoming a member). What are the three things you would like them to think about that experience? Don't spend more than a couple of minutes on this and then set those three things aside for later review.

Step 3:

On a whiteboard or piece of butcher's paper, draw a large bullseye that looks like Figure 2.1 (opposite).

It may look a little complicated, but taking it step-by-step, you should find this quite a simple process.

Step 4: The outer ring

On a brand bullseye, we work from the outside in. In our version, this outer circle is for perceptions—how people perceive your event or organisation, whether they are involved in it or not. We want you to fill up this outer circle with perceptions. These perceptions may be good, bad or ugly, accurate or untrue, complimentary or painful to admit. The point is, you want to capture it all.

You will notice that there is a horizontal line cutting your bullseye in half. The upper part is for emotional aspects, the lower part is for functional aspects. Do your best to put every perception into the correct half of the bullseye, as this will assist with your analysis later. A few examples are below:

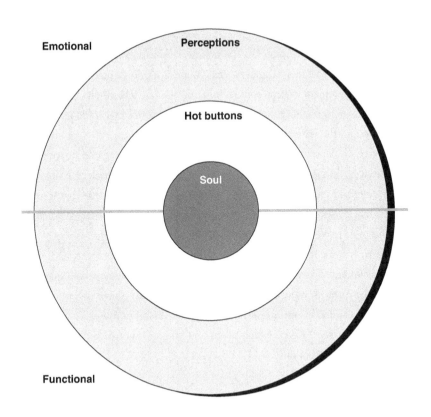

Emotional

Perceptions

Hot buttons

Soul

Functional

Figure 2.1
Brand bullseye example

Figure 2.1
Brand bullseye example

Functional	Emotional
Expensive	Elitist
Good entertainment	Inspiring
Family oriented	Quality family time
Boating	A dream/aspirational
International	Eye-opening
Disease	Depressing
Safe for kids	Peace of mind

You will notice that some of your functional aspects are also related to the emotional aspects, as with most that we've listed here. In some cases, you may even find an aspect that sits comfortably in both halves, like 'inconvenient'. That's fine. You can put it on the line, write it twice or indicate that it is in both with arrows—whatever works for you. The point here isn't that it's neat—in fact, the best bullseye brainstorms end up very messy!—but that what you capture is as complete and powerful as possible.

You also want it to be very specific. There are some aspects of your event that may well be true, but they aren't very useful. The end result of this exercise is that you will have a brand definition that really captures what your event or organisation is all about, creating a strong differentiation from competitors. You will not achieve that if you allow yourself or your team to populate your bullseye with bland terms that could be used to describe hundreds or thousands of other events. Some examples are 'fun', 'community', 'excellence/excellent', 'entertaining', 'family' and 'exciting'. Again, these may be true, but they aren't really that useful. It's like sending someone to the airport to pick up your brother and describing him as a male wearing blue jeans. It may be true, but it's not going to help that person locate your brother. And neither are generic terms going to get you to the most powerful and useful brand definition.

If your team is stuck in these generic terms, just keep asking questions until they get specific. For instance, if someone wants to put 'fun' on the bullseye, that's fine, but be sure to ask the team for more detail. Ask, 'What kind of fun?', 'How do people feel when they are having fun at our event?', 'How does our brand of fun differ from, say, going to a baseball game?' Keep drilling down and you will start to get much more powerful and specific perceptions.

Step 5: The middle ring

Once you've captured as many perceptions as you can in the outer ring, it's time to move in. The middle ring is for hot buttons—the aspects of your event or organisation that actually motivated people to get involved, attend, buy a ticket, donate, volunteer, change their behaviour (e.g. eat more vegetables or stop wasting water), or whatever you are trying to get them to do.

If you are struggling to understand the term 'hot button', try this:

1   Think of the last time you went to an event (not one of your events!).
2   Why did you attend that event and not some other event? What was the experience you wanted to have? Write down as many reasons as you can in one minute.
3   Now, circle the absolute most important one or two—the ones that really led you to making that choice. Those were your hot buttons.

The fact that a charity is tax deductible makes it a reasonably financial decision to donate to anyone. But why do you choose to donate to the one(s) that you do? Again, those reasons are your hot buttons.

Many of these things will be the same or related to perceptions in the outer ring. Use arrows to 'move' perceptions into the middle ring and write anything else that comes to mind. If you get stuck, pretend your team are a bunch of people who had just attended, donated, or whatever you wanted them to do, and ask them why they did it. Those were their hot buttons.

Step 6: Take it all in

Before moving to the centre, take a look at what you've accomplished. The bullseye you have just created will be invaluable in developing many aspects of your marketing plan, but should be telling you a few things already:

➤ **Functional hot buttons are threshold needs.** The items that appear as functional hot buttons may be important, but they are probably not the primary reason someone got involved. For instance, your event may be safe, local and have good parking—all important to parents of young children, and reasons for them not to go if you didn't have those things covered—but they are not compelling enough to have made them choose your event over going to another event, the park or some other safe, local, convenient activity.

➤ **The real motivations are emotional.** Once you have ticked all of the functional boxes (the threshold needs), people make decisions about their time and money for emotional reasons.

➤ **People make their decisions to attend your event, donate, or whatever it is that you want them to do, for very different reasons.** This should be telling you that there is no one-size-fits-all marketing message, and the message that works on one group won't even register a blip with another.

➤ **Part of your job as a marketer is to manage the negatives.** If there are negatives that are turning off key parts of your target audience, you need to determine if their perception is founded in reality. If the negative is a real problem with your event, you need to fix the problem and communicate that in your marketing messages ('Twice as much parking this year!'), if not, you need to address the misconception ('100% of funds raised benefit Canadian communities').

➤ **You could do an even better job creating a bullseye if you got feedback from your actual audience.** We're sure you've done a great job, and the bullseye you have created is probably miles ahead of your current brand understanding, but no one can tell you about their perceptions and motivations better than the audience itself. Resolve to spend a few hundred dollars (up to a couple thousand) for some focus group or interview research after your next event. Use the feedback to augment what you've already done and finetune it going forward.

Step 7: The centre

The centre of your bullseye is where you define the soul, or the essence, of your event. The 'soul' of your event will consist of a maximum of three aspects or concepts around your event that capture what it is about in powerful, specific wording. Now is not the time to fall back on generic terms, like 'fun' and 'family'. Imagine if you were trying to capture the essence of your very best friend using just three concepts; would you say 'fun, smart, female'? Unlikely. We bet it would look more like, 'irreverent, whip smart, fashion mad'—much more specific and much more powerful. That's your aim.

After all of the fast-paced brainstorming leading up to this point, there is a tendency to rush this part of the process, but we don't recommend it. If there is something that obviously needs to go in the centre, by all means put it there. If you agree that a concept is 90% there, but not quite, put the concept in there with a question mark, so it operates as a placeholder while you mull it over. Even if they are all placeholders, put two or three concepts in the centre and agree that you and your team will keep working on it.

Even if all you've got are placeholders, compare the bullseye to the three things you wrote down and put aside back in Step 2 of this process. We've found that there is usually a marked difference in the before and after. If not, you are more in touch with your brand essence than most.

As an example, have a look at the brand bullseye developed by New Zealand Fashion Week in a brainstorming session with their sponsors. As the focus of that event has shifted from an industry-only event to one that involves the fashion-loving public, their brand has also changed. What you will notice is that the bullseye takes into account a variety of perceptions, opinions and hot buttons—some counter to each other—all contributing to a brand soul and an understanding of their target markets that is far deeper than they had previously. For more about New Zealand Fashion Week, see <www.nzfashionweek.com>.

Step 8: Get more input

Post the bullseye somewhere obvious and invite anyone in your organisation or visiting your offices to add their thoughts. Do this for a week and we're 99 per cent sure your 'soul' will have developed to a point where it really reflects what your organisation does and who you are, powerfully and in a way that differentiates you from all or most of your competition.

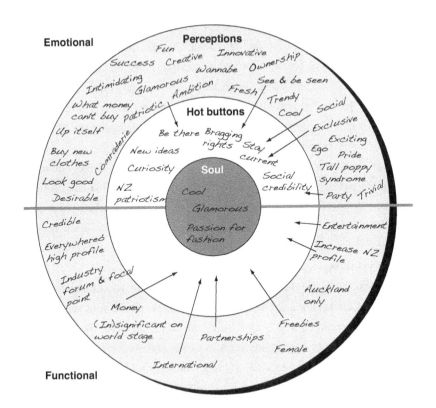

Emotional

Functional

Figure 2.2
New Zealand Fashion Week
bullseye

Defining your target markets

It is often a temptation to define your target market as a 'general audience'—you *want* everyone to come to your event and you are sure that if they do they will enjoy themselves. You may even receive government funding or a grant that tells you that your event/organisation or whatever has to serve the whole community.

Unfortunately, in a marketing sense, virtually no organisation has the money or other resources to reach the entire marketplace effectively. The job, then, becomes how to determine and prioritise your target markets so that you maximise the effectiveness of your marketing program. Your target markets, sometimes called 'segments', are determined by two general criteria:

1   **Demographics.** This is the hard data about a person or marketplace, such as age, sex, marital status, whether they have children, where they live, income and employment status, as well as more specific information, such as whether they own a computer, how old their car is, or how often they travel on business.

Target markets
must be
defined both
demographically
and
psychographically.

2 **Psychographics.** This is the softer data on your market and relates to why people do what they do, what motivates them to prefer one product to another and lifestyle questions. Examples of words used to describe a marketplace psychographically include 'active', 'value-for-money oriented', 'quality oriented', 'feminist', 'risk taker', 'strong environmental responsibility', 'macho', 'saver' and 'adrenalin junkie'. Psychographics have clearly overtaken demographics as the most important factor in defining a target market.

A target market is a group of people with very similar demographic and psychographic profiles. You will probably have several target markets, some of which will be very different from each other. All of your target markets put together are called your audience. Try not to confuse these terms, as the distinction will become very important when it comes time to targeting potential sponsors.

There are also two types of target market:

1 **End users.** These are the people we normally consider as customers—the people who come to the event or venue, buy tickets or use your service. These people could also be exhibitors, in the case of an expo, show or convention, or event participants, such as runners registering for a marathon. The target market exercise below will help you to prioritise these markets.

2 **Intermediary markets.** Intermediary markets are the organisations that the end user will go through or take the advice of in order to participate. These are many and varied but could include:

   (a) ticket sellers

   (b) exhibition space sellers

   (c) venues

   (d) retailers (e.g. 'get your entry form at Foot Locker')

   (e) convention and visitor bureaus

   (f) schools

   (g) reviewers

   (h) public transportation and/or parking facilities.

The importance of intermediary markets will vary from one event to another. If you have a large number of intermediary markets, it may be useful to prioritise them using the target market exercise below.

Target market assessment worksheet

Using your brand bullseye as a starting point, look for related terms in the the emotional perceptions and hot buttons and pull out three or four types of people who attend your event. As an example, people who attend the Melbourne Cup or the Kentucky Derby could be segmented by the following perceptions/motivations:

➤ Segment 1—See and be seen, ego, elite, bragging rights, 'in' crowd

➤ Segment 2—Excuse to party, social, drinking, group bonding, pilgrimage

➤ Segment 3—Gambling, money, best races, best horses, winning

➤ Segment 4—Glamour, fashion, excuse to shop, competitive (fashion-wise)

Using your brand bullseye as a starting place, segment your audience using their primary motivation(s) as the main differentiating factor (not factors such as gender or age). You should complete an assessment worksheet for each group, whether they are end users or intermediary markets. Leave naming your target market segments until last.

What is the prime motivation for this segment to attend your event?

....

....

What else makes your event appealing to this segment? (Note: Oftentimes, something that is a primary motivation for one target market will be a secondary motivation for another. Don't worry if there is some crossover.)

....

....

What proportion of your audience does this segment make up? (Estimate, if required.)

....

....

Is this segment growing or shrinking? What is its potential for growth?

....

....

Who will this segment attend with (if it is an event)?

....

....

Does this segment influence the attendance or participation of others? (For example, highly social, well-connected people who will encourage their friends to donate.)

....

....

Do geographic or logistical challenges affect the appeal of your event to this segment? Get specific.

....

....

Example: One-person description

Steven is a veterinarian in inner-suburban Manchester, specialising in small animals. He has an unassuming but successful practice and is known for the genuine affection he shows for the animals under his care, as well as for their concerned owners. He lives not far away with his partner, Donald, in a terminally half-renovated 18th century cottage. He drives a new VW Beetle convertible and always has a fresh flower from his garden in the flower holder. Although only 41, he has a love of old soul and R&B and has caused more than one snicker with his penchant for singing R-E-S-P-E-C-T and other classics at the top of his lungs while driving to work. He's stylishly dressed, without being flashy—you'd have to look closely to notice that his watch is a Tag. Steven has a wide social circle and enjoys trying —and critiquing— new restaurants and bars. He and Donald love to travel and have seen most of Europe, but never during football season—Go Man U!— although he always worries about his patients when he's gone.

What are the five things that have to go right in order for this segment to consider their experience to be a success? (Note: You do not necessarily have control over every one of these things.)

1 _____

2 _____

3 _____

4 _____

5 _____

Describe this segment as if it were one person. Be complete—name, job, family, lifestyle, etc. Don't make it just a list of attributes. Tell a story, such as the example in the margin. The more fun you have with this, the better. Really let yourself get to know this person.

....

....

....

....

....

....

....

What media are likely to appeal to this segment—specific newspapers and sections, radio and television programs, speciality pay TV channels, magazines, websites, e-zines?

....

....

....

What message(s) will this market be receptive to (what will make them attend)?

....

....

....

....

Name this segment. Make it something that has meaning to you and something that you and your staff can use to refer to this segment.

....

....

....

Once you have completed these questions and analysed your customer markets in depth, including research, you should have a more complete understanding of your current and potential customers. There are a number of ways to segment a marketplace. Some organisations see clear divisions between segments, while others see a lot of overlap.

Below is an abbreviated sample of how a football team may segment and define its target markets. As you can see, the motivations and interests are very different from one segment to another. People don't experience your event in the same way or for the same reasons, nor can you effectively reach them all with the same marketing message or mechanisms.

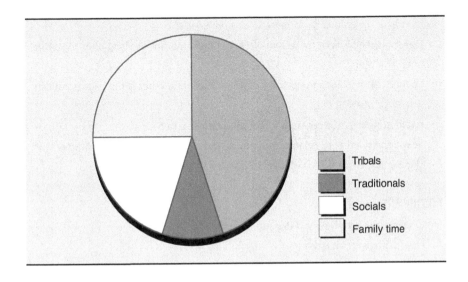

Figure 2.3
Target markets of a football team

Tribals
Traditionals
Socials
Family time

Tribals—45%

➤ Motivated by atmosphere of the game

➤ Love being part of the crowd

➤ Very emotional about their experience

➤ Opportunities for participation are important, such as singing the team song

➤ If not at the game, prefer to view it in a crowd atmosphere, such as a pub

➤ Fickle—lose interest if the team doesn't perform

➤ Equally divided between males and females

Traditionals—10%

➤ Supporting the team is a family tradition passed down from one generation to the next

➤ See attending and/or viewing the game as a duty

➤ Support the team through good times and bad

➤ Know a lot of detail about the team and the game

➤ Skewed towards male and older people, often having shifted over time from being Tribal or Social

➤ Strong loyalty

➤ Acknowledgment of their long-term support is very important to this group

➤ Interaction with the team and coaches is a big hot button

➤ If not attending game, tend to watch at home

Socials—20%

➤ Use games as an excuse for a social day with friends

➤ Day starts well before the game, often at a pub, and finishes long after the game, often at a pub

➤ Logistics of meeting and getting from one place to another is the biggest concern

➤ Attend games in groups

➤ If not attending, watch games in groups, often at a pub

➤ See strong team performance as a bonus, not a requirement for a good day

➤ Skewed to people who are male and under 35

Family time—25%

➤ Quality time with family is the strong motivating factor

➤ Have school-age children

➤ Attend games with family only, or possibly with another family

> Watch games together at home

> Make an effort to make games a 'special time' for the family

> The whole experience is important, no matter where they see the game

> Cost is important—they see a cost approximately equivalent to a family movie pass and associated concessions as being acceptable

Prioritising your target markets

We have found the following exercise useful in prioritising the key target markets that make up your audience.

Step 1

Try to imagine that the entire marketplace is represented by the graph shown in Figure 2.4. You will see three things:

1   There is a certain percentage of people who will always come to your event—they just need to know when and where it is and they will be there.

2   There is also a certain percentage of people who will never come, no matter what you do.

3   The people in the middle—the people who can be convinced—are your opportunity. They haven't made up their minds yet, so you can influence their decision. This is still a lot of people, though, so it needs to be assessed and prioritised.

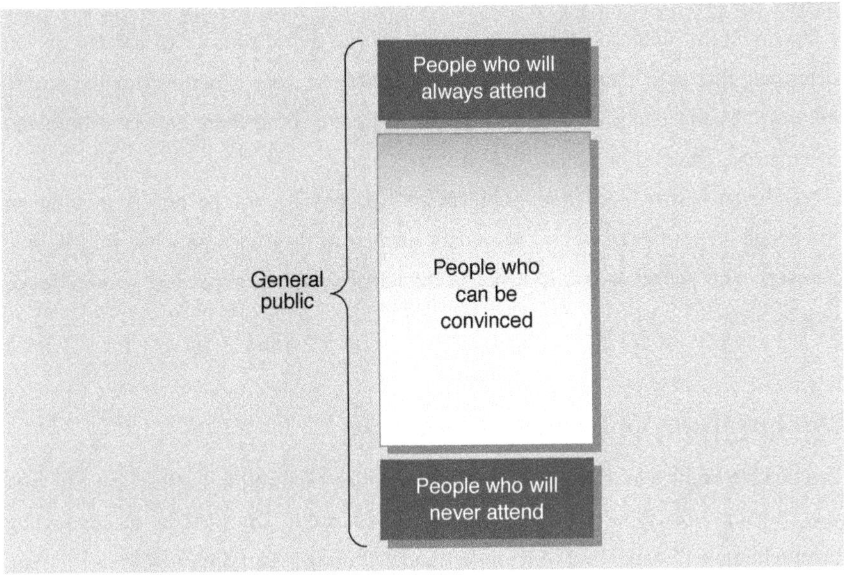

All of your target markets put together are called your 'target audience'.

Figure 2.4

People who will always attend

General public

People who can be convinced

People who will never attend

Some of these people can be convinced relatively easily. It makes sense that it is most cost effective to address your marketing activities to this group first. The less likely people are to come, the more difficult and expensive it will be to market to them. You may choose not to market to people who probably won't be convinced at all.

Step 2

Imagine that the 'always' group is already at your event. In front of you is a ballroom full of people—100 people from each of the target market segments that you've defined and they haven't decided whether they will go to your event or not. It will cost you $100 for the opportunity to speak to one of those target markets to convince them to attend. Which segment would you choose—the one where it will be easiest to convince all of them to attend or the one where you will be lucky to get 10% of them to attend? If you're trying to get the most people to your event, you'll pick the easiest to convince. That is your primary target market.

Step 3

Congratulations, the whole group has been convinced and they are off enjoying themselves at your event. Now you can talk to another target market group of 100 but it will cost you $200 for the privilege. Which target market would you choose this time? This is your 'secondary market'.

Step 4

Keep doing this until you reach a point where you either run out of money or you determine that your marketing efforts will probably be very expensive for the return, in terms of participants. Usually, you will hit this point somewhere between three and five markets. This is your 'tertiary market'.

The goal is that, over time, your 'always' group will grow by pulling in some of the people in your primary and secondary markets as they become what we call 'true believers'. This will allow you to invest in the tertiary markets, expanding your audience year by year.

Researching your target markets

You need to know a lot about your audience in order to reach them effectively. The best way to gather that type of data is very simple—ask them. The benefits of conducting comprehensive research and truly understanding your markets are twofold.

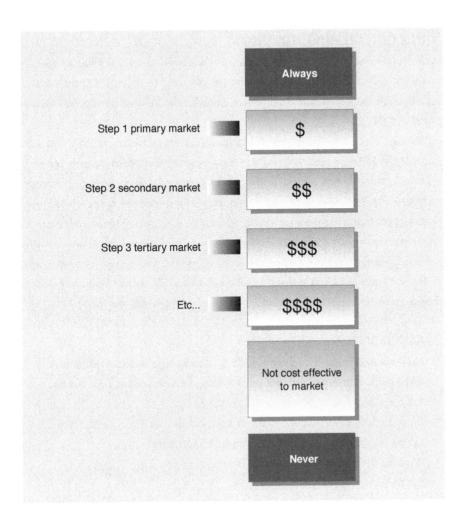

Figure 2.5 Prioritising your markets based on relative costs

1 **Marketing plan.** The research will give you not only an understanding of who your audience is but also of what motivates the different segments of it. This will enable you to create a marketing plan that will reach them effectively and at the lowest possible cost because you won't be paying to reach people who are not in your catchment groups.

2 **Targeting sponsors.** The most powerful things you can deliver to a sponsor is your audience and information about how they can connect to the various target markets. Thus, it follows that the better you know your audience, the stronger your understanding of your audience, the more valuable that sponsorship will be to a sponsor. This will help you to target your sponsors more effectively.

What do you need to know?

When conducting research of your market you will need to ask a number of specific questions to obtain the type of information you will need to know. The questions you ask may relate to information from current customers and potential customers on any number of things.

We have divided this list into psychographic and demographic factors, which are both important for different reasons. Understanding a target market's psychographic profile is essential in knowing how to market to them—to convince them to do what you want them to do—and providing meaningful opportunities for sponsors to connect with them. Demographic factors are great for excluding markets. If you are trying to get people to have regular mamograms, it is unlikely that your target market will include men; if you're running a local festival, it's probably a waste of time marketing to people overseas or even in the next state; and if you're trying to sell tickets to a $1500 a plate fundraising dinner, there is no use in targeting people who could never afford to pay that much.

Psychographic

> How would they describe themselves? (A valuable open-ended question best asked in qualitative research, but possibly using multiple choices on a survey.)
> Top three priorities in their lives? (Ditto above.)
> What do they do for recreation and/or hobbies?
> Do they donate or volunteer? How much and to whom?
> What are their travel and vacation preferences?
> Are they investors, savers or spenders?
> Are they trendsetters/opinion leaders or followers?
> Are they fashion-conscious?
> Are they sports fans? Favourite teams?
> Are they involved in their community? How?
> Are they interested in gardening or do-it-yourself activities?
> Are they fit and healthy? Do they exercise?
> What is their interest in the arts?
> What is their attitude toward corporate sponsorship
> How would they describe your event to a friend or colleague?
> Why did they or didn't they attend your most recent event?

The last two are very important to understand a target market's specific perceptions and motivations concerning your event. Again, this is probably a quantitative question, but far too valuable not to ask.

Demographic

- age and/or lifestage (kids in school, grown up kids, retired etc.)
- marital status
- income
- renter or homeowner
- number and ages of children
- occupation
- education
- car ownership—age of car, make and model
- location (often the easiest way is to get a postcode)
- length of time at present address
- Internet use and type (dial-up, broadband, wireless)
- mail order and online buying
- television viewing preferences
- club, organisation and affiliation memberships
- public transportation use
- purchasing habits
- frequent flyer membership
- pet ownership
- political activity
- movie or theatre going habits
- beverage preferences
- food preferences.

Remember that information on product usage, propensity to buy and sponsorship attitudes may greatly assist your sponsorship sales process. If you can demonstrate that your customers actively seek out a sponsor's product, a potential sponsor is likely to be far more interested in you. If you approach a car manufacturer with research on the average age of your customers' cars, their car purchasing habits and their attitudes towards the car manufacturer, your potential sponsor is far more likely to consider your proposal seriously.

Primary and secondary sources

So, how do you get all of that information about your target markets so that you can create the strongest possible marketing plan? There are two main sources—primary and secondary. We will look at each separately.

> Develop a strategy and budget for your research program, as the task can be both time consuming and expensive.

Before conducting your research, you must understand that it will require an investment of time, money or both. Once you have decided what information you are seeking, be sure to create a strategy and budget to achieve your research goals.

Primary information

As we stated earlier, if you want information about people in your target markets, ask them. Your potential audience is the best possible source for information about what will appeal to them and what kind of marketing will interest them enough to bring them to your event. This is primary information.

Primary information can be obtained by conducting: interviews with participants (such as runners in a 10 km race), attendees and potential attendees; surveys, including mail and telephone surveys, entrance and exit surveys, sponsorship awareness surveys, customer satisfaction surveys and focus groups.

Sponsorship surveys

Sponsorship surveys are a useful tool for determining your customers' attitudes towards sponsorship in general and your organisations' sponsors in particular. Sponsorship surveys can be done before, during or after an event to measure retention of specific sponsor marketing messages, whether the sponsorship has changed their attitude toward a sponsor and their propensity to buy a sponsor's product.

Entrance and exit surveys

Entrance and exit surveys are used to gather demographic and psychographic data, and other sponsorship-related data, as outlined above.

Focus groups

Focus groups are a highly effective method for gaining qualitative information on target markets and they are really easy and inexpensive to do. They involve getting together a group of 10 to 18 people who are representative of your target audience and asking them a range of questions about their opinions, preferences and lifestyles. This is a goldmine for information that will help you to develop your brand (and fill in your brand bullseye). If you do embark upon a program of focus groups, be sure to enlist an experienced moderator and pre-plan all questions to ensure you find out everything you need to know.

If you want information about your target markets, ask them.

Templates for an Audience Profile Questionnaire and a Sponsorship Impact Questionnaire can be found on pages 37 and 41.

Interviews

Conducting a series of interviews with competitors, peers, industry specialists and individual customers is a valuable way of gathering primary information on your markets that will assist in the development of your brand, your event, your overall marketing plan and your sponsorship strategy.

How to get primary information

A well-executed survey program need not be expensive. One of the cheapest ways to gather information is to utilise the services of a class at a business school or university. As part of their studies they need the opportunity to gather and analyse data, as well as presenting it, and you can provide that opportunity. The key here is not to treat them like research slaves but to work with them on both the methodology and reporting of results.

Another very inexpensive way to gather information is to run a simple drawing for a prize, asking pertinent questions on the entry form. This can work well but you will miss a whole segment of your market that is not motivated by that type of activity.

Secondary information

Secondary information is any information that you get about your audience that does not come directly from your audience.

If you are trying to define your target markets and will not have the opportunity to research your audience directly, secondary information is the only way you will be able to gain an understanding of your markets. Secondary information can include information from:

> sponsorship, marketing or advertising publications and reports
> business information resources
> government bodies
> industry bodies.

Where to get secondary information

Many secondary resources are available that can be a goldmine of information that will assist you in defining your target markets. In Appendix 2 of this book you will find a detailed list of resources, including associations, organisations and websites that will be useful sources of market information. Below, we have overviewed a few types of information resources.

> Contact your local university or technical college marketing department. Often there are students interested in a market research project.

Sponsorship, marketing and advertising

Getting market information from a sponsorship, marketing or advertising source is probably the most user-friendly way to get it. By its very nature, it will be marketing oriented, offering some direction as to how to reach your target markets. These resources can include:

- professional associations
- publications
- reports
- media guides
- sports or arts governing bodies
- local or state special events offices (some cities/states have them, some don't).

Government sources

Government sources are many and varied and mostly free. Contact your local reference library, state or federal publications area and/or census department to find out what is available. Many governments also publish lists of the available publications on the Internet. The type of government reports you could use include:

- American Statistical Index
- Australian Bureau of Statistics publications
- US Industry Outlook
- Census data.

Business information sources

Depending upon what type of markets you are targeting, business information sources can be very useful for gaining market information. They are also good for obtaining background information on potential sponsors:

- *Who's Who of Business*
- Standard and Poor's industry surveys
- Hoover's online *Business Periodicals Index*
- *Statistical Reference Index*
- Dun and Bradstreet products.

Industry sources

Industry sources can also be very useful, particularly if your event or organisation targets primarily businesses and businesspeople. Such sources include:

- trade, industry and professional associations
- chambers of commerce.

Audience profile questionnaire

 Research1.doc

Here is an example of a survey that could be carried out on people who have just attended a women's professional basketball game to determine the demographic and psychographic features of the audience market.

1 Is this your first visit to a women's professional basketball game?

- ❐ Yes
- ❐ No

2 How many games have you attended this season?

- ❐ This is my first
- ❐ 2–4
- ❐ 5–10
- ❐ More than 10

3 Where did you hear about tonight's game? Check all that apply:

- ❐ I have season tickets
- ❐ Friend or relative
- ❐ Radio ad
- ❐ TV ad
- ❐ Newspaper ad
- ❐ Internet
- ❐ Another sporting event

- ❐ TV or radio program or print article (please specify).....................................
- ❐ TV
- ❐ Radio
- ❐ Press
- ❐ Magazine
- ❐ Other (please specify) ....

4 What did you think of the stadium? Check all that apply:

- ❐ Good visibility
- ❐ Comfortable
- ❐ Easy to get to
- ❐ Good food/drinks
- ❐ Too many sponsor signs
- ❐ Not enough food outlets or staff

- ❐ Parking difficult/expensive
- ❐ Public transportation difficult
- ❐ Food/drinks too expensive
- ❐ Food/drinks poor quality
- ❐ Adequate food outlets and staff

5 What are the top three reasons you decided to attend this game?

- ❐ Atmosphere at the game
- ❐ Quality of play
- ❐ Good day/night out
- ❐ Good value for families
- ❐ I follow a particular player (please specify)...............................
- ❐ I just wanted to check it out

- ❐ I like to support women's sport
- ❐ Rivalry between the teams
- ❐ Easier/cheaper to get tickets than for men's games
- ❐ I came as a favour to someone else
- ❐ Other (please specify) ....

6 Did the game live up to your expectations?

- ❐ Yes
- ❐ Mostly
- ❐ No

7 If you could change one thing about your experience, what would it be?

....

....

....

....

8 Including yourself, how many people are in your group today?

- ❐ 1
- ❐ 2
- ❐ 3–4
- ❐ 5–9
- ❐ 10 or more

9 Who are you here with?

- ❐ Family adult(s)
- ❐ Non-family adult(s)
- ❐ Child/children
- ❐ School group
- ❐ Other organised group

10 What is your post/zip code?

....

Questions 11–14 for Non-Tri-State residents only

11 How long are you staying in the Tri-State area?

....

12 Are you staying in paid accommodation?

- ❏ Yes
- ❏ No

13 What other activities have you done/do you plan to do during your stay?

- ❏ Attend another sporting event
- ❏ Football
- ❏ Baseball
- ❏ Ice hockey
- ❏ Other
- ❏ Attend a non-sporting event

- ❏ Basketball
- ❏ Visit a museum or gallery
- ❏ See a concert, play or show
- ❏ Sightseeing
- ❏ Shopping
- ❏ Other (please specify) ....

14 When was the last time you did the following for pleasure?

	In past week	1–4 weeks ago	1–6 months ago	More than 6 months ago	Never/do not know
Go to the movies					
Attend a professional sporting event					
Play sport or do an exercise program					
Eat out at a restaurant					
Go to a concert or play					
Garden or work around the yard					
Visit a museum, art gallery or exhibition					
Go to the beach					

15 For each of the following statements, do you agree or disagree that it describes you personally?

	Agree	Disagree	Don't know
I am very fashion conscious			
I want to achieve a lot			
I love sports of any kind			
I am really a homebody			
I will try anything once			
I hate getting dressed up			
I try to be environmentally responsible			
I like to garden and potter around the house on weekends			
I would rather watch TV on Saturday than go out			
I thrive on the company of other people			
I do not like sport, either watching or taking part in it			
I would rather take part in something than watch it			

16 Are you in paid employment? What is your occupation?

❐ Yes ❐ No

❐ Occupation ....

17 How old are you?

❐ Under 18 years

❐ 18–24 years

❐ 25–34 years

❐ 35–49 years

❐ 50+ years

18 What is the highest level of school you have completed?

❐ High school

❐ Trade/technical or business college

❐ University degree (undergraduate)

❐ Advanced university degree

19 Which of these categories does your total annual household income fall into?

- ❑   Under $25 000
- ❑ $25 001–$40 000
- ❑ $40 001–$60 000
- ❑ $60 001–$80 000
- ❑ $80 001–$100 000
- ❑   Over $100 000

20 How likely are you to attend a women's professional basketball game again in the next 12 months?

- ❑   Very likely
- ❑   Somewhat likely
- ❑   Not very likely
- ❑   Not at all likely
- ❑   Do not know

Thank you for your help.

21 Record gender of respondent

- ❑   Female
- ❑   Male

Date of interview .... I certify that this interview was conducted in accordance with briefing instructions and the Code of Professional Behaviour, and that the information gathered is true and accurate.

Signed by interviewer: ....

Sponsorship impact questionnaire

Research2.doc

Here is an example of a questionnaire that could be carried out on attendees at an exhibition of modern art award finalists to determine how effective the sponsorship program is.

PART 1 / PLANNING

1   Who are the major sponsors of the 10th Annual Contemporary Art Awards?

....

2   Can you name any other sponsors of the arts?

....

3   (If no alcoholic beverage specified) Can you name any alcohol or wine sponsors of the arts?

....

4   When did you first try California Blender's Choice Sparkling Wines?
   - ❏   Tonight
   - ❏   In the last month
   - ❏   In the last three months
   - ❏   More than six months ago
   - ❏   In the last year
   - ❏   I have never tried California Blender's Choice Sparkling Wines

5   Would you purchase California Blender's Choice Sparkling Wines in the future?
   - ❏   Yes
   - ❏   Likely
   - ❏   Perhaps
   - ❏   Unlikely
   - ❏   No

6   When is the last time you purchased wine?
   - ❏   In the last two weeks
   - ❏   In the last month
   - ❏   In the last three months
   - ❏   More than six months ago
   - ❏   In the last year
   - ❏   I have never purchased wine

7   Which brand or style of wine did you last purchase?
   - ❏   French Champagne
   - ❏   Other imported sparkling wine
   - ❏   California Blender's Choice

❐ Gallo of Sonoma

❐ Fetzer

❐ Robert Mondavi

❐ Berringer

❐ Other American wines

❐ Chilean wine

❐ Australian wine

❐ Other import (please specify) ....

8 Which brands or styles of wine have you purchased in the last six months? (Choose all that apply.)

❐ French Champagne

❐ Other imported sparkling wine

❐ California Blender's Choice

❐ Gallo of Sonoma

❐ Fetzer

❐ Robert Mondavi

❐ Berringer

❐ Other American wines

❐ Chilean wine

❐ Australian wine

❐ Other import (please specify) ....

9 What are the main reasons you purchase a particular wine for the first time? (Choose all that apply.)

❐ Recommendation from friend/family

❐ Expert recommendation (e.g. wine critic, wine steward)

❐ I've heard of it, but I'm not sure where

❐ Description on the label

❐ I had the opportunity to try it and liked it

❐ Brand supports the arts

❐ Trusted the brand

❐ I liked the bottle/label

❐ Price

❐ Other ....

10 Are you a member of a wine club?

❏   Yes

❏   No

❏   I was a member, but am not one at this time

11 How would you rate the Contemporary Art Awards exhibition?

❏   Excellent

❏   Above average

❏   Fair

❏   Poor

(Be sure to also include basic database generating questions.)

Developing the marketing plan

Now that you understand who your audience is, it is time to create a plan that will bring them to your event, venue, organisation or service.

SWOT analysis

SWOT stands for **S**trengths, **W**eaknesses, **O**pportunities and **T**hreats. The SWOT analysis is a tool that allows you to identify the internal and external issues that may impact on your ability to market your event or product.

Strengths and weaknesses

In order to identify the strengths and weaknesses of your event or products, you must examine the issues *within* your organisation that impact on your ability to sell your event or property to your target markets and to sponsors.

An important area to explore is how your organisation perceives the value of the event or product. If your organisation sees your event as a priority and an opportunity to raise the profile of the organisation, the event is considered a strength. However, if your board sees your event as a drain on resources, then the event is a weakness.

Strengths and weaknesses are generally issues within your organisation's control.

EXERCISE

Consider the following list of internal organisational factors and determine how these will affect the success of your event. For each factor, determine whether its effect is a strength or a weakness and place your specific factors under either the strengths or weaknesses headings in the **SWOT Analysis Worksheet** found on page 47.

The internal factors that may influence your event include:

- staff attitudes and opinions
- staff experience and expertise
- the organisation's track record in staging and promoting similar events
- booster clubs, membership programs, databases
- how your corporate plan and your corporate objectives impact on your event
- key stakeholder analysis
- resources—money, people, assets, facilities, volunteers
- existing media profile
- media partners
- new organisational initiatives
- board and/or head office support
- your location.

Opportunities and threats

The next step is to analyse all factors *outside* your organisation that may affect your event. The external analysis will assist you in identifying the opportunities and threats related to your event. Once having determined the threats to your event, you can then reassess the situation and analyse how you can make these threats into opportunities.

For example, if you are holding an outdoor children's community festival, the following external factors may influence your event:

- weather
- major sporting finals on the same day
- poor attendance at last year's event
- fewer children in the relevant age group in your community.

Every threat
provides an
opportunity.

EXERCISE

Look at the following list of external factors that may influence your event and consider how these offer opportunities and threats to your event. Place your specific factors under either the opportunities or threats headings in the **SWOT Analysis Worksheet** found on page 47. Keep in mind that threats can often be turned into opportunities.

The external factors that may affect your event may be:

- political
- environmental
- geographic
- demographic
- historical
- industrial
- international
- local

- competitor related
- customer perception related
- economic
- consumer confidence related
- technological
- legal
- natural

> Generally, threats are beyond the control of your organisation. You can anticipate and even plan for them but there is little you can actually do to stop them happening.

EXERCISE

Look at the list of threats you have compiled in the **SWOT Analysis Worksheet** (page 47). Determine which of these threats require your attention. What do you need to do in order to maximise or minimise the effects of each factor?

It is imperative that you address each threat to your event when conducting your planning to ensure the success of your event. Each threat can be further categorised into one of four types of threat to help you determine its importance to your event's success. Categorising the threat determines how you will respond to the threat to minimise its effect.

1   **Monitor.** Threats that you decide to monitor only are those for which there is little that you can do to change or plan for, nevertheless you want to know what is happening. Examples might include any low-risk threats.

2   **Monitor and analyse.** Those threats that you decide to monitor and analyse are also ones that you can do little to reduce but you need to determine how they might impact on your event.

3   **Prepare contingency strategies.** Threats that you decide to prepare a contingency strategy for are those of which you can reduce the impact with planning. For example, if bad weather is a threat to your outdoor event, you can determine how you will handle it—postpone the event, move to an indoor facility or take out insurance.

4   **Prepare in-depth analysis and strategy development.** Those threats for which you decide to prepare an in-depth analysis and strategy development are those that have the greatest likelihood of impacting on your event. Technological, competitor and legislative factors are examples of threats that may require more detailed analysis and strategy development.

SWOT analysis worksheet

Strengths

....

....

....

....

....

....

Weaknesses

....

....

....

....

....

....

Opportunities

....

....

....

....

....

Threats

....

....

....

....

....

You are competing for your audience with anything they could do with their leisure time and money.

Competitor analysis

As with any company, you have competitors. It used to be that events only really competed for their audience against other events but, as more leisure options have come into play and leisure time has become more limited, this is no longer the case. In fact, you are competing against anything that a potential customer could do with their leisure time and money.

Use the following worksheet to analyse your competition.

1 Who are my direct competitors (similar events or organisations)?

....

....

2 Who are my indirect competitors (other activities or events that are compelling to your audience)?

....

....

3 What do my potential and existing customers like about my competitors' events, products and services?

....

....

4 How much are customers paying for my competitors' events, products or services?

....

....

....

5 What makes my competitors successful and why? What are they doing right?

....

....

....

6 How do my competitors communicate with their customers?

....

....

7 How do my competitors position their events, products and services within the market?

....
....

8 Who are my least successful competitors and why? What are they doing wrong?

....
....

9 What are my competitors' major strengths and weaknesses?

....
....

10 Are my competitors implementing any changes to their fees, products, marketing programs or operations?

....
....

11 Who are my potential competitors in the short and long term?

....
....

12 How does my product or service differ from my competitors' events, products and services? This is your unique selling point! A great way to find it is to do a quick competitor footprint.

....
....
....
....
....

Competitor footprint

Create a Venn diagram with your organisation and your two biggest competitors (you can add other competitors later) showing attributes you share and those you don't. We recommend that you use butcher's paper—you need some space—and work in a group setting. You already have most of the content for this—just pull the information straight off of your brand bullseye to start.

What this process will show is whether you are marketing yourself in ways that you share with your competitors, or whether you are (or could be) marketing yourself based on your unique selling points.

Figure 2.6
Competitor footprint

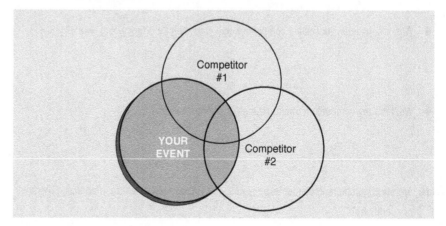

Marketing strategies

Now that you have completed your SWOT analysis and you know who your competition is, it's time to plan your marketing strategy.

In order to ensure your marketing strategy remains on track, you need to include the following information:

➤ objectives

➤ rationale for each objective

➤ strategies for achieving each objective

➤ measurement mechanisms to determine the outcome of each objective.

Objectives

Your objectives indicate what you want to achieve. They should be SMART objectives:

Specific

Measurable

Achievable

Results oriented

Time bound.

For example, if your stated objective is to obtain media coverage of your event, you have not been specific enough. Try, instead, 'to obtain a major article in *The Daily Express* and two major news stories on Channel 8 News and Radio Station 9CN by the second week of the festival'.

Rationale

The rationale must be a brief statement outlining why a particular objective or strategy has been chosen.

Strategies

Strategies indicate how you will meet an objective. Strategies are the specific actions that will be undertaken to achieve a desired outcome.

Measurement mechanisms

Measurement mechanisms are ways in which you will determine whether you have achieved your objectives and your customers' critical success factors. Measurement mechanisms may include, but are not limited to:

- sales figures
- sales growth
- quality of media coverage
- number of attendees
- customer opinion and satisfaction
- sponsorship success data
- propensity to buy data
- reports
- number of events held
- number of sponsors
- number of new names for databases
- sales leads
- profit or revenue
- advance ticket sales
- wholesale ticket sales
- number and quality of cross-promotions
- customer propensity to return to the next event.

Sample

Objective

To obtain a major article with a colour photo in *The Daily Express*, as well as two major news stories on Channel 8 News and Radio Station 9CN during the second week of the festival.

Rationale

This will achieve an 80% market penetration in our target markets and will give an added boost to ticket sales beyond the opening week rush.

Strategies

➤ Create a media kit for distribution to local media representatives.

➤ Create media interview opportunities with celebrity festival guests.

➤ Provide DVDs of last year's event and highlights of the first week to local television stations for ease of coverage.

Measurement mechanism

➤ Quality and acceptance of media kit.

➤ Number of media interviews.

➤ Number of broadcasts that utilise DVD material.

Strategies worksheet

As you start working out your objectives and how you will achieve them, this exercise may help you to understand the process behind their development.

1 What are my marketing objectives? For the purposes of this exercise limit yourself to no more than five objectives.

2 Provide a brief rationale for each objective.

3 For each objective, provide specific steps or strategies that you will undertake to meet the objective.

4 Record the relevant measurement mechanisms for each objective.

Sample worksheet

Complete this sample worksheet to develop your marketing plan.

Objective one

....

....

Rationale

....

....

Strategies

➤

➤

➤

➤

➤

Quantification mechanisms

➤

➤

➤

➤

➤

Resources

All plans require resources. The resources required to implement your plan might include information, time, advertising expertise, graphic design skills, media talent, equipment, office space and staff, as well as funds.

In many cases, your marketing and promotional plans will be designed with a specific budget in mind.

Ask yourself the following questions to ensure you have addressed all your resource requirements.

1   What resources do you need to implement the marketing strategies? Sponsors can often provide non-monetary resources to a project. These should be clearly identified in your marketing plan.

2   How much funding do you require for these items? Include the number of hours, space required, training and administration support when budgeting for resources. Some examples include:

- staff time (include overtime)
- advertising
- equipment
- office space
- maintenance and storage.
- printing
- distribution
- volunteer costs
- travel

3   What sources of information, data, knowledge and research do you need?

> Remember to keep your objectives SMART—Specific, Measurable, Achievable, Results oriented and Time bound.

Develop an action list

Having a plan does not mean anything unless you put it into action. These points are designed to enable you to create a master timeline and action list for your marketing plan.

1   Phase the strategies and timeline for each and every strategy. Ensure that each strategy has specific start and stop dates.

2   Identify who will be responsible for each step of every strategy.

3   Determine how each strategy will be evaluated, measured and reported. Identify who will be responsible for these tasks. Schedule all evaluations, approvals, meetings and reports into your master timeline and action list.

Remember to consider reports, in-house experience, surveys and consultant studies that already exist within your organisation. No one needs to reinvent the wheel.

Marketing plan template

 Market1.doc

This template can be used to develop your own marketing plan. In the worksheets in this chapter you have been asked key questions and should have answered them comprehensively. If you haven't, go back to these worksheets and your research and do so now. Summarise and transfer this information by answering the questions in this template to develop your marketing plan.

Background

Why are we preparing this document? What do we want this document to achieve?

Target audiences

Who are we trying to reach? What do we know about them?

Critical success factors

What are the key things we need to achieve in order for this plan to be a success?

Market research

What are our strategies based on? (Summarise your research in dot points.)

Internal analysis

What within my organisation can affect this plan, both positively and negatively?

Case studies: Gaining marketing value from sponsors

Sponsors can be a great marketing resource. A strong sponsor leverage program can augment or even replace a lot of your marketing expenditure. Some examples:

Kids Help Line, a crisis hotline initiative of Boystown Family Care, is a great service for Australia's kids, but not enough of them knew about it. Boystown worked with Kellogg's to create a multifaceted marketing campaign that they could never have afforded on their own. Millions of cereal boxes featured the Help Line phone number, as well as tips on such subjects as bullying, and a dual-branded television commercial ran during family programming, with the result that more kids called, more families knew about the service (and donated to it) and Kellogg's scored some major points with parents.

Six Flags theme parks primarily targets families and wanted a cost-effective way to reach them. They struck a deal with family-oriented America OnLine whereby AOL promotes the theme parks to over 20 million members. In return, AOL gets to provide added value to its members by offering discounts to the parks.

The Heart Research Foundation in Poland partnered with numerous media organisations and two mobile phone operators in an effort to raise its profile and dramatically increase community donations when government funding dried up. Both mobile phone companies make a donation to the foundation every time someone sends an SMS message reminding someone of the initiative.

Chevrolet, a division of General Motors in the United States, has developed a partnership with 14 of the country's top ski resorts, which it uses to anchor cold weather promotions for its range of sports utility vehicles (SUVs). They chose top ski resorts that pull a large proportion of their market from the local/regional area (i.e. they are not solely tourist-oriented). The most interesting thing about this deal is how they have paid for it, which is primarily in contra. Instead of running a standard SUV media campaign during the colder months, Chevy incorporates promotion for each of the ski resorts in its core geographic markets. As these resorts generally don't have the budget for big media campaigns, this has extremely high value for them.

Environmental analysis

What factors in my environment can affect my purpose? What changes must we plan for? (State the assumptions you are making about the future.)

Competitor analysis

Who are our competitors?

Marketing SWOT analysis

What factors are hindering or restraining our purpose? What environmental factors are driving or assisting our purpose? (List here your strengths, weaknesses, opportunities and threats.)

Marketing objectives

Where do we want to go?

Marketing strategies

How are we going to get there? (Put these in dot points underneath your objectives; follow the sample on page 51.)

Evaluation

How will we know that we have achieved our objective? (Indicate how you will evaluate, measure and report against your key quantification mechanisms.)

Master timetable and action list

When will we get there? (Complete the following table to assist you in your planning.)

Strategy	Time frame	Action officer
Objective 1: (provide details)		
Strategy 1 detail	Start and completion date	Person responsible
Strategy 2 detail	Start and completion date	Person responsible
Strategy 3 detail	Start and completion date	Person responsible
Objective 2: (provide details)		
Strategy 1 detail	Start and completion date	Person responsible
Strategy 2 detail	Start and completion date	Person responsible
Strategy 3 detail	Start and completion date	Person responsible

Resources

How much is it going to cost us to get there? (The following sample may be used as a format to assist your planning.)

Objective 1: Research current customers

STRATEGY 1

Survey subscription ticket holders to determine sponsorship attitudes and awareness levels.

Needs

Survey forms	$3 500
Development of database (software, hardware upgrade)	$2 000
Contract researcher (20 hours @ $45 per hour)	$900
Processor (40 hours @ $22.50 per hour plus overheads @ x 1.9)	$1 710
Total for strategy 1	**$8 110**

STRATEGY 2

Survey users of website services and information.

Needs

Post survey form on website and remove at conclusion of survey (outside of current contract)	$2 500
Processor (10 hours @ $22.50 plus overheads @ x 1.9)	$428
Total for strategy 2	$2 928
Total cost to achieve objective 1	**$11 038**

Follow this format for all objectives until you have costed all aspects of fulfilling your marketing objectives.

Review the marketing plan

Now that your plan is complete, you need to look back on it to double check that you have covered all of the key aspects. Consider the following questions as you review your marketing plan. Do you have a clear vision of what the completed marketing campaign will look like? Have you identified the critical success factors and measurement mechanisms? Have you identified the key elements that need to be organised within your master timetable and action plan? Have you clearly identified all resources, including financial, human and training, that need to be planned for? Do you have a contingency strategy if parts of the plan don't work? Have you addressed all possible threats to your plan and event? Have you identified internal communication strategies within your plan? How will you report on progress to staff, members and your Board?

Continually reassess

A marketing plan is a living document. Ensure that you have scheduled review periods into your plan so that you can finetune your plan throughout the implementation phase.

Calculating overheads

When calculating your staff costs, you need to take into account your additional overheads. Adding these to the salary or hourly rate will give you the 'real cost' of employment.

You have two choices for calculating these costs. One is to calculate actual costs for all overheads (rent, equipment, utilities, insurance, etc.) and divide these by the number of staff and their hours. This is very time consuming and generally unnecessary.

The other option is to use a standard multiplier on salary or hourly rates. Most companies that approach real costs of employment this way use a multiplier between 1.4 and 2.6. In our example, we have used 1.9, meaning that if an activity will take an employee paid $10 per hour 100 hours to complete, the real cost of those hours will be $1900.

Chapter 3

Implementing the marketing plan

You have written your marketing plan and it's looking good. Now we need to make that plan work for you.

Although there may be a number of other aspects to implementing your marketing plan, the most common components are:

➤ media promotion

➤ online promotion

➤ publicity

➤ database/loyalty marketing

➤ signage.

We have included information about each of these components.

Media promotion

Although you can go out and simply purchase media, like any other company, this is not all that common, primarily because it ignores the fact that you have a lot to offer a potential media partner. Instead, most sponsees embark upon media promotion to achieve their objectives without spending a fortune.

Generally, media promotions are created with one or more media partners. You provide them with co-ownership of the promotion and either a paid schedule or sponsorship of your event (and all ensuing benefits), and they provide several times that investment in media value. This can be an extremely cost-effective way for you to get your message out into the marketplace.

Who should create the promotion?

Generally speaking, the sponsee is much more likely to achieve its goals if it is intrinsically involved in creating the promotion. See **The Nine Steps of Promotional Media** (page 61) for some hints.

Do you go to one or more media outlets?

If you have determined that you can achieve your objectives with either of two competing media outlets, our suggestion is that you brief them both on the promotion and ask them both to come back to you with a package that meets the brief.

If you have determined that there is only one media outlet that will suit your needs perfectly, you should negotiate closely with them to create a partnership. Do not let them hold you to ransom—you can always walk away and rethink your approach for a different type of media.

How much value should you get?

If your proposal is structured correctly (see **The Nine Steps of Promotional Media** on page 61), you should be receiving substantially more value from the media partner than the funds you invest. This is usually expressed as a value-to-cost ratio.

The table below outlines some value-to-cost ratios and what that value includes.

Media	Target value-to-cost ratio	Value includes:
Television	3:1 to 8:1	Paid spots
		Bonus spots (confirmed)
		Bonus spots (space available)
		Promotional spots (co-branded by the television station)
		News coverage
		Other editorial coverage (lifestyle, sporting or news magazine programs)
		Advertising production
		Use of on-air personality for endorsement, appearances, voice-overs or as a spokesperson
Radio	3:1 to 10:1	Paid spots
		Bonus spots (confirmed)

(Cont.)

Media	Target value-to-cost ratio	Value includes:
		Bonus spots (space available)
		Pre-recorded promotional spots (co-branded by the television station)
		Live promotional spots
		Live liners (very short promotional spots)
		News coverage
		On-air interviews
		Remote broadcasts
		Advertising production
		Use of on-air personality for endorsement, appearances, voice-overs or as a spokesperson
Newspaper	3:1 to 8:1	Paid advertising
		Bonus advertising (confirmed)
		Bonus advertising (space available)
		Insertion of program, poster or other promotional material that you supply
		Printing and/or design of program or poster
		Special supplement (can often be used as the official program)
		Advertorial coverage
Magazine	2:1 to 5:1	Paid advertising
		Bonus advertising (confirmed)
		Bonus advertising (space available)
		Special section
		Insertion of program, poster or other promotional material
		Advertorial coverage
Outdoor	2:1	Paid advertising
		Bonus advertising

Is there any downside to media promotions?

Sometimes there can be a downside to media promotions. If you work with, say, one radio station, it will provide much greater value for your investment if you agree not to work with any other radio stations. But this could severely limit the amount of people in your target market that you can reach. In that case, you have two choices:

1. Offer paid and promotional exclusivity to the one radio station and get maximum value from it. Use other types of media to increase your reach.
2. Offer promotional exclusivity but not sales exclusivity, explaining that in order to achieve your objectives you need greater numbers than it can deliver alone. You will probably get less value from it as a result.

The nine steps of promotional media

Buying promotional media is very much the same as any other kind of marketing transaction. It is part science, part street smart, part creative and a lot of commonsense. Here are nine easy steps to make the task easier.

1 Set your objectives for media

Establish your specific goals. What are you trying to do? Are you promoting an event, selling tickets or building up your profile? Know what you want to accomplish, who you want to communicate with and how much you have to spend before you begin the media buying process.

2 Target your media correctly

As with above-the-line media, the key to success is to choose the media partner(s) that will deliver the largest portion of your target market for the least amount of money. For instance, the number one radio station may deliver you 115 000 listeners in your target market but you will pay to reach their total audience, which may be many times your core market.

On the other hand, if you select a lower rating radio station, magazine or television program where *their* core market is *your* core market, the likelihood is that:

➤ you will spend less money to reach more of your core audience with less media coverage waste
➤ their listeners/readers/viewers will be more receptive to your marketing message.

3 Understand why media run promotions

Competition within the media for the attention of consumers is increasing exponentially and the fact is that most media are virtually interchangeable, in terms of content.

In addition to making a sale to you, most media groups want one or more of the following things from a media promotional opportunity:

> to create a point-of-difference from their competition through the creative use of promotions. This will attract more listeners/viewers/readers and make them more attractive for regular advertisers. Creative is the key word here—if it looks or sounds like every other enter-to-win promotion in the marketplace, it isn't worth anything in a media negotiation

> to increase the profile of their shows, personalities, stars etc.

> to create new advertising vehicles. An example would be a newspaper creating the official program for your event in exchange for the right to sell advertising in it.

4 Create a proposal that helps them to achieve that goal

In order to maximise the media value you achieve for your investment, it is imperative that you go to your target media with a plan that will achieve your objectives and will create a strong point-of-difference for them and assist them with attracting their audience. Do not fall into the trap of thinking that your promotional spend is their driving force, because it is not.

5 The more creative the better

Think outside the square, push the envelope, think laterally—whatever you call it, it is about thinking creatively.

Make your proposal relevant to the audience—really think about what this audience is interested in and what they want, and then give them that and more.

Ensure your proposal really is creative. Sure, everyone wants a vacation but open up any magazine and you can enter five different contests to win a holiday at a beach resort and, with discount travel packages in every newspaper, most people know that it is not that great a deal. Be sure that what you offer is special—go to the extra effort to make this something that they could not do without you.

6 Involve your advertising agency

This is really your call but we strongly suggest that you utilise the creative resources of your advertising agency to ensure that what you propose to your target media is fully developed and creatively executed.

7 Negotiate for control of scheduling

Negotiate for time slots in programs that consistently deliver ratings and the demographics you are seeking. Bargain for newspaper and magazine placements in sections that have proven circulation and the readership demographics you need.

Many media sponsorships provide advertising time at the discretion of the station. This is of absolutely no value to you. If you can't match the demographics of your audience with programs and publications that deliver to these groups, the sponsorship is of little value to you or other sponsors.

8 Never pay more than your volume rate

There are some media groups that will tell you that, since they are giving away a lot of unpaid promotion, the buy must be made at casual or 'rack' rates, even if you are a regular advertiser who normally gets a discount. This is a lot of rubbish.

If you structure your promotional offer correctly, you are actually doing them a favour—you are helping them to create a strong point of difference and paying their costs to do it. You should never pay more than the rate negotiated by you or your media buyer for the paid portion of the deal.

9 Keep your ear to the ground

Make time to meet and network with people in the media industry. These people are approachable. Learn the lingo, read industry publications and speak to your contacts to find out about the media buying process. If there is a media campaign that you feel has been particularly successful or innovative, contact the organisation and arrange to discuss the campaign with the relevant people.

Keep your ear to the ground on how radio, television and newspapers are performing. Listen to the radio and keep an eye out for industry trends, new programs and industry developments. Become an active media watcher.

A **Media Planning Worksheet** is provided below to assist you with the planning and evaluation of your media campaign.

Media planning worksheet

 Market2.doc

This worksheet is designed to assist you with the planning and evaluation of your media campaign. The items in this worksheet should be confirmed if at all possible prior to developing your sponsorship proposal. The evaluation of each type of media should be highlighted in your sponsorship proposal.

Media lingo

Although some of this terminology is specifically about television, most of the terms can be applied to other media (e.g. print, radio) as well.

Rating
A measure (expressed as a percentage) of viewers watching TV within a specific demographic.

Target Audience Rating Point (TARP)
A measure of audience level at a given time on TV. This is expressed as a percentage of the potential audience available of a given demographic.

Example: If there are 1 million adults aged 25–39 in your market and 250,000 of them see your advertisement, then you have reached 25% of the potential audience and the spot would have a TARP of 25.

Gross Rating Point (GRP)
This is a summary of all TARPs on a TV schedule and can also be referred to as total TARPs. Often, your media plan may state that you will purchase, for example, 250 TARPs per week. This figure is an expression of GRPs and will comprise a number of separate advertising spots.

Audience Share
This is often quoted by TV networks to express the percentage of people

(Cont.)

Total media budget

	Cost	Value
Television		
Radio		
Newspaper		
Magazines		
Outdoor		
Total		

Breakdown by media type

Television

Campaign to commence *X/X/X* and conclude *X/X/X*.

Total cost: $*X*

Total value: $*X*

Value-to-cost ratio: *X*:1 (target between 3:1 and 8:1)

	Dates	Number
Paid spots		
Bonus spots ('freebies')		
Promotional spots		
Production		
News coverage		
Celebrity/on-air personality appearances		

Radio

Campaign to commence *X/X/X* and conclude *X/X/X*.

Total cost: $*X*

Total value: $*X*

Value-to-cost ratio: *X*:1 (target between 3:1 to 10:1)

	Dates	Number
Paid spots		
Bonus spots ('freebies')		
Pre-recorded promotional spots		
Live liners (short, live promotions)		
On-air interviews		
Remote broadcast		
Celebrity/on-air personality appearances		

Newspaper

Campaign to commence *X/X/X* and conclude *X/X/X*.

Total cost: $*X*

Total value: $*X*

Value-to-cost ratio: *X*:1 (target between 3:1 and 8:1)

	Dates	Size
Paid advertising		
Bonus advertising (confirmed)		
Bonus advertising (space available)		
Program insertion (you supply the program)		
Special supplement (can be used as program)		
Advertorial coverage		

Magazine

Campaign to commence *X/X/X* and conclude *X/X/X*.

Total cost: $*X*

Total value: $*X*

Value-to-cost ratio: *X*:1 (target between 2:1 and 5:1)

Media lingo (Cont.)

using television that watched the particular program or event. Remember—it only refers to percentage of those watching any TV and not potential of a demographic. You can have a TARP that is different to the share figure.

Reach/Coverage

The percentage of total potential audience reached over a given period of time.

Frequency

This refers to how many times the people see the advertisement. Frequency is often measured in 'bands'. These numbers will often be quoted as being 1+, 2+ or 3+ which refers to people who have 'been reached' one or more times, two or more times, or three or more times.

	Dates	Size
Paid advertising		
Bonus advertising		
Advertorial supplement		
Insert		
Other		

Outdoor

Campaign to commence *X/X/X* and conclude *X/X/X*.

Total cost: $*X*

Total value: $*X*

Value-to-cost ratio: *X*:1 (target 2:1)

	Dates	Location
24 sheets (regular sized billboards)		
Supersites (giant billboards)		
Taxis		
Buses: inside		
Buses: outside		

Online promotion

Within this section, we are addressing primarily web-based promotion, but also need to keep in mind the increasing amount of content being made available to mobile phones, MP3 players and who knows what other technological must-haves in future!

Your website

We are assuming that your organisation or event already has a website. If not, you really need to set one up. The web is now a major, and for some, the primary, tool for gathering information on topics of interest, events, causes and more. If you're not online, you're not in the game. In addition, your online presence, and how it is presented, says a lot to sponsors about your professionalism.

At a minimum, your website should feature the following:

- what the event or organisation is and what it's about
- location
- dates and times
- pricing
- transport and parking information
- schedule of events (if applicable)
- special offers
- sponsor recognition (at *minimum*, logos linked to their sites)
- logos of all endorsing bodies (linked to their sites)
- key marketing messages—tell visitors how this event relates to them. Push those hot buttons!

How you feature all of this is very important, and although we make no claim to being website gurus, we do have a few suggestions:

- Get the website professionally designed and built. A good web designer will know where to put the most important information, how to make it user friendly, and will be able to make the whole thing reflect your image.
- It doesn't have to be huge—a credible-looking 2–3 page site with the right information is much better than a 20-page site with lots of content and none of it compelling.
- It also doesn't have to be flashy (literally). You don't need Flash animations, music or other purely cosmetic content to make the website work. They look good, but do cost more to implement, so if cost is a factor, just stick to great content.
- If there is content that would be useful for people to have around or bring with them to the event, such as an event map or schedule of activities, either provide a printer-friendly version or create a downloadable PDF.

Other websites

Be sure to get your event or program listed on complementary websites. These will vary greatly from one event to another, but here are a few suggestions:

- convention and visitors bureau schedule of events
- city council schedule of events
- governing body schedule of events (e.g. if it is a golf event, ensure that your state and national endorsing golf bodies list your event on their calendar)
- newspaper 'what's on' sites (some radio and television stations have this type of listing on their sites, too!)

➤ your sponsors' websites

➤ sites specific to your target market (e.g. gamers, football fans, retirees).

Search engines

The fact that 'google' is now officially a verb should tell you how important search engine positioning is. Again, we're not experts, but have some suggestions.

➤ Submit your site—go to the websites for at least five or six of the biggest search engines (Google, Yahoo!, AOL etc.) and follow the directions to submit your website. This will go a long way toward ensuring that it will list your website when people search for the keywords you specify.

➤ Up your positioning—if you get your event listed *and* include a link to your home page, on a number of complementary websites, you are far more likely to come up higher in a search engine result list.

➤ Familiarise yourself with metatags—these are 'tags' built into the programming on your website that search engines see and use to determine what your site is about. Your visitors will not see the metatags. Do a brainstorm and then cull, so you use specific keywords. There are also lots of free search engine optimisation tools online that will help you pick keywords. Whatever you pick, get your website developer to put them into your metatags.

➤ Consider search engine advertising—products like Google's AdWords allow you to pay for advertising alongside searches for keywords you specify. If you specify 'cancer research', then whenever someone searches for that topic, your ad will come up. You can target specific geographic regions and only run the ad during certain time frames or times of day. It works on a pay-per-click basis and is a science unto itself, but gets easier pretty quickly.

If all of this is starting to sound like gobbledygook, don't despair. Every half-decent website in cyberspace has gone through the same thing. There are plenty of good books available, including 'For Dummies' books on both Google and search engine optimisation, and lots of online tutorials. That's how we did it!

Emails

Email marketing can be very powerful, or it can be perceived as very annoying. It is, basically, database marketing, but the immediacy and personal contact has its own benefits.

If you want to get into email marketing and have absolutely no experience, you will probably want to find yourself an expert to develop the strategy and help you build your list. Whether you are currently doing email marketing or not, we do have a few suggestions:

➤ Give away information—a great way to get people to welcome contact from you is to ensure you are giving them useful information, such as how-tos, checklists, articles and white papers, and more. An excellent format for this strategy is an e-newsletter.

➤ Focus on the customer—when you are trying to market something (sell tickets, increase donations, etc.), talk about the specific benefit to the customer. Email is personal. Keep the message personal, as well.

➤ Don't broadcast—be absolutely sure your email list falls into one of the following two categories:

  • Best: People who have asked and/or given permission for you to contact them.

  • Okay: People who are interested and active in the specific area in which you operate. Do not ever send to a generic list just because you *think* they should all care about your cause. You will burn bridges!

➤ Segment your list—categorise the people on your list based on various factors, so you don't send every communication to every person. If you've got a community event in Texas, they don't need to hear about it in Connecticut. If you are selling tickets to a $1000-a-plate dinner, your $15 one-off donors probably don't want to know about it.

➤ Respect your customers—do not ever, ever loan, sell or rent your list. Also, if someone doesn't want to hear from you by email, be sure they are removed permanently from the list and apologise for any inconvenience.

The Holy Grail of marketing is something called 'going viral', and it happens most often via email. This is when what you send, or what somebody else sends, about your event gains a life of its own. People love the idea or the concept or the joke or whatever and send it to everyone they know. It spreads 'virally'. There is a great book about viral marketing called, *Unleashing the Ideavirus*, by Seth Godin.

Podcasting

Whether this pertains to your event or not depends entirely on the scope of your event. But if you've got content that people want to see or hear, this is a very interesting marketing medium that is only set to grow.

The gist of it is that you can create content, put it on the iTunes site, other MP3 sites or your own site, and people can download it and listen or watch on their MP3

> Use technology to extend the event experience for your audience and your sponsors.

player. This is not just limited to music—if you can record it in audio or video format, it can be downloaded into an MP3 player.

Below are just a few examples of content that might be compelling. Many of these could be done in serial form.

- business advice from a professional association
- training program from a marathon organiser
- concert footage from a concert promoter or band
- infant first aid basics from a children's hospital
- how to fix a flat tyre from a racing team.

You can charge for the content—possibly using it as a fundraiser—or let it out there for free. The key is to make it compelling and credible.

Mobile phone content

In recent years, mobile phones have morphed into something that only slightly resembles the first mobiles we all had, and this is only set to continue. Now, making a phone call is just a small portion of what that little machine can do, and depending on what content you've got, you might have something that people want.

From wallpaper to ringtones to games to videos, they can all be downloaded into a phone. You could also use phones as a promotional tool, creating text-to-win competitions, forums for people to post short videos (from their phones) about or at your event, and much more. Use your imagination. This can be a powerful tool for the right event.

Publicity

Publicity includes editorial media coverage in newspaper and magazine articles, and television and radio coverage. It is also known as public relations. Public relations will probably be very important to your event. That said, publicity is the only facet of a marketing plan that is out of your control—you can't make the newspaper write what you want them to write—so be sure that PR isn't your only marketing strategy. There are also … some key strategies that you can follow that will help you gain better results from your activities.

- Be sure that your public relations program is handled by a reputable public relations professional, preferably a member of your national public relations institute. Hiring an independent public relations professional is probably a lot less expensive than you think. Do not dismiss spending this money until you have analysed the value against the cost.

> If you are handling public relations internally, do ensure that whoever handles it is an active member of the public relations community.

> Whether internal or external, be sure your publicist understands what is expected, the resources available to him or her, and how success will be judged. A **Publicity Brief Template** can be found below.

> Understand that not all media are equal. One spread in a national magazine could be worth dozens of smaller placements.

> Understand that, in order to get coverage, an event has to be newsworthy. Spend some time developing a variety of interesting angles. This will not only increase your potential for coverage, but it will also allow you to go to the same media outlets again and again with different stories.

> Do not discount the value of smaller, more targeted media outlets. They may be more receptive to your story and the readers may be more avid.

Whether your publicity is handled internally or externally, be sure to brief them fully in writing.

Publicity brief template

 Market3.doc

This is the type of document you should use when briefing a publicist (internal or external). It can also be very useful as a tender document for competitive pitching. The specifics shown here, such as media emphasis, are only to be taken as an example. This document will need to be customised to meet your needs.

Desired result

1   Strong media relations campaign supporting the launch of [*your event*].
    (a) Coverage across all media, with emphases in the following areas:
        (i)   general interest
        (ii) family interest
        (iii) children/teenagers.
    (b) Close contact with targeted media to ensure the best possible coverage and story angles.
2   Increased awareness of [*your sponsors'*] sponsorship of [*your event*].
3   100 000 attendees at [*your event*].
4   Hospitality opportunity for key customers and selected staff.

Guidelines

1 Your responsibilities for the media launch are:

   (a) Creating, mounting and tracking a top-quality publicity campaign across all media.

   (b) Working with [*your event*] to create an effective media kit.

   (c) All creative and administrative aspects of the media launch to the following rough guidelines:

   Timing: to be determined

   Location: to be determined

   Theme: to be determined

   Featuring: celebrities, demonstrations, etc.

   (d) Development of a guest list and invitations (in conjunction with the above). Invitees will include:

   (i)   the media

   (ii) celebrities

   (iii) sponsors

   (iv) representatives of [*your event*]

   (v)   Parliamentary Minister of X

   (vi) sponsor's costumed character.

   (e) Coordinating photographic opportunities, interviews and other special requests as they pertain to publicity.

   (f) Full and accurate accounting of expenses and fees.

2 Timetable

   (a) Preliminary publicity plan to [*your event*] by [*date*].

   (b) [*Your event*] to open lines of communication between publicist and sponsors/ celebrities when publicity plan is approved.

   (c) Publicist to enact publicity plan and begin campaign (to magazines, television and other alternative media that need longer lead times) by [*date*].

   (d) The launch is planned for [*date*]. Time of day to be determined but suggest late morning.

3 Communications

   (a) We will expect weekly updates on publicity progress, including a list of placements, confirmation that placements have been clipped and compiled, and responses to invitations.

   (b) We will include publicist on all pertinent communications.

   (c) Specific requests for information, both ways, should be put in writing.

[*Your event*] resources

1 Information available:

    (a) background information on the *X*-year history of the event

    (b) examples of media coverage in past years

    (c) biographies of celebrities

    (d) overall marketing plan

    (e) implementation timeline

    (f) budget.

2 Information to be confirmed:

    (a) celebrities available for launch

    (b) sponsors/staff to be invited.

3 Materials currently available:

    (a) creative look developed by [*designer or advertising agency*]

    (b) completed advertisements

    (c) bromides of event and sponsor logos

    (d) photographs of celebrities and VIP guests

    (e) biographical sheets for all celebrities

    (f) a range of banners and flags

    (g) T-shirts and caps.

4 Materials in development:

    (a) creative piece for media launch invitation

    (b) sponsor utilisation of sponsorship (main media support).

5 The team

    Although there are many other people involved in this event, the team includes the key contacts.

    (a) Jane Chen, Marketing Manager for [*your event*]. Overall responsibility for the project. Phone (852) 2555 5555, fax (852) 2555 5551.

    (b) Larry Lunar, Marketing Coordinator of [*your event*]. Providing assistance in the planning, coordination and implementation of the sponsorship and supporting marketing activities. Phone (852) 2555 5554, fax (852) 2555 5551.

6 Celebrities available

    List celebrities, athletes or other well-known participants.

7 Budget

    There will be an absolute ceiling of $*X* for all costs associated with this publicity campaign, which cannot be overrun.

8   Evaluation to be based on:

(a) weight of the campaign and balance of media gained

(b) impact and innovative style of media launch

(c) management process and communication.

Source

[*Your name*]

[*Your event*]

[*Full address*]

[*Phone, fax, email*]

Database marketing

You probably have more access to databases than you realise.

One of the best ways to communicate large amounts of information to a specific target market is to embark upon a campaign of database marketing.

Databases come in all shapes and sizes and you probably have access to several. Below we have listed several sources, in order of their probable receptiveness to your marketing message:

1   members

2   season ticket holders

3   previous attendees or ticket purchasers

4   people who have signed up for your mailing list

5   databases provided by industry organisations (e.g. your local arts governing body)

6   databases that you rent from outside sources (demographically and geographically targeted).

Once you have settled on the database(s) to be used for your communications, you will need to determine how you will reach this group. Keep in mind that different types of databases represent different groups that may be receptive to varying methods of communication. You have many options for communication, including:

➤ email announcements and e-newsletters (ensure your list is highly targeted, ideally opt-in and run in an ethical manner)

➤ newsletters or other publications

➤ putting information in regular mailings

➤ special mailings (specific to this event)

➤ telemarketing

➤ promotional material in member gathering places (clubhouse, etc.).

In addition to informing them about your event or organisation, you may also want to include some type of enticement for them to attend. Some suggestions include:

➤ priority seating

➤ early ticketing

➤ special pricing or offers

➤ merchandise discounts

➤ invitations to special events.

Signage

Signage includes signs that are made specifically for an event, such as banners, A-frames and scoreboards. Pre-event and event signage can be a strong communication vehicle. Think broadly about your options, which could include:

➤ venue signage (facing a roadway or public area)

➤ signage on your office building (if it is in a good location)

➤ street banners or flags around your town

➤ electronic billboards (many cities and towns have electronic reader-boards that show upcoming events)

➤ signage at convention and visitor bureau kiosks

➤ perimeter signage

➤ airport signage

➤ vehicle signage.

Any surface that can be painted, bannered or hung from can support signage.

Part 2

sales

The sales process

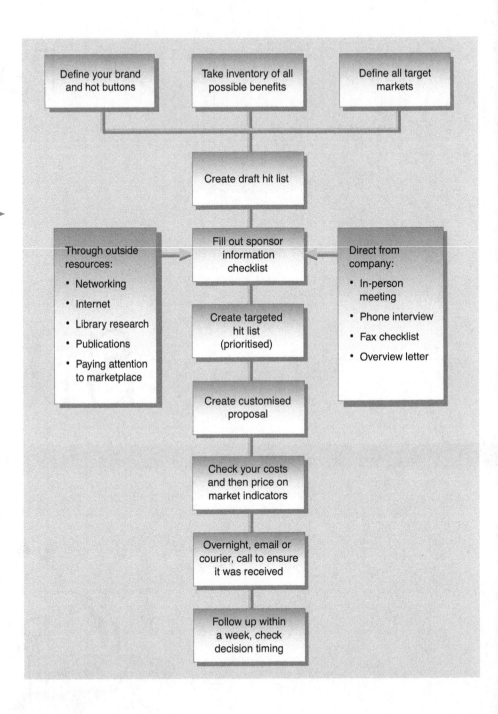

Chapter 4

Understand what you have to offer

When most sponsorship seekers, particularly non-sporting organisations, are asked to define what they have to offer, they either start listing all of the places where they can place a sponsor's logo or they talk at great length about all of the good corporate citizenship a company will foster by supporting them. Either way, it's the wrong answer.

In general terms, a sponsor wants three things from a sponsee:

1   To use the sponsee's brand attributes and hot buttons to underpin or introduce those attributes within the sponsor's own brand. (Note: this is about reinforcing authentic sponsor attributes, not making them look like something they're not.)

2   To access one or more of the target markets of a sponsee and to connect with these people in a meaningful way.

3   To gain a range of tangible benefits from the sponsee, ensuring that the impact of the previous two points is maximised and providing mechanisms and tools to achieve specific marketing objectives.

If you want to maximise your chances of creating a strong match with a sponsor, it is imperative that you understand fully what you offer in each of these areas. The more precisely you can define these benefits, the better.

Define your brand and hot buttons

The good news is that, if you've created a brand bullseye to better market your organisation or event to your potential audience, you've already defined your brand and hot buttons. This time, though, we are going to look at the bullseye as a *sponsorship* tool.

If you haven't created a brand bullseye yet, now is the time to do it. The information it will provide will assist you to:

➤ identify potential sponsors

➤ create a compelling and creative offer

➤ provide the sponsor with ideas and insights that will help them get the most from the sponsorship.

Define your audience

You have already defined your target markets when you developed your marketing plan. Now, you need to re-look at your target markets from the sponsor's perspective.

Your marketing objective is to get people to your event. This is quite different from the sponsor's marketing objective, which is to effectively connect with as many target markets as possible. Thus, when defining your target markets in terms of what you can offer a sponsor, you need to look at the audience in terms of the people who will be receiving your (and, subsequently, your sponsor's) marketing message.

When you look at target audiences in terms of what you have to offer a sponsor, be absolutely certain that you don't fixate on the people who actually come to your event. No matter how many people attend, or how well suited they are to your potential sponsor, they still reflect only a fraction of the sponsor's target marketplace.

Through your marketing efforts, you will reach a lot of people who will not attend your event for one reason or another but who are still receptive to the marketing message. These people could include people who see or hear:

➤ pre-event advertising

➤ pre-event promotions (direct marketing, Internet sites, sponsor promotions, etc.)

➤ pre-event publicity

➤ street, venue or event signage

➤ media or online coverage of the event

➤ word of mouth recommendations

➤ post-event wrap-up coverage.

Take inventory

In order to understand the full range of tangible benefits your organisation has to offer, you need to prepare an inventory of your assets. Make a list of every promotional and marketing opportunity that could possibly be of value to a potential sponsor. List

> Define your audience in terms of everyone who will receive your marketing message, not just the people who will attend.

everything, even if you wouldn't sell it. This helps you to think expansively and you can sort them out later.

During this process, you need to look at your organisation as a sponsor would. You will no doubt be astounded at the wide range of benefits that you have to offer that you have never thought of before. This should allow you to showcase the value of your organisation to a much broader range of sponsors.

Once you have prepared this list, do not make the mistake of offering your entire inventory to sponsors (we have seen this done before). Instead, think of your inventory as your kitchen. It is a list of everything you have in your kitchen that could be used to make a meal—the food, the spices, the utensils, appliances and even the electricity in the wall. Imagine what a mess you would get in if you tried to make a meal using everything in your kitchen. That's the same kind of mess you will get in if you try to create an offer using every item on your inventory. What you need is a recipe and we'll provide you with one.

A **Generic Inventory** can be found below to get you started. Just keep adding to and subtracting from it, as well as finetuning specific benefits, until it reflects what your organisation has to offer. Remember, this is a living document—update it regularly.

Do not delete items from the inventory just because it might be unlikely that you'd offer those benefits. We recommend using the 'million dollar rule': if you would at least consider providing that benefit (or figuring out how you could provide it) if the perfect sponsor offered you a million dollars, then leave it on the list. You still may never offer it (but you never know!), but keeping the list big, creative, and even a little outlandish, will spark even more creative new ideas into the future than if you made the list very conservative. Sponsors love creativity, so you need to work at keeping an open mind.

> Never offer a sponsor everything on your inventory.

> When creating your inventory, use the 'million dollar rule'.

Generic inventory

 Sales1.doc

What follows is a generic inventory. This is a starting point for you to prepare an inventory of your own property. The point of this exercise is to ensure you catalogue everything that you control which could be of value to a potential sponsor. You will probably not use all or even most of these items but it creates a menu from which to develop customised proposals for your potential sponsors.

The types of benefits that are most valuable to smart sponsors who take a best-practice approach to connecting with their target markets—the blue-chip benefits that create win–win–win sponsorships—are marked with an asterisk (*). This is not to say that the other benefits should be ignored or minimised, but that you should endeavour to include at least some blue-chip benefits in every proposal.

Sponsorship types

- Naming rights sponsorship (perceived 'ownership' of the event)
- Presenting sponsorship
- Naming rights or presenting sponsorship of a section, area, entry or team
- Naming rights or presenting sponsorship of a day, weekend or week at the event
- Naming rights or presenting sponsorship of an event-driven award, trophy or scholarship
- Naming rights or presenting sponsorship of a related or subordinated event
- Major sponsorship
- Supporting sponsorship
- Official product status
- Preferred supplier status

Exclusivity

- Category exclusivity among sponsors at or below a given level
- Category exclusivity among sponsors at any level
- Category exclusivity in event-driven advertising or promotional media
- Category exclusivity as a supplier or seller at the event

Licence and endorsements

- Use of sponsee logo(s), images and/or trademark(s) for the sponsor's promotion, advertising or other marketing activities
- Merchandising rights (the right to create co-branded merchandise to sell)
- Product endorsement (your organisation endorsing the sponsor's product)

Contracts

- Discounts for multi-year contracts
- First right of refusal for renewal at conclusion of contract
- Last right of refusal for renewal at conclusion of contract (not recommended)
- Performance incentives

Venue

➤ Input into venue, route and/or timing
➤ Use of sponsor venue for launch, main event or supporting event

On-site activities

➤ Creating a promotion that showcases the sponsor product (e.g. if you have a 3G mobile with Company X, you can send in a text with the word 'Robbie' and get an exclusive 30-second video interview with Robbie Williams sent to you as soon as he goes off stage)*
➤ Sampling opportunities*
➤ Demonstration/display opportunities
➤ Opportunity to sell product on site (exclusive or non exclusive)
➤ Coupon, information or premium (gift) distribution
➤ Merchandising (sponsor selling dual-branded products)

Signage

➤ Venue signage (full, partial or non-broadcast view)
➤ Inclusion in on-site event signage (exclusive or non-exclusive)
➤ Inclusion on pre-event street banners, flags etc.
➤ Press conference signage
➤ Vehicle signage
➤ Event participant uniforms/pinnies/number tags
➤ Event staff shirts/caps/uniforms

Case studies: On-site sales

Don't limit yourself to food and drinks. Many other types of companies are using sponsorship to sell or demonstrate their products on-site.

• Pharmacia uses on site tents to promote arthritis drug, Celebrex, at PGA Seniors Tour events.

• Federal Express sets up shop at every CART motor race so that the teams and officials have a handy and fast way to send and receive critical packages.

• An increasing number of companies are using events to attract new employees through information distribution and setting up recruiting booths.

Hospitality

➣ Access to or creation of what-money-can't-buy experiences*

➣ Development of customised hospitality events to suit the interests and priorities of the target market (e.g., hot laps in a NASCAR for adrenaline junkies or a barbecue and a chance to 'meet the drivers' on practice day for family-oriented customers with younger kids)*

➣ Tickets to the event (luxury boxes, preferred seating, reserved seating or general admission)

➣ VIP tickets/passes (backstage, sideline, pit passes, press box etc.)

➣ Celebrity/participant meet and greets

➣ Event related travel arrangements, administration and chaperone (consumer prizes, VIP or trade incentives)

Information technology

➣ Provision of exclusive, meaningful content for sponsor Internet site (e.g. advice, celebrity blog, behind the scenes info or images, etc)*

➣ Provision of web 'events' for sponsor Internet site (e.g. chat with a star, webcast, webinar)*

➣ Licence to produce event-oriented electronic media for promotion or sale (e.g. DVD, CD, screensaver, game, ringtone, voicemail, video message)*

➣ 'Signage' on event Internet site

➣ Promotion or contest on event Internet site

➣ Links to sponsor Internet site from event Internet site

➣ Naming rights (perceived 'ownership') to event Internet site

➣ 'Signage' or promotion on event electronic media (e.g. CD, DVD, screensavers, games)

Loyalty marketing

This section is about providing benefits that the sponsor can pass on to its target markets in order to reinforce their relationships.

➣ Access to event, parking or merchandise discounts for a specific customer group (e.g. frequent flyers, Gold Card holders)*

➣ Access to event, parking or merchandise discounts or other perks for any customers (usually by showing proof of purchase)*

➣ Exclusive access to an event, area, contest/prize, service, celebrity or experience for all or a specific group of consumers*

➤ Early access to tickets (before they go on sale to the general public)*

➤ Block of tickets, parking etc. that the sponsor can provide to loyal consumers. These can be provided with or without naming rights to that section (e.g. the Acme Energy Best Seats in the House or MaxiBank Express Lane event entry)*

Case studies: Loyalty marketing

Think about benefits you can offer that would make the event even better for the sponsor's customers.

• In Sydney, there is a summer-long outdoor movie series where people sit on the ground to watch new releases and classics. Attendees just have to turn on their mobile phones to show they are with Vodafone and they get a cushion to sit on. At another Australian out-door movie festival, customers of St George Bank get exclusive access to the best viewing area in the park.

• Also in Sydney, if you drive a Lexus, you get free valet parking at the Sydney Opera House.

• The Arkansas State Fair provided Southwestern Bell with the opportunity to distribute lost kid tags for children to wear while they are at the fair. Parents can write their mobile phone number on the tags so that fair staff can immediately contact them if their child is found.

Database marketing

➤ Unlimited access to event generated database(s) (e.g. member lists) for direct marketing follow-up—be careful not to breach privacy laws

➤ Opportunity to provide inserts in event-oriented mailings

➤ Rental or loan of event database for one-off communication

➤ Opportunity to run database-generating drawing or contest on site

➤ Opportunity to run database-generating drawing or contest on site as a requirement for attendee admission

Employees/shareholders

• Participation in the event by employees or shareholders*

• Access to discounts, merchandise or other sponsorship-oriented perks*

• 'Ownership' of part of the event by employees (e.g. creating an employee-built and -run water station as part of a marathon sponsorship)*

• Provision of a celebrity or spokesperson for meet and greets or employee motivation*

• Creation of an event, day or program specifically for employees*

• Creation of an employee donation or volunteer program*

• Opportunity to set up an employee recruitment station

• Distribution of employee recruitment information

Public relations

➤ Inclusion in all press releases and other media activities

➤ Inclusion in sponsor-related and media activities

➤ Assistance with developing a PR campaign that is aimed at the sponsor's particular target market (consumer or B2B)

Ancillary or supporting events

➤ Tickets or invitations to ancillary parties, receptions, shows, launches etc.

➤ Signage, sampling and other benefits at ancillary parties, receptions, shows, launches etc.

Other promotional opportunities

➤ Custom design of a new event, program, award or other activity that meets the sponsors' *and their target markets'* specific needs and interests*

➤ Proofs of purchase for discount admission*

➤ Proofs of purchase for discount or free parking*

➤ Custom design and administration of media promotions

➤ Custom design and administration of sales promotions (consumer and trade)

➤ Assisting sponsor with trade sell-in

➤ Design, production and distribution of POS

➤ Design of on-pack promotion, liaison with factory (packaging and distribution)

➤ Securing and administration of entertainment, celebrity appearances etc.

➤ Provision by sponsor of spokesperson/people, celebrity appearances, costumed character etc.

➤ Proofs of purchase for premium item (on site)

➤ Online, phone or SMS proof redemption

➤ Opportunity to provide prizes for media or event promotions

➤ Couponing/advertising on ticket backs

➤ Discount admission coupons for customers (distributed in pack or POP)

Case study: Creating something new

The Wildlife Conservation Society partnered with Jaguar Cars to create the Save the Jaguar program and its website, www.savethejaguar. com. This has provided Jaguar with additional appeal to a younger demographic while providing real benefit to the WCS through donations linked to merchandise sales. Jaguar hosts WCS expert lectures in both dealerships and zoos. Jaguar also makes a $5 donation for each prospect that completes and returns a buyer survey, resulting in a much higher than average response rate.

Media profile

➤ Inclusion in all print, outdoor and/or broadcast advertising (logo or name)

➤ Inclusion on event promotional pieces (posters, fliers, brochures, buttons, apparel, etc.—logo or name)

➤ Ad time during televised event

➤ Event-driven promotional radio or television schedule

➤ Event-driven outdoor (billboards, vehicle, public transport)

➤ Sponsor/retailer share media (themed display ads, 30/30 or 15/15 broadcast)

➤ Ad space in event program, catalogue etc.

Research

➤ Access to pre- and/or post-event research (quantitative or qualitative, attendees or target market)

➤ Opportunity to provide sponsorship- or industry-oriented questions on event research

Pass-through rights

➤ Right for sponsor to on-sell sponsorship benefits to another organisation (this is always pending sponsee approval)

➤ Right for retailer sponsor to on-sell sponsorship benefits to vendors in specific product categories

---

Case studies: Pass-through rights

Mastercard passed on benefits of their World Cup Soccer sponsorship to banks around the world, with dozens of them developing major promotions and creating World Cup affinity cards.

The timing of the ASA motor race, the Tecumseh 300, coincides with the annual International Lawn, Garden and Power Equipment Expo, the largest trade show of its kind in the US. Tecumseh, a major manufacturer of engines for lawn machinery, use the race for a key customer hospitality program with a twist. They have also negotiated pass-through rights, allowing twenty of their customers to sponsor a top 20 race car for $1500. For their small investment, they get branding on the car and an appearance by the driver at their show stand. Many spend more to upgrade their branding and get extra tickets and commentator mentions.

As part of their major stage sponsorship, Milwaukee's Summerfest provided supermarket chain Piggly Wiggly with the opportunity to create an on-site supermarket and bring in a partner, Kraft Foods. Kraft provided staffing and on-site giveaways, and shared the cost and benefits of both the sponsorship and leverage program.

Contra

➤ Opportunity to provide equipment, services, technology, expertise or personnel useful to the success of the event in trade for part of sponsorship fee

➤ Opportunity to provide media value, in-store/in-house promotion in trade for part of sponsorship fee

➤ Opportunity to provide media at sponsor-contracted discounted rates in trade for part of sponsorship fee

Production

➤ Design and/or production of key sponsor events (hospitality, awards etc.)

➤ Hiring and/or administration of temporary or contract personnel, services and vendors for above

➤ Logistical assistance, including technical or creative expertise

Cause tie-in

➤ Opportunity to involve sponsor's preferred charitable organisation or cause

➤ Donation of a percentage of ticket or product sales to charity*

Media production

This is generally only an issue if the event is run by a media company.

➤ Production of event-driven broadcast or print advertising

➤ Production of event-driven video for promotion, training or documentation

Expertise

➤ Opportunity to provide expertise that will improve the sponsor's performance, products or image (e.g. an environmental organisation providing advice on conservation)

➤ Provision or assistance in the development of a training program related to the sponsee's expertise

Vesting

Please note that providing a sponsor with an equity stake is not very common. If you do it, be sure to get qualified legal advice.

➤ A portion of overall net profits

➤ A portion of gross revenue

➤ A portion of proceeds from a part of the event (ticket sales, concessions, parking, exhibitors etc.)

Case studies: Creative sponsorship benefits

- As part of Honda's sponsorship of the alternative rock group Blink-182's concert tour, the band designed a one-of-a-kind car for the winner of a consumer promotion.
- At some of the many equestrian events they sponsor, Mercedes bring a fleet of their four-wheel drives so that attendees can test drive them on an off-road obstacle course.
- Several outdoor events in skin cancer-prone Australia now give sponsors the opportunity to provide attendees with UV-sensitive plastic bracelets. When the bracelet turns colour, it is time to cover up or get out of the sun.
- The Montreaux Jazz Festival provided Oldsmobile with access to artists for a special edition CD, which they gave away to people who provided contact details and demographic information.
- Heavy metal festival Ozzfest provided retail sponsor Hot Topic with Ozzy Osbourne's throne as the top prize in their event-driven promotion.
- The du Maurier Downtown Jazz Festival in Toronto provided Canadian coffee chain Second Cup with the opportunity to create an on-site café and host post-show autograph sessions with major artists.
- The European Snowboarding Tour provided Swatch with the opportunity to create and sell a watch featuring a chip that gives wearers free admission to 31 European ski resorts.
- Orange UK sponsors several youth-oriented music festivals across the country with a key part of the deals being that they can create an Orange Station where revellers can recharge their mobile phones. Through these sponsorships, Orange also gains access to musicians who record messages for fans to be played exclusively on Orange's information hotline.

Chapter 5

Creating a hit list

Once you understand your target markets and what you have to offer, you should start developing a preliminary hit list of potential sponsors. In fact, you will often start thinking of companies when you go through the previous exercises.

When creating a list of potential sponsors, be sure to pay attention to *specific brands, products* or *services*, not just the overall corporation. We cannot emphasise this enough. There are three reasons for this.

1 Very few companies have only one product or brand and, where there are multiple brands, they are often very different from each other. Their differing attributes and target markets will fit with varying types of sponsorships.

2 Corporate sponsorship departments are usually the first place that sponsees go with their proposals and hence they are inundated with requests. Going directly to a well-matched brand area can minimise the competition you will face for both attention and money. Plus, many sponsorship departments do not have the authority to make major sponsorship decisions. More and more, that authority is falling to the brand team anyway.

3 The brand areas will almost always have their own marketing budgets and those budgets are often reasonably flexible. These areas are most closely accountable for the performance of their brands, rather than where the money is spent, and are often willing to put marketing funds that are not specifically committed to something else into sponsorship if they believe they will get a positive result.

> When looking at potential sponsors, look at specific brands products or services, not just the corporation.

Sponsor matching

A good hit list will be based upon matching your event or property with a sponsor. There are three ways of doing this:

➤ by target markets
➤ by objectives
➤ by attributes/values.

The power is where two or more of these matches intersect.

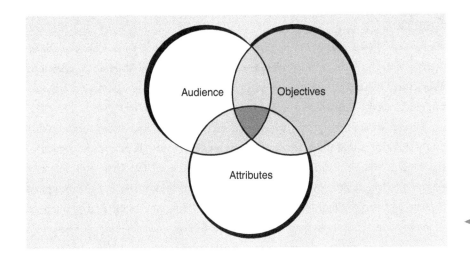

Figure 5.1 The best sponsorships are matched three ways

Audience matching

The starting point for sponsor matching is ensuring that your event or product targets one or more of the sponsor's core audiences. The more of your target markets that match the sponsor's target markets, the more potential there is for a strong sponsorship. If you don't match any of the potential sponsor's target markets, then it does not matter how well you match objectives or attributes, you are wasting your time.

There are several types of sponsor audiences that you could match:

➤ current customers

➤ potential customers that fit one of the sponsor's current customer profiles

➤ newly targeted potential customer groups

➤ intermediary customers (retailers, trade, distribution)

➤ internal customers (sponsor employees and/or shareholders).

There is one common pitfall surrounding newly targeted customer groups. Often, sponsorship seekers will realise that their event does not target any of a company's different markets. Instead, they try to make a case that they can deliver new markets. Although this approach is very proactive, it rarely works.

When a company targets a new group of customers, the initiative is usually developed through market research and accompanied by a comprehensive marketing campaign. If the company has not already identified your marketplace as having a potential for them, it is unlikely that they will be receptive to your approach, particularly within your time frame. In addition, one sponsorship on its own is unlikely to deliver the critical mass of people needed to make the new marketplace desirable for the potential sponsor.

Exercise

We have developed an easy way to develop your hit list based on target market matching. Starting with the 'one person' descriptions from your **Target Market Assessment Worksheet** (Chapter 2), for each of your segments, write down any brands or categories of product/service that would feature reasonably prominently in their lives.

Aim for a big list—at least a couple of dozen brands for each target market. What you will notice is that the better and more complete your one-person description is, the easier it will be to find potential sponsors for your hit list. There will definitely be some red herrings on your hit list, but don't be deterred. This is a brainstorming exercise and you will find some genuine prospects. Plus, you will be finding out a lot of information about these potential sponsors before approaching them. If they aren't right for your organisation or the event, it will be obvious long before you commit yourself to anything.

Objective matching

This type of matching does not always happen but it can be a very powerful tool for gaining sponsorship if it does. Objective matching happens when you and your sponsor share actual objectives, such as 'promoting good health and nutrition to primary school students', or when your objectives are mutually complementary.

Attribute matching

Strong attribute matching is one of the hallmarks of great sponsorship. It creates relevance between the sponsor and your event, which carries through, creating relevance and interest in the sponsorship to your target markets.

Look at the brand bullseye that you prepared in Chapter 2. Just as there are different levels to your organisation's personality, there are also different levels in how you can match with a potential sponsor.

➤ Your 'soul', in the centre circle, is the core of what you are about. Matching one or more of these with a sponsor is absolutely essential in order to create an authentic match that a sponsor can use to underpin their own brand.

➤ Attributes, found in the 'perceptions' and 'hot buttons' part of your bullseye, are the areas where you can define yourself to best match a potential sponsor. This is where you can be somewhat of a chameleon, creating a strong and relevant appeal to a wide range of potential sponsors.

When identifying potential attribute matches, remember that there are two different ways of matching:

1 **Attribute equals attribute.** For example, a women's contemporary art exhibition has the attributes of being smart, strong, sexy and original. This may be a good match with Calvin Klein fragrances, which market itself in the same way.

2 **Sponsor attribute solves sponsee attribute.** For example, being a member of a rally driving team has to be one of the world's dirtiest occupations. This may be a good match for a laundry soap, car wash, personal care products or Black and Decker's Dustbuster.

Promoting a strong attribute match can be a big selling point. When used in an interesting or humorous way, attribute matching can lead to new approaches to creative advertising and is a great way for a company to cut through the clutter of a heavily sponsored event.

Keep in mind that who you don't target can be just as important as who you do. Be sure you take into account the impact on your organisation's image and target market before you approach any potential sponsor.

Example: The bank and the show

An established overseas ice show is touring New Zealand for the first time. It has a substantial media budget to promote ticket sales but its experience elsewhere has been that, the more different ways it can speak to its target market of families with children aged 2–10, the better result it gets.

A major New Zealand bank with branches throughout the country is facing increased competition from new entrants into the home loan market. It is particularly feeling the pinch with younger, first-time home buyers who are being attracted by the lower interest rates offered by the new competition. It is also losing current customers, who are switching away to the competition's lower rates. The bank has countered this by creating a range of innovative home finance products. It is looking for ways to entice current and new customers to look into the new products and understand how they work, as well as to add value to its relationship with existing customers.

The show and the bank were able to achieve objectives for each other in a number of ways:

- The bank created displays in every branch across New Zealand, including monitors playing a promotional video of the show for people waiting in line. This ran for a month prior to and through the tour.
- The bank promoted the show on all ATM screens for the same time period.
- The bank included fliers for the show in customer statements, offering priority ticketing as an added value for all customers.
- The bank promoted to current and potential customers that they would get one free child's ticket for every adult ticket purchased if they filled in a questionnaire and ran a computer model of how their home loan would work using the new home loan product. This could take place either in the branch or on the Internet.
- The show provided a list of all ticket buyers to the bank after the tour. The bank knows that families with young children are prime candidates for home loans and used this list for database marketing.

Case study: The International Chili Society and Procter and Gamble

The International Chili Society holds cook-offs around the world, culminating annually in the World's Championship Chili Cook-off, an enormous festival of hot food enjoyed by tens of thousands of people.

One of our all-time favourite sponsorships featured a company that was not a huge sponsor of this event but the attribute-driven shock value provided an impact that far outstripped many of the other, larger sponsors.

Just imagine some of the attributes of chili. Delicious as it may be, there are some rather specific traits that can be often be attributed to eating the stuff, some of them problematic—heartburn and indigestion.

So, who was that sponsor that everyone remembered? Procter and Gamble's Pepto Bismol Antacid.

A case in point is the National Education Association in the United States. The NEA decided against accepting sponsorship from Hyundai, as most of the teachers who make up the membership are unionised and Hyundai is not. The NEA realised that taking sponsorship from a non-unionised manufacturer would undermine its credibility with its membership and could spark a major backlash.

Get referrals

If you have happy sponsors, ask them for referrals.

A lot of corporate sponsors know each other and you should use that to your advantage. If you've got happy sponsors, ask them for referrals to other potential sponsors. Just use the direct approach, and ask if they know of any other sponsors that would be a good match for your organisation. Some sponsors won't be a lot of help, but others will be a wealth of information, not only about who may be interested, but what their hot buttons are and how best to approach them.

If you have any doubts as to the satisfaction level of a sponsor, don't ask them for a referral. You will only make yourself look silly. Take some time to improve your relationship and their results before you ask.

Research your potential sponsors

If you ask a sponsor, any sponsor, what they want from a sponsorship proposal, they will invariably say one thing: 'We want a proposal that is tailored to our needs'. The big question is how do you know what they need?

Now that you know how you can match with a potential sponsor, you need to get the information that will allow you to assess their suitability—do you match?—as well as allowing you to create an offer that meets their needs.

Your *job* as a sponsee is to assist your sponsor in meeting their needs. In order to do that, you should know your potential sponsor's:

- long-term marketing objectives (over twelve months)
- short-term marketing objectives
- product or brand attributes
- target markets
- needs—absolute requirements
- wants—these are things that would be nice
- exclusions—many companies, for instance, will not sponsor individuals, and some will not be involved if an alcohol company is a prime sponsor, so you need to know these things
- special emphases—basically everything else, such as new product launches, new services being offered, a new logo, their competitive situation.

In Chapter 4, when we discussed creating an inventory of your assets, we compared the inventory to a kitchen. Well, the research you gather about your potential sponsor is your recipe.

A **Sponsor Information Checklist** can be found on page 98 and this will help you to compile and organise this information. Completing this checklist will provide you with a strong understanding of what a potential sponsor requires from a sponsorship investment. It should be completed in full prior to developing your offer.

As you complete the checklist for each of the companies on your preliminary hit list, you will notice that a number of potential sponsors will emerge as being very strongly matched with your event, some less so, and many companies will be excluded altogether. This process will save you a lot of time, as you will then only approach the most likely sponsors. It will also demonstrate to potential sponsors that your primary aim in sponsorship is to understand what they need to achieve and to help them achieve it.

The ways of obtaining the information for the **Sponsor Information Checklist** are listed in the table overleaf.

Outlined below are these sources in the order in which they should be utilised or approached.

> Do not develop your offer until you have completed the Sponsor Information Checklist for your potential sponsor.

From the sponsor	From other sources
Sponsorship guidelines	Networking
Website	Internet
In-person meetings	Library (ABI/Inform Full-Text Online – see Appendix 2 for details)
Telephone interview	Publications
Annual report	Publications and websites (marketing and business resources, as well as resources aimed at their industry, such as the Australian Banker's Association website)
	Paying attention to the marketplace

Other sources

Before you even bother picking up the telephone to call a company, you need to research them thoroughly through other sources. If you have a list of prospects, a couple of afternoons spent on the Internet and at the library can provide you with a lot of information.

Use this information to fill out, as completely as possible, the **Sponsor Information Checklist** for each of your potential sponsors.

A range of research, news and networking resources is included in Appendix 2.

Annual report

If your potential sponsor is a publicly listed company, its annual report must be made available to anyone who asks. The usefulness of information in annual reports varies but can include some or all of the following:

> an understanding of the corporate culture, mission and vision
> a list of all products and brand lines
> the overall financial performance of the company (and often specific product categories)
> annual expenditure on sponsorship
> a list of all (or sometimes only major) sponsorships
> new company initiatives
> income and expenditure trends.

You should review the annual reports of any potential sponsors prior to creating an offer but do remember that this is only a starting place. You need to know much more specific information to create an effective proposal.

Request annual reports from the public affairs area, not marketing.

Annual reports are usually available for download from company websites. This is not only convenient but can be a great resource when you are researching a multinational company with an overseas head office, as it allows you to get not only a national but also a global understanding of their culture, direction and priorities.

Sponsorship guidelines

The fastest, cleanest and usually most complete way to get the required information from a sponsor is to request a copy of their **Sponsorship Guidelines**. This is (usually) a short document that outlines all of their needs, exclusions, target markets and the process by which they make investment decisions.

This can be a fantastic resource for you but beware of preprinted, glossy brochures. Sponsors' needs change all the time and they can sometimes be out of date. We advise sponsors to update them regularly and make them widely available, such as through their website. This method may be less slick but the information is often more reliable.

Although **Sponsorship Guidelines** are gaining popularity with sponsors, not all companies have them. If you come across one that does not, you can make yourself look great and add value to your relationship by providing our version of this valuable tool to them. Clearly, the **Sponsorship Guidelines** that we have provided on page 102 are just an example that the sponsor will need to customise to reflect their unique needs and positioning.

In-person meetings

No matter how much information you find about a company from other sources, it is always ideal to meet with a potential sponsor prior to developing a proposal. There are several reasons for this:

➤ you will gain a lot more insight from a conversation than from even the best proposal guidelines

➤ you will develop a personal relationship with the brand or sponsorship manager

➤ your enthusiasm and belief in the project will often be infectious

➤ it is more difficult for someone to brush you off if you are sitting there in person.

Be sure to do your homework before your in-person meeting. You should endeavour to fill out as much as possible of your **Sponsor Information Checklist** before making contact. This will allow you to demonstrate your professionalism and commitment to understanding their needs. You can also use what you know about the company and its sponsorship program to find out what has and has not

Use the Internet to research overseas corporate headquarters of your potential sponsors.

Do your homework
on the company
before the
meeting.

worked for them in the past, how sponsorships were utilised and other pertinent pieces of information. For specific meeting techniques, see the **Sales Checklist** on page 124.

Telephone interview

If you cannot have a meeting in person with the potential sponsor, a telephone interview is definitely the next best thing. Again, it is absolutely imperative to do your homework prior to picking up the telephone or you could do more harm than good.

Do make an appointment for the interview, just as if you were there in person, and stick to your allotted time.

Case study: PBS and Georgia Pacific

The Public Broadcasting Service's recent hit history television show *Frontier House* took three American families out of their comfortable 2002 lives and placed them in Montana circa 1880. The three families lived for five months in frontier Montana with only the tools and technology of the 1880s and a few weeks of basic provisions.

One of the series' sponsors was paper manufacturer Georgia Pacific. PBS disallows all commercial advertising and thanks sponsors in a short non-commercial acknowledgment screened prior to the program. The acknowledgment featured one of the young participants running to the authentic outhouse. Shot in the manner of the series, it provided documentary-style shots of the inside of the outhouse and included a frame of rags on hooks where we might expect to see a roll of toilet tissue. The voice-over spoke of Georgia Pacific, manufacturer of a range of paper products including Dixie cups, Bounty paper towels and toilet tissue, and their support for the program series.

Although PBS doesn't allow commercial messages, the way the spot was put together allowed Georgia Pacific to hit home with a clear message about the comfort and convenience of their products.

Sponsor information checklist

 Sales2.doc

The idea of the Sponsor Information Checklist is to provide you with a format so that you can obtain as much information about your target sponsor as you possibly can, by giving you all of the clues you need to make your best shot at gaining their sponsorship. Do not worry if you cannot get all of the information but do try to get most of it before creating your offer.

If you speak to your potential sponsor, be reasonable about the amount of information you request and the time you need to gather this information. Know the basics and ask the questions below that are in italics first. Also, get the correct address, name and title from the receptionist or secretary, not your target contact.

Sponsor: ....

Address ....

Phone ....

Website ....

Contact name ....

Contact phone ....

Contact email ....

PA name ....

First step, review the potential sponsor's website.   ❏ Done

Key brand/product attributes:

1 ....

2 ....

3 ....

4 ....

5 ....

Objectives:

1 ....

2 ....

3 ....

4 ....

5 ....

Relevant product lines and target markets:

Product	Target markets

Have they recently or are they planning to add to or extend their brand lines, change their logo, re-launch a product, merge with another company or enter into a new or distinctive marketing campaign? Please describe.

....
....
....
....
....
....
....
....

Key direct competitors in their category.

1 ....

2 ....

3 ....

4 ....

5 ....

Key indirect competitors (other categories that may compete with their category).

1 ....

2 ....

3 ....

4 ....

5 ....

How do they utilise their sponsorships?

....
....
....

Has this company ever sponsored a similar property? Can you get any information on how that
went? (Speak to the other sponsee if you feel it is appropriate.)

....
....
....
....
....

Is there any national or overseas precedent for a relationship such as this? Have you got a copy of any supporting magazine or newspaper articles?

....

....

Do they have any exclusions in the area of sponsorship?

....

....

How long should approval take and what is the approval procedure for sponsorships?

....

....

....

Date: ....

Information gathered by:...

Sponsorship guidelines

 Sales3.doc

Hawk Brewing receives dozens of proposals every year, many of which we reject because they do not adequately meet our needs. We have developed this document to make our requirements clear to potential sponsorship seekers and to encourage the presentation of proposals that meet those needs.

General

➤ We will consider proposals in all categories except [*insert exclusions here*].

➤ We require sponsorship and sales (if applicable) exclusivity in the category of beer and pre-mixed alcoholic beverages.

➤ We generally need a minimum of six months lead time to effectively plan and implement our leverage activities.

➤ Logo and/or name exposure is considered a bonus but is not the primary goal of sponsorship.

➤ We prefer to invest in sponsorships that carry out audience research during and/or after the event, including questions relating to our industry, and provide results to Hawk Brewing.

➤ We expect that our sponsorship partners will invest a minimum of 10% of the total value of the sponsorship to proactively add value to the sponsorship.

[*Sponsor*] brand positioning

Here is a short overview to assist you in understanding our brand positioning. Our goal is to partner with organisations and events that are a strong, natural match to at least some aspects of our brand positioning.

➤ 'Not everyone can be a Hawk' (tag line)

➤ premium beers (including brands for true beer connoisseurs)

➤ smart, witty, irreverent

➤ cool, sexy

➤ an American status product

➤ 'Drink Responsibly' message

As we expand overseas, our goal is to become known as an American status brand that retains its desirability independent of any prevailing or cultural attitudes toward America (think 'Levis').

Target markets by product

Beer	Target
Hawk Beer	Males, 18–30, highly social, into music and sports, consider themselves to be 'cool'
Light Hawk (low alcohol)	Primary—designated drivers, responsible, socially oriented, consider drinking a premium light beer to be a good compromise Secondary—women 18–34, single, active, tomboyish, highly social, out and about, somewhat fashion conscious
Raven Ale	Males 25+, upscale, status and quality oriented, highly brand aware, want to be seen with the coolest brands
Raven Special	Upscale bars, pubs and restaurants, available east coast only
Mad Vulture	Males and females, 18–24, single, music and fashion oriented (pop culture), party/rave oriented, not generally alternative types. Introducing new flavour in October 2008

Sponsorships must provide *at least* six of the following

These should be tied to both your overall objectives and key attributes/values, and should number 10–15.

➤ A natural link with our brand positioning (see above)

➤ Provision of exclusive and meaningful content for our Internet site

➤ On site sales

➤ Exclusive event, access, or area for members of Hawk's Hawkeye Club (1.2 million members worldwide, 84% in North America)

➤ Opportunities to host pre- or post-event parties, concerts or other over-21 social activities

➤ Celebrity appearances at key pubs and clubs (or 'virtual' appearances in video webchats or webcasts)

➤ Other event-related benefits that we can pass along to a large proportion of our customer base (both consumers and trade). Feel free to use your imagination

➤ Access to premium event-driven content so we can develop premium online content and in-pack CDs, DVDs, or CD-ROM games

➤ Ticket discounts, premium tickets, or access to an exclusive ticket line for customers with proof-of-purchase

➤ Ability for Hawk Brewing staff to participate in a meaningful way

To be considered, proposals *must* include

➤ Key details of the opportunity

➤ Overview of your marketing plan—including what is and is not confirmed

➤ List of sponsors who have committed to date

➤ Comprehensive list of benefits, including how they relate to us and our products

➤ Creative ideas as to how we can use this sponsorship and those benefits to connect with our target markets

➤ Timeline, including important deadlines

➤ Credentials of your company and key subcontractors (publicist, event producer etc.)

Process for consideration

➤ All proposals are reviewed by the Sponsorship Manager to assess suitability, feasibility and resources required (human and monetary)

➤ Recommended proposals are presented to [*insert title*] for approval

➤ Sponsee is notified of the disposition of the proposal within X weeks

Submit proposal to:

[*insert full contact details*]

Chapter 6

Proposals

We'll now go back to our kitchen analogy. You have an inventory of all of your ingredients, the **Sponsor Information Checklist** has provided you with a recipe, so now it's time to start cooking!

What to include in a proposal

In order to give the sponsor enough information to make a decision, a proposal must contain the following points.

Overview

Paint the picture, tantalise the sponsor with both what your organisation is about and how you can benefit them.

Event/property details

This is really an event FAQ, listing dates, times, locations, projected attendance, ticket costs, membership numbers, etc.—all the hard data. The information provided here could vary widely depending on the type of property. The idea is that you don't want your potential sponsor getting three-quarters of the way through the proposal and not knowing when the event happens, where or other key pieces of information.

Target markets

If a sponsor is going to consider your event, one of the first things they need to know is who you are targeting. Showcase your target market segments, using both psychographic and demographic information. Ideally, you will be able to support this section with comprehensive market research information, but even if you don't have that (yet!), try to be as complete as you can be. You may want to consider including your 'one person' target market descriptions (from Chapter 2—Marketing plan). If they have helped you to understand your market segments, they may also help a potential sponsor.

Do not ever use phrases such as 'lovers of art', 'museum goers' or 'general audience'. These types of phrases are too general and indicate to sponsors that you know nothing about your audience.

You can address your target markets as a separate part of the proposal or you can incorporate them in your marketing plan overview, outlined below.

Marketing plan

This is an overview of the marketing plan you have already created. It outlines exactly how you will be marketing yourself to your target markets, the value, reach and audience of all marketing components, which media you are using and your publicity plan.

Creative ideas for leverage

This is where you get to strut your stuff and demonstrate your understanding of your potential sponsor's needs. Tell them how they can use this sponsorship to solve their problems. Tell them how they can use this sponsorship to achieve their goals. Throw out the rulebook and get creative. Use great resources, like ABI/Inform (see Appendix 2) for fantastic ideas and precedents from around the world. You know the potential is there—flesh it out for them! There is nothing that will help sponsor say 'yes' to a strong sponsorship opportunity more than that.

There are some people who will say this is dangerous; that sponsors will steal your creative ideas and do them with someone else. Yes, that is a possibility, but it doesn't really happen that often. Use confidentiality wording (see below) and include the ideas. In many cases, creative ideas for leverage will be the difference between 'yes' and 'no'.

Comprehensive list of benefits

This is where you list the benefits that you will provide as part of this offer. These should be taken from your inventory and reflect a comprehensive package, but should never include everything in your inventory. Tailoring the list is absolutely essential.

Use bullet points and, depending upon how long the list is, you may want to categorise the benefits as they are categorised on your inventory.

Investment

This should reflect the total investment, including:

> cash

> contra or in-kind investment

> promotional support that directly benefits your organisation.

You should also include payment due dates and any performance incentives in this section.

Bonuses

Your case for investment will be a lot stronger if you can provide the potential sponsor with a precedent as to exactly how this has worked for other companies like them and/or a precedent as to exactly how your other sponsors have achieved a commercial return (in other words, used their sponsorship to change the perceptions and behaviours of their target markets). If you have this information, put it in a section before the 'Comprehensive list of benefits'.

How long should it be?

As a rough guideline, in order to get all of the information into the proposal that the sponsor will need, you are looking at a minimum of four to five pages. If you have a lot of promotional concepts, research, precedents or a very comprehensive marketing plan, you could go up to about twelve pages. Any more than that and you risk losing your reader.

More important than size, however, is that it is easy and fast to read. This will be more a testament to your ability to format the proposal nicely and use concise wording than the actual amount of information included.

The teaser

You may want to create a two- to three-page proposal summary of the property, target audience, key marketing and promotional strategies, and key benefits. We have found it very effective to use the summary to tease out prospective sponsors, which can greatly assist you, particularly if time is of the essence. Do be prepared to customise this summary wherever and whenever possible and ensure you include contact details and deadlines for decisions.

Using the sponsorship proposal template

We have included a **Sponsorship Proposal Template** on page 118 for you to use as a guideline. Clearly, you will need to adapt this to your own property and style but this should give you a good place to start. For best results, you may want to consider the following suggestions:

➤ You must include all of the information in the template in order for a sponsor to be able to make a decision.

➤ We prefer a proposal that positions each of the proposal headings onto its own page or at least separates them clearly, keeping it easy and straightforward to read.

➤ Do not use an executive summary—your contact will tend to read that and not get to the meat of the proposal. Instead, use your cover letter to tell the contact very briefly what it is about and how it relates to them (see the **Proposal Cover Letter** on page 132).

➤ If you already have other sponsors committed, highlight this in your cover letter.

➤ If at all possible, include existing audience research.

➤ A major selling point for sponsors is that research will be done during the course of the sponsorship and provided to the sponsor, including at least a couple of questions provided by the sponsor. The perceived value of this to the sponsor is much higher than it may cost you. (See Chapter 5 for low-cost research strategies.)

➤ Create a proposal with an eye for detail and presentation. The more professional it looks, the more credible you are. Use the magic that technology offers to its fullest potential—insert photos, maps, artwork or whatever is appropriate into your proposal document and print it in colour. Keep it professional and don't go overboard, but do use technology to help you build the atmosphere and personality of your event within the proposal document.

➤ Include such items as brochures and calendars of events for review by the sponsor but do not make the sponsor search for pertinent information in these documents. If it is important (such as key dates or locations), it must be included in the proposal itself, ideally in the event details section.

➤ In this day and age, many proposals are submitted in PDF form via email or an online submission mechanism. There is no reason you can't include supporting artwork or other documents—either as an attachment or to dress up the proposal itself (they can click on small artwork to see it bigger). If you are submitting it in hard copy, either comb bind your proposal or neatly staple it and enclose it in a presentation folder.

➤ Do not send a DVD or CD-ROM with your proposal. It wastes money and sponsors almost never look at them. If you are invited to make a presentation, you may want to show a video and then offer to leave a copy at that time if they want it for further review. Our insider tip: most won't.

Confidentiality

Unfortunately, we have all heard of cases where a sponsee went to a company with a great idea for an event but was turned down, only to see their idea implemented directly by the company a few months or a year later. This is not the norm but it does make sense to protect your ideas.

If the proposal includes any of your creative ideas, it should include a legal statement that all concepts included are your property. A sample can be found below. This should be placed *before* the body of your proposal, such as at the bottom of your title page.

> © *Copyright* [organisation name] *2008. This publication is copyright and remains the intellectual property of* [organisation]. *No part of it may be reproduced by any means without the prior written permission of* [organisation].

Depending upon the confidentiality of it, you may also want to include this wording:

> *The information contained in this proposal is confidential and no part of it may be copied and/or disclosed to any person without the express permission of* [organisation].

Pricing

While developing your sponsorship proposal, you also need to address pricing. This is no doubt the most vexing area of creating a proposal and, unfortunately, we cannot offer any hard and fast rules. We can, however, offer a few strategies that should help.

First and foremost, the total fee must be less expensive than if the sponsor were to run the event on their own. The overall package must represent value for money.

No matter what, never tell the potential sponsor how you are going to spend the money! This undermines your value and indicates your need rather than your worth. It also undermines the perception that you are a professional, viable organisation whether they participate or not. It is not unusual for a sponsor to request a breakdown of marketing and promotional expenditure.

It used to be that you could use equivalent advertising costs as a benchmark, but the sophistication of most sponsors has grown to such a point that they identify that sponsorship is a unique marketing medium, offering a degree of relevence and connection with people that precludes any direct comparison of costs. Unfortunately, that just makes pricing more difficult. There are no hard and fast rules, but we do have some guidelines that should help you get there.

> Never tell the potential sponsor how you are going to spend the money.

Remember, your baseline fee is *only* a baseline, not your final price.

Calculating your baseline fee

When calculating your price, you must firstly understand that a significant chunk of the sponsorship fee will go towards providing the promised benefits, as well as paying for the sale, servicing and administration of the sponsorship. The difference between those costs and the fee is your profit—the amount that you will actually be able to put towards increasing your revenue base.

> Cost of providing benefits offered
> + Staff and administration costs
> + Sales costs
> + Servicing costs
> ———————————————
> = Your total cost

Once you have calculated the total cost of providing the sponsorship, you need to add in your profit. Your profit is the money you get to use as income to underwrite an event or program, or simply to add to your bottom line. As a rough guideline, your baseline fee will be two to three times your total cost, for a profit of 100–200%.

> Total cost to deliver the program
> + 100–200% profit (revenue for your event)
> ———————————————
> = Your baseline fee

Once you know your baseline fee, you need to stack it up against market indicators. These indicators could show that you are in the right ballpark or, more likely, they could show that you are significantly under- or overpriced. If your baseline fee is overpriced against the market, you will have to readdress the benefits package and/or how it is delivered to ensure that it provides adequate income for your event. There is no use going to all the trouble to sell and service a sponsorship if it's not providing you with any benefit, or worse, if it costs you more to provide the sponsorship than you charge for the package.

No sponsorship should be valued solely on what you need.

Determining market price

Once you have determined your baseline fee, you need to adjust it to reflect the marketplace in which you operate. Ask yourself the following questions.

➤ What is the cost of similar sponsorship products on the market? Corporate sponsorship managers talk to each other and know the price of similar sponsorship packages. You need to have that same understanding.

➤ How does your product stand up? If similar events are offering the standard 'tickets and logo exposure' package and you are offering a creative and multi-faceted marketing opportunity, then you can promote your product as having a much higher value.

➤ How does your sponsorship servicing measure up? If you are constantly willing to go the extra mile to make a sponsorship work, then you will be consistently adding value to the package.

➤ Are there any other variables that might affect your price? What if your team wins the national championships? What if you lose your star player?

➤ How much is your potential sponsor likely to invest? Precedent is not always a reliable indicator but if you know a sponsor has never invested more than $20 000 in a sponsorship program and you are approaching them with a package valued at more than $100 000, you need to understand that you will probably encounter some resistance. You will need to build a strong case for that level of investment, as well as possibly being prepared to negotiate for a lower level of benefits.

No sponsorship proposal should be valued solely on what you need to make the project work.

The above questions should get you pretty close to the market value of your event. In order to double check yourself, you should do the following:

➤ Pay attention to the marketplace—read sponsorship publications, join a sponsorship or marketing association, extend your network.

➤ Use your network—we know people who won't send out a proposal without running it past three trusted colleagues first.

Equivalent opportunity cost

When calculating your price you also need to understand what you are competing against in terms of media—the 'equivalent opportunity cost' as media buyers put it. This is particularly the case if you are approaching a brand manager, as they will likely have to reallocate money from some other media to your sponsorship if they commit.

If you are seeking money for a sponsorship, you need to understand how a sponsor *could* spend this money. You need to understand that you are not only competing with other sponsorship seekers but you are also competing with the main media, endorsements and sales promotions.

Questions you need to ask to determine how else a sponsor could be spending their money include:

➤ How many television commercials could they buy in peak viewing with that investment?

➤ How many black and white pages in metropolitan daily newspapers?

➤ How many colour pages in mainstream or targeted magazines?

➤ How many weeks of 30-second spots, at a rate of thirty per week, on metropolitan radio?

➤ How many billboards?

You should be able to get these costs from your advertising agency or media placement company. If you don't have either of these, you will need to secure price lists (which can often be found online) from key media throughout your marketplace and make an educated estimate.

If your event or program is national in scope, get national figures. If it is limited to one city or region, then get figures specific to that region. And remember to use figures that are representative of the discounts given to large advertisers, not casual rates, which will be much higher.

In addition to giving you an understanding of your competitive position, knowing what a sponsor could get for their investment can really help you during the sales process, particularly if your event or program offers strong benefits over time.

Imagine being able to make a case for your highly targeted, strongly matched two-month event, offering a whole range of benefits to meet the sponsor's objectives versus them placing five advertisements during *60 Minutes*. Used judiciously, this can be a very powerful argument but you must be absolutely confident in the value of your offer.

Proposal issues

There are a number of issues that come up over and over again around the creation and presentation of sponsorship proposals. We have addressed some of the most common ones here.

Should we offer different sponsorship levels?

A lot of sponsorship seekers offer levels to their potential sponsors—gold, silver and bronze levels are very popular (and overused to the point of being a cliché). The main problem with this approach is that, without realising it, most sponsees formulate the packages so that all of the levels get access to the best benefits, with the main difference being that the lower levels get less of the supporting benefits.

Clearly, this is not an approach that is conducive to creating strong, high-level sponsorships. It undermines the true value of the relationship, creating instead a bargain hunter's paradise.

At the same time, everyone likes choice, including sponsors. So the trick is working out how to offer sponsors a choice without undermining your value and potential revenue. We have identified two good ways around this: 'The apple and orange approach' and 'The up-selling approach'.

The apple and orange approach

This approach revolves around the strategy of offering two packages that are completely different from each other, each emphasising a differing set of sponsor objectives. You don't want the potential sponsor to be able to compare them on a benefit-for-benefit basis, so you create an apple and an orange. Ideally, the packages should be priced similarly, but even if they aren't, this strategy can work very well.

This is very different from the above 'levels' strategy of offering three different-sized apples. If all the potential sponsor wants is an apple, they will almost certainly take the smallest, cheapest one.

The following is a very generalised example of two packages that a basketball team could offer to a potential confectionery sponsor—same sponsee, same sponsor but very different outcomes.

Offer 1: emphasis on VIP hospitality

➤ Naming rights to team mascot
➤ Use of private box (seating 12) for eight featured games
➤ Autographed team merchandise for all sponsor guests
➤ Post-game player meet-and-greets in the box for each game (one or two players, as available), as well as team mascot
➤ Inclusion of VIPs' children in half-time activities (as appropriate)
➤ Thirty pairs of premium tickets to other games
➤ VIP tickets and travel for six to an all-star game

Offer 2: emphasis on new product launch

➤ Naming rights to team mascot
➤ Naming rights to a feature game
➤ Media launch for new product at the game
➤ Attendance at launch by coach and mascot
➤ Half-time on-court product launch stunt and audience contest
➤ Exit sampling of new product for all attendees of launch game
➤ Use of hospitality room for VIP guests at featured game (seating 50)

➤ Consumer raffle boxes located around venue

➤ Twenty-four pairs of reserved seat tickets to future games for use in consumer raffles

The up-selling approach

Another strategy that we favour is offering one highly tailored package, with an optional upgrade available at extra cost. Our experience is that, in a high percentage of cases, once the potential sponsor is sold on the concept of a partnership with a sponsee, they look at the upgrade as an opportunity to maximise the sponsorship and take it up.

Do remember to go through the pricing exercise for both the offer and the upgrade to ensure that you are covering all of your costs.

Below, we have provided an example of the offer and upgrade prepared by the same basketball team to the same confectionery company potential sponsor.

Sponsorship offer

➤ Naming rights to team mascot

➤ Naming rights to a feature game

➤ Media launch for new product at the game

➤ Attendance at launch by coach and mascot

➤ Half-time on-court product launch stunt and audience contest

➤ Exit sampling of new product for all attendees of launch game

➤ Use of hospitality room for VIP guests at featured game (seating 50)

➤ Post-game player meet-and-greet in the hospitality room (one or two players, as available), as well as team mascot

➤ Consumer raffle boxes located around venue

➤ Twenty-four pairs of reserved seat tickets to future games for use in consumer raffles

Optional VIP hospitality upgrade

➤ Use of private box (seating 12) for six additional featured games

➤ Inclusion of VIPs' children in half-time activities (as appropriate)

➤ VIP tickets and travel for six to an all-star game

How do we define category exclusivity?

The only rule of exclusivity is: the more exclusivity is granted, the more valuable it is.

There are three types of exclusivity:

➤ sponsorship

➤ signage (in cases where the venue may have existing, conflicting signage)

➤ sales

Most exclusivity is granted on the basis of categories and is often referred to in proposals and contracts as 'category exclusivity'. This usually refers to the category of business that a company is in, e.g. airline, carbonated soft drink, ice cream, beer. You can make this exclusivity more valuable and attractive to your sponsor by extending across competitive categories.

An example of this would be to grant Pepsi sponsorship and sales exclusivity across categories such as carbonated soft drinks (their true category), non-carbonated soft drinks, sports drinks, fruit juices, fruit and iced-tea based drinks, flavoured milk and water.

When preparing an offer, you need to balance the degree of exclusivity you offer the sponsor with the financial impact on your organisation. If you granted Pepsi the exclusivity outlined above, you will surely get more money from them for the sponsorship, but it also cuts out a lot of other potential sponsors and the revenue they could bring in.

On the other hand, if you are having a hard time selling a category, you could consider breaking it into smaller, more affordable chunks. For instance, you could divide the IT category into hardware, software, ISP and peripheral categories. The Atlanta Olympics famously broke up the automotive category after being unsuccessful in selling it to one manufacturer, and sold separate sponsorships in categories including 'official pick-up truck' and 'official luxury car'. This can be effective, but it can also be confusing, so you will need to work closely with sponsors in similar categories to ensure that they either work together (as IT sponsors often do) or stay well out of each other's way.

Do we need a glossy sales brochure or video?

Unfortunately, when it comes to selling sponsorship, a lot of sponsees rely on flash over substance. They produce glossy sales brochures outlining the sponsorship packages (often laid out in levels). While these brochures are often beautifully prepared, they lack what sponsors want most—customisation.

Rather than going to the effort and expense of creating slick sales materials, put that effort into researching your potential sponsors and creating highly customised proposals. Every one of the sponsors we have polled has supported this contention. Your proposal should be neat and professional—do put it on letterhead and bind it. That is all the sponsor expects from the presentation.

Do not rely on flash to sell a proposal.

What is useful to sponsors is providing examples of all of your event promotional materials from previous years, if you have them. If not, you could include one or two mock-ups of the planned materials for the current event. This will showcase the style and degree of professionalism that your organisation has, as well as add colour to the presentation.

Do you need a video? In a word, no. Sponsors never watch them—most sponsorship managers have a shelf full of videos they have never seen. And if you bring one along with you to your meeting, you can be virtually assured that something will go wrong with the audiovisual. A well-planned and enthusiastic verbal presentation will give you a lot more mileage.

Photographs and diagrams are a different story. If your event is extremely visual, such as an art exhibition, photographs are a must. If your event is an expo of some type, a map or other diagram will give the sponsor an opportunity to understand your vision and their place in it.

Should we go to one company at a time or can we go to several?

In a perfect world, you would only go to one company in any given product category at a time. But, as you have already gathered from reading this book, creating relationships takes time. You are highly unlikely to have enough lead time before your event to research, approach and negotiate your sponsorships using this approach.

In reality, it is perfectly alright to have several offers out at one time. If you have done your background research, this should not exceed 10 or 12 companies and the offers will most likely be very different from each other, reflecting the different needs of the various companies.

How much lead time does a potential sponsor need?

Most sponsors set their larger sponsorship expenditures as part of their marketing budget, 12 to 18 months before the events. They will often have an additional amount of money set aside for opportunistic spending if something else comes up. This amount is usually, but not always, fairly limited and will not accommodate major sponsorships. Only if something really extraordinary comes along will they breach this plan.

In addition, companies need time to maximise sponsorships. Usually, the more product lines, customer types, distribution channels and so on that they have, the longer it will take them to make the most of their sponsorships. This should be as important to you as it is to them because a happy sponsor is a good sponsor.

It is imperative that you ask the question about lead times when doing your background research on potential sponsors. Only then will you know for sure what their policy is. As a very rough guideline, we have found the following time frames to be common across a lot of companies.

18–24 months

➤ Major sponsorships (often national and/or televised)
➤ Multinational sponsorships
➤ Multi-year events

12–18 months

Most sponsorships come under this time frame.

6–12 months

If you go below 12 months, you may still have some success at creating major sponsorship relationships. Most likely, however, you will start having to undercut the value of the sponsorship because the sponsor won't have time to maximise the program fully. You will also start running into budget problems and may have to get creative with pricing and payments.

If you are looking for a smaller investment (under $100 000 or so), you can often have success without undercutting your value right down to six months.

If you have missed the budgeting time frame, you will probably be accessing a limited pool of opportunistic funds. You can sometimes increase your chances by going directly to the product marketing areas, as they often have opportunistic funds that are not specific to sponsorship and can make decisions with a somewhat shorter lead time if they can be directly tied to product objectives.

Under 6 months

These investments are reserved for surprise or unanticipated events.

Unanticipated events are events such as a major sporting team winning the championship. Around that one unanticipated event, a wide range of other sponsorable events could crop up. These are the only type of events that we recommend sponsors should consider with less than six months' lead time.

If you are trying to sell sponsorship for a planned event with less than six months' lead time, you are extremely unlikely to be successful. Not only do you hit obstacles such as the sponsor not having enough time to maximise the sponsorship or

the budget already being set, but it also smacks of desperation and could undermine your credibility as a strong and highly sponsorable organisation for years.

When is the best time to approach sponsors?

The best time to approach a potential sponsor is before they have set the marketing budget for the year in which your event or organisation is seeking sponsorship. It is as simple as that. Again, you need to ask the question of the potential sponsor when you are doing your preliminary research—well before providing them with a proposal.

There is one timing long shot that you can try, however. If you have a smaller sponsorship on offer, you may want to approach a potential sponsor within six to eight weeks of the end of the financial year. If they have any unspent funds in their sponsorship budget for that year, you may be able to access them. Extra funds are usually as a result of the above-mentioned opportunistic budget not being fully utilised over the course of the year.

Sponsorship proposal template

 Sales4.doc

Australiana Airways
and
The Sydney International
Fishing Expo

Date

Use your own judgment when doing the title page, but do show the sponsor name and your name together using the word 'and' or 'presents' or, if you are selling the naming rights, show the name of the event as it would be if they took up the sponsorship was taken up.

Always date your proposal and always put it on a professional lettterhead.

2

'The worst day fishing
is better than the best day
working'

Anonymous

Use this page to set the stage. We like using a relevant quote—funny, inspirational or something that just says it all. Your challenge is to really get to the core of what your event is about—the beauty of flowers, the spirit of competition, the dignity of the underprivileged. There are lots of good quote sites on the Internet.

If your event is very visual, an image of something relatively simple—one flower, a pair of dancers—can be very powerful, on its own or with a quote.

Give a good overview of what this event is about and how being involved will benefit the sponsor. At this point in the proposal, your appeal is basically emotional. You want your target to be able to visualise the event and how its involvement will look and feel.

Use emotional wording—a lot of strong adjectives (use a thesaurus).

As a general rule, two-thirds of this page should be devoted to visualising the event, and the remainder to visualising the sponsorship.

3

Overview

In November 2008, the Darling Harbour Convention Centre will throw open its doors and welcome 85,000 enthusiastic fishermen and women to the Sydney International Fishing Expo.

They will be treated to more than 100 demonstrations and activities for all types and levels of experience. They will enjoy more than 450 exhibitors from Australia and overseas and will have the opportunity to try out their gear on the largest indoor trout lake in the world. And as high consumers of fishing tourism, they will flock to our brand new Fishing Adventures area and can even book their trips on site.

Approximately 40% of Australian men fish at least once a year, with a quarter of them fishing at least once a month. These men love their sport and they make sure that they are equipped for it to be as successful and enjoyable as possible. On average, these fishermen and women spend more than $150 each at the Expo.

Where does Australiana fit in? Based upon our visitor survey last year, more than 65% of fishermen fly to a fishing destination at least once every two years, with the average size of their group being 4–6. This is broken down very evenly between overseas and rural Australian destinations, allowing Australiana to showcase not only major international destinations, but your extensive regional network as well.

As a major sponsor of the Sydney International Fishing Expo and naming rights sponsor to our new travel area, Australiana Fishing Adventures, complete with exclusive on-site booking facilities, Australiana will enjoy a major profile with this lucrative market. You will also have the platform to create meaningful promotions, cementing your relationship with these consumers, tourist boards, adventure travel specialists and travel agents.

4

Event details

Dates and times:	Friday, 21 November 2008, 1:00–10:00 p.m. Saturday, 22 November, 10:00 a.m.–6:00 p.m. Sunday, 23 November, 10:00 a.m.–6:00 p.m.
Location:	Darling Harbour Convention Centre, Sydney
Attendees:	We are targeting 85,000 attendees over the three-day show. This is a projected 7% increase on 2002. Attendance has increased by an average of 5–10% over each of the past five years. A full list of target market segments can be found on the following page.
Cost:	$22 adults, $15 for children under 12, $50 for a family of four. This is consistent with charges for similar shows and is a $1 increase on the adult fee from 2007.
History:	The Sydney International Fishing Expo has been going for 17 years and has never grown by less than 4% in attendance in any year.
Parking and transportation:	There are 5000 parking spots at the Convention Centre ramp. In addition, we have arranged for a free shuttle bus service from the Casino parking ramp. The Convention Centre is accessible by bus and light rail, as well as by ferry from Circular Quay.

This is where you list the hard information about the event. Be straightforward and completely unemotional. This will not only answer a lot of questions your target sponsor may have, but is also your opportunity to show how organised you are.

If the sponsor's primary target market is your secondary or tertiary target market, be sure to emphasise the marketplace(s) that are most relevant to them.

5

Target markets

Based upon audience research (attached), our media and promotional campaign is aimed directly at the following demographic and psychographic groups.

1. Fishing enthusiasts—people from all walks of life who fish more than 20 times per year. Tend to be boat owners and trade their boats in every 5–7 years. Based on audience research, these people make up 23% of our audience, and accounted for 47% of all product sales in 2007.
2. Fishing adventurers—upscale males, 28–45, who generally take one major fishing trip per year, generally travelling in groups of 4–6. Low consumers of fishing products, high consumers of fishing tourism. These people make up 19% of our audience, and average $4500 per year expenditure on fishing tourism.
3. Social fishermen—occasional to regular fishermen, tend to fish in groups of family or friends, see fishing as a quality time activity for families, and in particular, to bond with their children or grandchildren. View the Fishing Expo in the same manner—as an opportunity to spend time with the kids. Heavily into participation aspects of the Expo, particularly ones that are kid-friendly. Particularly high consumers of 'starter' equipment for kids and grandkids, as well as small upgrades for their older boats or other equipment. Make up approximately 40% of the audience.
4. Flashy fishermen—a small, but big spending market. Tend to be successful business owners and/or people who have recently had a windfall. Want a boat and want the best of everything. In addition to spending up on equipment, they love expensive, high adventure trips—anything where they get a big story to tell!

As with the previous five years, we will be embarking upon comprehensive market research again in 2008. We are happy to include up to four travel-related questions on Australiana's behalf and will provide Australiana with the full results of the research.

Write one paragraph outlining your television advertising and promotion, as well as any sponsorship deals you have with a television station that might increase the value of your media further. Be sure to note what is and is not confirmed. Do not mislead your sponsors. Take the same approach for each media vehicle.

Marketing plan

Based upon target market research, we have created a media plan that will generate interest in and awareness of the Expo, while specifically targeting our key markets.

Main media

Our total budget for paid and promotional media is $150,000, and with that we have been able to negotiate $450,000 in media value. A full media schedule and an audience profile are attached in the Appendix.

Television

Our comprehensive television campaign focuses on two main areas—people who are into fishing and people who are into fishing (or other adventure) travel—with separate promotions and advertisements targeting each of them.

- Two four-week media promotions, run in conjunction with Channel 8 programs 'Lon Davies' Fishing World' and 'Great Vacations'. 'Fishing World' reaches 100,000 avid fishermen and women in the greater Sydney area every week. 'Great Vacations', Channel 8's new vacation program, reaches 350,000 people, mainly active travellers, each week.
- Paid media schedule on Channel 8, supported by tactical advertising on Channels 7 and 10. These schedules will run for four weeks prior to and through the Sydney International Fishing Expo. Placement will determine which of the two ads will run at any given time.

Radio

We have negotiated a three-week drive-time promotional schedule on 2UW running prior to and through the Expo. The schedule is anchored by a major fishing vacation promotion. This station matches our core audience profiles almost exactly.

This schedule will be augmented by two-week limited schedules on NNN and 2SS, reinforcing the messages on the other two stations most listened to by our audience and ensuring that we get the most complete coverage of our key markets in the lead-up to the Expo.

Newspaper

The Sydney International Fishing Expo is sponsored by the *Sydney Mirror*. As part of that partnership, we have negotiated a series of five advertisements per week, including 1/6th page ads in the Friday What's On section and page-dominant ads in the Saturday Travel section.

Magazines

We are embarking upon a limited magazine campaign, with placements in *Travel and Leisure* and *Fish Lover*'s magazines.

Other event promotion

In addition to paid and promotional media, we will embark upon a comprehensive publicity and non-media promotional campaign.

Publicity

We have engaged the services of one of the country's top publicists, [*insert publicist or company name*], who has/have designed a campaign targeting both general and niche media. This campaign will kick off with a fishing-themed media launch (complete with rods) on a boat in the Harbour on 13 October and will continue through the Expo.

We will be providing media access to top experts and celebrities, including Lon Davies and the cast of 'Great Vacations' for interviews, photos and expert commentary.

As this is the first year for the Australiana Fishing Adventures area, we will be concentrating a large portion of our publicity effort on the promotion of this part of the Expo. Australiana will benefit greatly from the promotion of travel destinations and packages, a key part of this strategy. We are also very happy to assist Australiana in developing a publicity plan that targets your specific consumer and intermediary markets.

Website and e-marketing

We have a year-round website—www.fishexsydney.co.au—generating 1,480,000 hits annually, with 37% of those hits in the month prior to the Expo. The website includes a wide variety of information about the show, its sponsors and exhibitors, and is featured on all appropriate media promotion and publicity.

After huge success in 2007 with creating a little bit of how-to content and comedy on the website in the lead-up to the Expo, we are pulling out all the stops and will be creating content including:

- How-to articles x 3 by Lon Davies
- Humorous how-to articles x 3 by sports comic, Steve Sando (example: 'How to get a girly-girl to go fishing')
- Recommended plan of attack for finding what you're after at the Expo
- Best fishing joke contest
- Prizes for worst fishing photo and fishing photo taken in the most unusual or remote place

Driven by promotions and e-newsletter sign-ups, we have a database of more than 88,000 interested fishermen and women. We will be sending them a pre-launch announcement of dates, including a code to pre-order their Expo tickets at a significant discount from Ticketek.

7

Leverage ideas

Based on our research and a subsequent phone meeting with Australiana, we understand your key objectives in the upcoming year are as follows:

- Increasing revenue, particularly for higher profit products
- Promote high-quality (high profit) holiday travel to frequent business travelers and groups
- Extend the success of your endorsed gourmet tourism packages into other areas
- Provide added value to higher level frequent flyers
- Showcase new services and packages to key travel agents
- Fly the flag to grassroots Aussies in the face of increasing foreign airline competition
- Showcase your new business class service.

Using the tools and benefits provided by The Sydney International Fishing Expo, we have come up with a number of ways that Australiana Airways can achieve these objectives.

Travel industry hospitality

On Saturday night, 22 November, we will be throwing a travel agents-only cocktail party in the Australiana Fishing Adventures area. Australiana will be promoted as the host of this party and you are welcome to invite up to 100 agents on top of the 250 core adventure travel specialists identified by the Expo.

A number of our celebrities and demonstrators will be on hand to discuss these destinations with agents. A feature will be a fishing 'tournament' where agents will compete for a number of travel prizes by casting their line into the trout lake (which borders the Australiana Fishing Adventures area). To keep it light, prizes will be awarded for biggest fish, smallest fish, prettiest fish, most stylish cast, etc.

You are welcome to showcase your newly designed business class seats and other amenities at the cocktail party and throughout the Expo. You may also want to promote the new business class as the ideal option for discerning leisure and adventure travelers.

Finally, as part of your package, we will provide Australiana with 2500 double passes to the Expo, so that you can provide added value to your core business travellers.

Travel packages

Lon Davies and the cast of 'Great Vacations' have committed to nominating their favourite fishing destinations in Australia and overseas. Australiana will have exclusive access to these lists, which can be used to develop 'endorsed' fishing travel packages for sale at the Expo, on your website and through your travel agent network.

On-site sales

As naming rights sponsor to the Australiana Fishing Adventures area, you will be located in a large, central area, themed to resemble a fishing cabin. Arrangements have been made to provide this area with power and other cabling necessary to run an Australiana reservations area on-site. Australiana will be the sole air travel company represented at the Expo.

As this is the first year for the Australiana Fishing Adventures area, there is little direct precedent, but similar areas at the Great Adventure Sports Expo and Harbour Golf Show have resulted in on-site bookings valued at between $10–12 per attendee. At a projected 85,000 attendees, this equates to on-site sales valued at between $850,000 and $1 million.

To ensure the greatest possible opportunity for Australiana to develop travel packages with our other travel exhibitors, we will provide Australiana with an exhibitor list and contact details no later than eight weeks prior to the Expo.

Frequent flyers

We are happy to offer pre-ticketing and a ticket discount to your frequent flyers. We will provide you with artwork and the Ticketek code and you can forward that by email to the appropriate customers.

In-flight

You could turn the favourite fishing destinations lists from Lon Davies and the 'Great Vacations' crew into an in-flight video and/or magazine feature. This is included in our partnership agreement with them, as it also promotes their shows. The producers of each show have indicated that they will assist however they can, but if you need their on-air personalities for a video, that would be a separate contract.

We strongly suggest that you utilise this sponsorship across your range of customer publications, including *Australiana Club News*, your frequent flyer newsletter, and your in-flight publication, *Go Australiana*. These could feature a range of subjects, including:

- Fishing destination profiles
- Fishing tips from our experts
- How to pack your fishing gear for air travel.

We will provide all required assistance to develop content for these publications and have a number of exhibitors who are already interested in advertising and/or developing co-promotions with you.

You may also want to consider contracting Steve Sando to do a humorous, fishing-themed segment for your in-flight programming. Note that Steve has indicated that he is open to this, but again, would need to be contracted separately.

Australiana Club promotion

We suggest that you run a simple enter-to-win promotion for your highest-value customers, members of the Australiana Club. As these members are generally in the higher socioeconomic bracket, it would be important to ensure that entry is easy and the perceived value of the prizes is high.

The grand prize winner would receive a group fishing package for six to an exotic international location. The Cook Islands Tourist Board has expressed interest in providing hotel accommodation and daily top-level fishing trips (both deep sea and inland) if you think this destination is appropriate for your core customers.

A second place winner would receive a group fishing package for four to one of Australia's top regional fishing destinations. Again, the Snowy Mountains Tourism Council has agreed to provide lodge accommodation, meals and fishing trips, including a full day at a destination so remote it can only be reached by helicopter. If you would prefer to feature another destination, we are happy to work with you to arrange the ground portion of the package.

2,500 third prize winners will receive a complimentary double pass to the Sydney International Fishing Expo (provided as part of your sponsorship package).

Entry will be in Australiana Club lounges, and could be as simple as swiping their club membership cards (as you did last year for the Indy Car promotion).

If hospitality is a major factor in the package, outline all hospitality opportunities here. If it is a minor factor, move this back towards the benefits section.

If on-site sales, preferred vending status or product demonstration is a big factor, you will also want to include a section on sales, vending and display in this area of your proposal.

Note: Information shown is just an excerpt. More detail is provided on the CD-ROM.

Benefits

As a major sponsor of the Sydney International Fishing Expo and naming rights sponsor of the Australiana Fishing Adventures area, you will receive the following comprehensive package of benefits:

Sponsorship

- Naming rights sponsorship of the Australiana Fishing Adventures area, incorporating the Australiana logo in all signage and promotional material
- Major sponsorship of the Sydney International Fishing Show (we are limited to three major sponsors)
- Official airline partner status
- Sponsorship and sales exclusivity in the category of air travel

On site

- 10 m x 10 m site in prime, central location in the Fishing Adventures area. This site has a themed 'fishing cabin' structure on it and is fully cabled for computers and electricity access
- Opportunity to book air travel and packages on-site
- Logo acknowledgment on all 'Sydney International Fishing Expo' signage

Hospitality and networking

- Host status for Saturday evening travel agent cocktail party
- Ability to invite up to 100 additional travel agents (on top of the 250 adventure travel specialists we have already identified)
- Introduction to all Fishing Adventures exhibitors a minimum of eight weeks prior to the Expo
- Facilitation of travel cross-promotions and packages with other exhibitors

Access to intellectual property

- Exclusive use of 'favourite fishing destinations' lists developed and endorsed by Lon Davies and the cast of 'Great Vacations' for in-flight and club magazines, in-flight entertainment and web promotions
- Exclusive licence to create and sell travel packages based on the 'favourite fishing destinations' lists

Media profile

- Use of Australiana as an intrinsic part of all travel-oriented publicity activities (promoting travel packages, destinations, on-site booking etc.)
- Logo/name inclusion in all paid and promotional media and publicity
- Assistance with developing and implementing a publicity plan for Australiana's key marketplaces

Tickets

- 25 VIP passes to the Expo
- 8 VIP car parking spaces
- 2,500 adult double passes to the Expo, for use in promoting the Expo to your business travel customers

We have only provided a sampling of the benefits that might go along with this package—ideally, this list should be at least a couple of pages long. Use your inventory and create a comprehensive list of real benefits. Depending upon how long the list is, you may want to categorise the benefits (like the inventory).

A hint to all of you—logo exposure is only a small fraction of a good benefits package.

This package must, must, must be customised to your sponsor's needs.

Outline how much this is going to cost in cash and contra. Be sure to include a proposed payment schedule. We also like to include a minimum promotional commitment, ensuring that they embark upon at least some activities to maximise the sponsorship, and that they are activities that will benefit you, the sponsorship seeker, as well.

One note on pricing, if your country has a goods and services tax or VAT, you need to indicate if that is included in the price or needs to be added on.

Investment

Your investment for this comprehensive sponsorship relationship will be:

- $160,000 cash (price does not include GST)
- $15,000 domestic air travel for use by event staff (to be used by 31 December 2008)
- Provision of return air travel for two to the Cook Islands, for use as a drawing prize facilitating our audience research (full credit for the prize will be given to Australiana)
- Provision of return air travel for two to Darwin, for use as the major prize for our promotion on 2UW (full credit for the prize will be given to Australiana)
- Commitment to strongly promote the Sydney International Fishing Expo to your Australiana Club members and frequent flyers, as well as in *Go Australiana* magazine

Half of the cash component will be due upon signing a contract, with the remainder due on 1 September 2008. The entire domestic air travel fund should be made available to the Sydney International Fishing Expo upon signing the contract.

Chapter 7

Sales process

Sales checklist

You have done your research, the sponsor is interested and there's no spinach in your teeth—it must be time for a meeting!

Prepare, prepare, prepare

It has been suggested that the sales process is 75% preparation, 10% sales pitch and 15% follow-up. If you have the opportunity to meet the sponsor in person, ensure that you know everything you can possibly find out about their company before you walk through the door. You need to know what matters to your potential sponsors and how they measure success. Are they after sales opportunities, launching a new product, preparing for a share issue or embarking on any of a myriad of other marketing activities?

Determine what you want to achieve from this meeting

Ideally, your initial meeting should be about gathering and confirming information. Both you and the potential sponsor want information. You want to create a customised proposal that addresses your sponsor's specific marketing objectives and you need to expand on what you know in order to connect me with an appropriate offer. On the other side, your potential sponsor wants to know about you and your event. Your counterpart will be asking you a few key questions:

➤ Who are you and why should I do business with you?

➤ What's unique about this event and can it connect me with the target markets I want?

➤ Why will people come to your event?

➤ What's in it for me?

➤ How much is it going to cost me?

It will increase your credibility exponentially if you can answer all of these questions before the sponsor asks them. You should be able to sum up your event, your expertise and your enthusiasm concisely, providing the key information to your potential sponsor, so that you can then get on with your own information gathering.

Check your vocabulary

It is important in sales meetings to talk the corporate language. This reminds your corporate contacts that you think like they do—in business terms. Start substituting corporate terms for terms that are often used by smaller sponsees and non-profit organisations (see below).

Instead of...	Use
'Awareness', 'exposure' or 'profile'	'Opportunity to connect with your target market' or 'opportunity to build relevance and relationhships'
'Small audience' or 'small audience of enthusiasts'	'Highly targeted', 'pure demographic' or 'niche market'
'Support'	'Invest'
'Cost' or 'fee'	'Investment'
'Donation' or 'gift'	'Investment'
'Donor', 'funder' or 'supporter'	'Investor', 'sponsor' or 'partner'
'Reaching a small audience'	'Narrowcasting' (the opposite of broadcasting)
'Surplus' (extra funds)	'Profit'
'Marketing dollars'	'Sponsorship' or 'investment'

Make contact with the right person

Establish who you should contact and make an appointment to see him or her. Ensure you meet with someone who has the authority to make decisions on sponsorships of your size.

Mind your manners

Be on time and keep the meeting on track and on schedule. Speak with confidence, smile and shake hands firmly. Speak clearly and remember you are there to gather and check information. Remember, you have two ears and one mouth for a reason—you need to listen twice as much as you speak. Whatever you do, don't go into hyper sales mode. And be sure to follow up the meeting with a personal thank you note (see sample on page 134).

Instead of 'awareness', 'exposure' or 'profile', use 'opportunity to communicate your marketing message'.

If you are a non-profit organisation, make it clear that you are not looking for a donation

Ensure that your contact knows that you are not asking for a donation because this will often be their assumption. It will be even more imperative for you to be very businesslike, using business vocabulary and discussing the project in terms of it being an investment.

Always focus on the sponsor's needs

Remember as you talk that these people are not interested in meeting your needs but in achieving their own business objectives.

On a related note, don't talk in depth about the connection between your organisation and the sponsor. They are much less interested in your organisation than they are in making a connection with target markets that interest them. Position your organisation as a conduit for building those relationships.

Don't discuss price

Do not talk about the price until after you have excited them about the idea. Avoid setting your price until after the initial meeting. It is acceptable to discuss a price range or an indicative amount but always follow that with the caveat that it is only an indication and that the fee will be set based upon the benefits package offered as a result of the meeting.

Be enthusiastic

Your enthusiasm is your greatest selling tool. Following the meeting, send a thank you letter outlining what you have discussed, answering any questions and indicating when they will receive your formal proposal.

Using a broker

No one can sell your organisation or its products the way you can. However, if your organisation lacks the skills, experience or the resources to sell your sponsorship property, hire a broker.

What to look for in a broker or an agent

Experience

Ensure your broker or agent supplies you with a list of clients (including the specific events or properties s/he has acted as a broker for), amounts raised for each, how long the sales processes took and references. If you are working with a larger sales agency, be sure to get references on both the agency and the specific person or team handling your event.

Understanding of the product

Does your broker understand and empathise with your project? Has s/he worked with similar properties?

Value added

Determine exactly what your broker will and will not do. A good broker will work with you to ensure the property, marketing plan and the offer work for potential sponsors.

Professional affiliations

Is s/he a member of at least one recognised sponsorship or marketing association?

Exclusivity

No sponsorship brokers worth their salt will handle a property unless they have exclusive selling rights. Tag teams are bad for them and bad for you. Have they insisted on exclusivity? For how long? It is not uncommon for a broker to request a period of three to twelve months for the securing of sponsorship.

Hunger

How hungry is your sponsorship broker? A good broker is hungry for the project. Is yours?

Presentation

How does your broker present him or herself? Is s/he professional? What are his/her meeting and presentation skills like?

How s/he works

Ask how s/he sells properties. What is his/her strategy and philosophy? If s/he takes an uncustomised, shotgun approach to sales, don't use him/her.

Marketing and business knowledge

Many brokers specialise in particular areas—sports, events, arts, community. Find out the areas of specialisation. Who are his/her contacts? What are his/her networks?

Follow-up and reporting

At the beginning of the contract period, establish how frequently you want the broker to report back, what information you need and in what format.

Fees and payments

Brokers work on a commission basis with the fees ranging anywhere from 10–30% or even more. Brokers are paid this commission only if they successfully negotiate

the sponsorship on your behalf. Brokers are responsible for producing their own sales material. However, if you want flash brochures, videos and whiz-bang presentation materials, you will be expected to cover production and printing costs. Also, you need to be clear on whether the commission is to be paid from the total amount sought or added to it. For example, if they are raising $100 000, are you paying them $20 000 of the $100 000 they raise or do they have to raise $120 000 to cover their own commission? The latter is becoming much more common and is usually more desirable for you.

Contracts and letters of agreement

Ensure you have one. The contract should include commission payable, reporting deadlines, clearances and sign offs, exclusions, time frame and amount sought. Also, include whether the commission is to be added to the total amount sought or paid from it.

Consulting assistance

If you need assistance determining the nature of the property, pricing and packaging or assistance in managing the sponsorship, the broker will charge an hourly fee or a project fee for these services. Fees range from $150 to $300 per hour.

Where to find brokers

Personal referrals are best. If you don't know anyone who uses or has used a broker, call your local marketing or sponsorship association and ask for a referral.

Other ways of selling

While we are big advocates of contacting a sponsor directly and tailoring an offer to their needs, this is not the only way to get your opportunities in front of the right people. Below we outline a number of other channels through which you can introduce your organisation and/or sell sponsorship.

Agencies

Many corporations employ promotions, advertising and public relations agents to handle various facets of their work. Ensure you take time to introduce your sponsorship properties to these agencies. The purpose is not hard sell but rather to show agencies how you can help them add value to their clientele.

Share Our Strength, a small US-based anti-hunger organisation introduced itself and its sponsorship opportunities to a range of PR agencies that represented major food manufacturers and producers. Eighteen months after these initial introductions, Gollan Harris Chicago invited Share Our Strength to pitch a sponsorship proposal to one of its largest clients, Tyson Foods. The pitch resulted in a multi-million dollar partnership.

Internet auctions

We are starting to see sponsorship being sold via Internet auction sites, such as eBay, with some packages being sold for well above the normal asking price. While this approach does get the sponsorship in front of a lot of potential buyers, the lack of discussion and customisation and the abbreviated decision time frame tend to create short-term transactions rather than long-term, marketing-oriented partnerships.

If you want to try this out, we recommend using it only for sponsorships offering a very limited array of benefits, such as hospitality packages or exclusive vending rights.

Matchmaking services

There are several websites offering sponsorship seekers the opportunity to list their opportunities on a database. The idea is that sponsors will search based on their needs and find a good opportunity. This approach is easy and cheap and would seem to be a good idea. Unfortunately, there are also some downsides. It is difficult to know how many sponsors will be searching the database during your window of opportunity, much less the number that will be appropriate to you. Our experience is that you will hear from far more companies trying to sell something to you than sponsors who want to discuss investing in your event. Finally, if you do have a strong partnership orientation, it will be very difficult to showcase that in this type of forum. The upshot is that if it is free or very inexpensive, give it a go, but expect to be inundated with junk mail.

Directories

A number of event directories operate in much the same way as the matchmaking services—dividing events mainly by type, time of year and region. The main difference is that these directories tend to be annual, established and have a wide, reliable readership of corporate sponsors. Sponsors often use these directories as a starting point to understand what sponsorships are out there. If they are interested, they then contact the property directly to discuss the opportunity and develop a partnership.

We recommend listing in established directories, particularly those published by sponsorship associations and publications, such as IEG (see Appendix 2 for contact details). Note, you will still get junk mail, but the potential of your listing contributing to a sponsorship deal is most likely a lot higher than with online matchmaking services.

Preliminary letter

 Letter1.doc

26 June 2008

Mr Andrew Tofte
Managing Director
ARN Australia Pty Limited
Unit A, 108 McEvoy St
Waterloo NSW 2017

Dear Mr Tofte,

I am writing to introduce the School Administrators Federation (SAF), to tell you about its services and to invite you to consider a sponsorship proposal.

When decisions affecting education and school administration are made, it is the SAF's business to understand all the issues involved. The Federation has unrivalled access to all aspects of Australia's school administration system, bringing together the interests of those who manage schools, those who work in them, those who design and build them and those who supply them with goods and services.

SAF is a non-profit national industry association of school administrators. Founded in 1989, SAF works to enhance the quality of school administration for public and private schools across the nation.

The Federation is recognised by governments, educational professionals and the teaching community as a national leader in the school administration industry and is well placed to give you access to all the important networks relevant to your marketing needs.

Our regular activities include:

➤ Annual Conference of School Administrators—our national conference brings together teachers, administrators, policy makers, purchasing officers and suppliers. The 2008 conference is to be held at the Adelaide Convention Exhibition Centre from Friday 14 November to Tuesday 18 November.

➤ Seminars—administration workshops and financial management and purchasing seminars are held throughout the year and enjoy sell-out attendance with over 15 000 participants annually.

➤ Publications—SAF produces a newsletter, Schools Administrator Today and an education administrator paper, Head of the Class, every quarter. Circulation for our publications is over 120 000.

➤ Awards—SAF recognises and encourages innovation and excellence in school administration with the National School Administrator of the Year awards.

➤ Industry information—SAF has access to a wide range of up-to-date national and international school administrator information and can assist suppliers, policy makers and educational professionals with industry research requests. We maintain an active database of over 25 000 purchasing officers and school administrators.

At SAF, we are committed to creating and maintaining win–win partnerships with industry suppliers. We have a number of sponsorship opportunities ranging from sales and exhibition properties to exclusive conference packages.

I have included a brochure on SAF for your interest.

I will ring your offices on Tuesday morning to discuss your specific marketing and sponsor-ship objectives and how we might tailor a proposal for you.

Sincerely,

Ernie Farley
Marketing Manager

Proposal cover letter

 Letter2.doc

15 January 2008

Miranda Morgan
Managing Director
Fresh Milk of Minnesota
3333 University Avenue SE
Minneapolis MN 55414

Dear Miranda,

Thank you for inviting me to discuss your sponsorship marketing objectives. I enjoyed our meeting and feel confident that we have developed a sponsorship proposal to meet both your immediate and long-term needs.

Your situation
[A brief overview of where they are at and what they want.]

Your objectives
As a result of our meeting, I have assessed that the specific sponsorship marketing objectives for your organisation are to:
[Briefly list specific objectives in dot points.]

The project/event
[Provide a brief overview of the project.]

Marketing and promotional benefits
[Provide a very brief overview of the type and value of benefits.]

Investment
Your investment in [event] will be repaid many times over as a result of your organisation's improved ability to identify and cultivate [clients, customers, sales].

The next step
I have attached a detailed proposal for [event]. Included in this document are the media advertising strategy and the public relations and promotional strategies.

Thank you once again for the chance to submit this proposal. We look forward to exploring a partnership with you and hope that we will have the opportunity to contribute to the success of your organisation over the long term.

Sincerely yours,

Davina Craft
Sponsorship Director

Meeting thank you letter

 Letter3.doc

26 August 2009

Kerry Gemmell
Sponsorship Manager
Positively Vodka Importers
17–23 Longbridge Street
Sydney NSW 2001

Dear Kerry,

Thank you for taking time from your busy schedule to meet with me today to discuss your marketing objectives and your sponsorship guidelines.

The Woolloomooloo Theatre Company is committed to producing contemporary theatre productions that reflect our audiences' expectations. We are a contemporary, cutting-edge company producing Australian theatre for Australian audiences. Like Positively Vodka, we are committed to building new audiences through carefully targeted sampling programs.

I am confident that a partnership with the Woolloomooloo Theatre Company will benefit both our organisations. Our upcoming subscription campaign targeting younger executives and opinion leaders provides a great opportunity for Positively Vodka to promote its newest range of flavoured vodkas.

I will forward a formal proposal to you on Friday. Thank you again for taking the time to meet with me today.

Yours sincerely,

Paige Kay
Marketing Manager

Rejection thank you letter

 Letter4.doc

24 February 2009

Olivia Charles
Marketing Director
Acme Toy Company
17 Smith Street
Toronto
Ontario M5E 1E6

Dear Olivia,

I appreciate your having taken the time to review our proposal.

As you might expect, I am disappointed that Acme Toys cannot sponsor our School Bike Safety Project. As we discussed, our project provides unique marketing and promotional opportunities and access to your target markets in a cost-effective and creative manner. However, we recognise that it is impossible for you to invest in every potential sponsorship proposal.

I would very much like to keep in touch with you. We are currently developing a range of educational projects that are specifically targeting young families and I feel confident that your marketing objectives can be addressed with one of our upcoming projects.

Thank you again for your considering our proposal.

Yours sincerely,

Mia Alexander
General Manager

Chapter 8

Special considerations for non-profit organisations

This is a new chapter in this third edition, and when we contemplated including it, we wondered if it was really necessary. In reality, sponsorship is sponsorship, and the approach and process for doing it well is exactly the same whether you are a European children's charity or an American university bowl game.

In the end, we realised that non-profit organisations do face a number of additional challenges and have some unique opportunities, so we decided to include this chapter to address those special considerations.

Rumour and innuendo

You may find yourself facing a lot of preconceived notions about what sponsorship of a non-profit organisation is about. You need to accept that, no matter how proactive and partnership oriented your organisation is, many others with less enlightened outlooks have gone before you, burning bridges as they went.

Below, we have outlined some of the more common attitudes held by sponsors, and a few techniques that can break you out of that pigeonhole.

You are looking for a handout

Corporate sponsorship of non-profits has not been around to any great degree for very long. In fact, when it all started, many non-profits simply changed from asking for a donation to asking for sponsorship, without changing any of the underlying structure. Sponsors would invest marketing money, be treated like donors, get no return and learn to be very sceptical of non-profits looking for sponsorship.

To counteract this, there are a few things you can and should do:

➤ Ensure you don't focus on your organisation's need, particularly in early conversations. Give them a thumbnail sketch and then move on.

➤ Use those early conversations to gain information from the sponsor on their overall marketing objectives and target markets, and how they see these changing in the future. Although they may have a non-profit strategy in place, asking those very objective-oriented questions, rather than asking them what they support, will position you as a potential commercial partner.

➤ Do not ever let your personal passion for your organisation's mission blind you to commercial realities. Your organisation may do amazing things, but that doesn't make you the perfect partner for every sponsor out there. Concentrate on finding the right fit and you will end up with a portfolio of fantastic partners that bring money, promotion, expertise and more to the relationship.

➤ Clearly acknowledge to the sponsor that while you are a non-profit organisation and clearly have funding needs and a social agenda, you understand that they need to be able to justify their investments and make a meaningful return.

➤ Do your very best to speak with a brand manager, if you can. The brand manager is the caretaker of brand health and often hasn't had the experience of being burned by non-profits in the past. If you approach the partnership strategically, they could very well be receptive.

➤ If you do all of the above and the sponsor still refers you to their (underfunded, fully committed) foundation, they really aren't seeing a lot of potential for the partnership. Keep in contact, as future projects may be a better fit, but it's probably better to just move on.

You don't know how to be a real partner

A number of times, we've asked non-profit audiences to define their 'dream sponsor'. Inevitably, someone will say, 'someone who gives us a lot of money and doesn't make us work hard for it'. Invariably, this comment is met by a roomful of nods of agreement. Again, this may not be your approach (and we hope it isn't), but there are a lot of non-profits out there defining the perfect sponsor as a virtual silent partner.

Managing this perception is about managing their fear, just like the 'handout' perception. We suggest that you do all of the above, and add a couple more:

➤ If you have current sponsors who are achieving a commercial return—that is, changing people's perceptions and/or behaviours—by all means, use them as case studies. The best way to prove you can be a real partner is to showcase the fact that you are one already.

➤ Ask your sponsors (current and any former sponsors with whom you parted on amicable terms) for references. In particular, ask them to outline some of the objectives they've met through the sponsorship. You get bonus points if they invite potential sponsors to contact them.

'Good corporate citizenship' and 'giving back' are euphemisms, not objectives.

They won't be able to achieve 'real' objectives using cause sponsorship

This perception has more to do with a sponsor's own lack of vision and leverage, but it is certainly something you will have to counteract at one time or another. Again, all of the above strategies will be helpful, but we would add one more.

If you have a potential sponsor that refers to non-profit sponsorship as 'good corporate citizenship', 'giving back to the community', 'warm fuzzies' or some other related euphemism, you need to dig deeper. These are not real objectives, they are camouflaging the real objectives—for you and for the sponsor. Ask them, 'If you are successful at being a good corporate citizen, what does that mean to your staff? Customers? How would it change what they think of you? Interact with you?' That's not a hard thing to ask, but the result is that they should tell you about the results they want to achieve—their real objectives.

It will be difficult to end the relationship if the sponsor's needs change

From time to time, a sponsor's needs will change and it will be time to drop a sponsorship and do something else. Non-profit sponsorships get dropped, too, but they can be so ungraceful about it that it's scary to contemplate.

We know of non-profits who have tried to pull rank—going to the chief executive, or even a government minister, to complain about being abandoned by a sponsor—as well as many who threaten to go to the media. A few even do go to the media, which can get really ugly.

Now, what kind of partnership is it when the non-profit organisation is ready to resort to threats of blackmail to continue getting the money? We'll tell you: one that is going to scare every other sponsor away for a good long time.

Never threaten a sponsor into renewing.

We're sure you would never do something so dastardly to a sponsor you have spent years valuing, but to be sure they know it, we suggest the following:

➤ From the very start, you need to tell the sponsor—and back it up with actions—that you will do everything you can to assist them in achieving their goals, but that you understand that it needs to meet their strategic needs, and if those needs change, you will understand.

➤ Ensure you are servicing your sponsors really well. In addition to staying abreast of their sponsorship plans, you should be asking about their forward planning and if any changes will affect the relevance of your organisation to their brand. That way, you should know as early as possible if a renewal isn't on the cards.

> If the sponsorship has high visibility, you should offer to issue a joint media release that positions the split as amicable, based on a change in strategy, and setting you up as a great partner to other sponsors.

> If their exit is really going to hurt, don't try to convince them to stay—that decision has been made. Instead, ask them to ease the transition. They could pay for you to attend a workshop, secure a consultant to assist you in finetuning your offering, or sponsor you for one additional year at a much lower level. Assuming they left because of a change in strategy, they may also be able to provide you with referrals to other sponsors who may be more appropriate.

Your real competition and your real edge

With the huge range of non-profits out there—from local to global, children to aged, education to environment, health to homelessness—it would be very easy to think that sponsors are choosing first to sponsor one or more non-profits, and then deciding which ones.

Not so! As sponsorship decisions are increasingly driven by brand management teams, you need to understand that they make their decisions based primarily on two things:

1   Brand fit—does it underpin any of the brand's values or attributes? Can it achieve a range of objectives?

2   Target market fit—is it relevant to at least one of the brand's target markets? Is there scope to provide the target market with a functional or emotional benefit?

What this means is that you are not competing against other non-profits, but against anything that brand could sponsor, plus advertising, sales and media promotions, online activities, endorsements and anything else they might do to market the brand.

Before you freak out about the huge amount of largely well-resourced competition, take a deep breath and hear this: there are some things on that list that a non-profit organisation will be able to do better than anyone else.

Non-profits tend to inspire deeply held passion and admiration in their supporters. The potential for providing a sponsor with an emotional added-value benefit for their customers is outstanding.

One of the major factors for success that we've seen over the years is the more individualised and real you can make the investment, the more relevant it will be—even to people who may not be fervent supporters:

➤ 'Every dollar donated will vaccinate X children from all major childhood diseases.'

➤ 'In 2007, our staff planted over 20 000 native trees with their own hands and donated enough to plant 55 000 more. That's almost 500 acres and three times as many trees as there are in Central Park!'

➤ 'A $20 donation could pay for the doorknob this family turns every time they walk into their first real home.'

➤ 'We didn't see a doctor to minimise scarring, we saw Green Plan. They showed us how we can cost-effectively rejuvenate retired mine sites, creating new habitats and dramatically reducing the long-term impact on Australia.'

The biggest thing to keep in mind, however, is that non-profits—and no one else—can provide a sponsor with an opportunity to make their customers and staff the heroes. Say that to them. It's very powerful.

Get the right advice

We would never say a bad word about fundraisers—a passionate, resourceful bunch working in a highly competitive field. What we will say is that there are not a lot of fundraising workshops, conferences, publications or other resources that are 100% up to date with best-practice sponsorship. It's a highly specialised, highly changeable industry and just not their core capability.

With that in mind, you need to be careful about where you get your information on corporate sponsorship. You need to be sure to get the information from organisations who do corporate sponsorship—not fundraising—as their core job.

➤ **Workshops**—Attend workshops aimed at both for-profits and non-profits. You need to understand and practice the process, and it's the same for everyone. Better yet, balance your training between the sponsee side and the sponsor side. It can be very enlightening to understand what sponsors are after from the sponsors' own mouths.

➤ **Conferences**—A non-profit conference with one session on sponsorship is unlikely to be your best source of cutting-edge information. Go to a conference serving the entire sponsorship industry and attend a range of sessions. You can learn as much from an astute motor racing team as you can from a successful non-profit organisation.

➤ **Associations and publications**—Read sponsorship industry publications, subscribe to industry websites and newsletters, and join industry associations.

To get you started, there is a huge range of sponsorship resources listed in Appendix 2.

➤ **Consultants**—If you decide you need strategic or brokering assistance from a consultant, again, try to secure a consultant that works across the range of sponsorship seekers, including non-profits.

There is nothing stopping you from being a member of fundraising associations or going to non-profit conferences, as you probably need a range of skills in your job. Just understand that you will probably need to augment those resources with some that are specialised for sponsorship.

Partnership options

Non-profits have more options for partnering with sponsors than any other type of sponsee. The most common structures are outlined below, but the key is that any of these can and should be leveraged by the sponsor as if it were a standard sponsorship.

➤ **Cause sponsorship**—This is the standard sponsorship structure. A sponsor makes an investment of cash, goods or services in a non-profit organisation and receives a range of leverageable benefits in return.

➤ **Cause-related marketing** (CRM)—The sponsor creates a sales promotion whereby it makes a donation every time a customer makes a purchase. For instance, you might buy recycled paper towels and every time you buy that brand, it donates ten cents to the Wildlife Conservation Society. There is often, but not always, a flat sponsorship or licensing fee paid to the non-profit organistion, and the total cause-related donation is almost always capped.

➤ **Donation facilitation**—This is where a sponsor creates an easy 'funnel' for donations, such as Qantas collecting loose change from passengers, in any currency, and donating it to UNICEF, to the tune of millions of dollars.

➤ **Donation matching**—This is similar to above, but the sponsor agrees to match all donations made, often to a capped amount.

The CSR trap

As corporations move toward 'corporate social responsibility' (CSR), two things have happened:

1 Some corporations have elected not to become more socially responsible in their environmental, workplace or other practices, and instead have elected to write cheques to non-profits.

> Non-profit sponsorship and corporate social responsibility are not the same thing.

2   Some non-profits have positioned writing that cheque as ticking the CSR 'box', further enabling the above, flawed, take on CSR.

CSR is a measure of how responsible a company is in the manner in which it carries out business and makes money, as well as the sustainability of those measures.

CSR is not a measure of how much money a company spends sponsoring or donating to non-profits. Sponsoring non-profits can be very powerful and, if authentic, a big statement about the values of a company and its brands, but it doesn't work if it's not authentic. Sponsoring environmental organisations does not undo continuing and unaddressed environmental damage. Sponsoring World Vision does not undo using subcontractors who engage child labour.

If there is an authentic match between a company's CSR initiatives and what your organisation does, they can certainly use the sponsorship to underpin those values. By the same token, if your organisation can provide meaningful assistance to them in achieving CSR targets—providing expertise, infrastructure or other means—then you can connect CSR and sponsorship.

However you look at it, always remember, running a business in an ethical manner and sponsoring your organisation are not the same thing. Writing you a cheque is not CSR.

Chapter 9

Negotiation

The object of the negotiation process is to create a win–win–win deal; that is, the sponsee wins, the sponsor wins and the target markets win. In order to achieve this level of partnership, both parties must be completely open about their objectives. This should be a fairly straightforward task if the development of the offer were done in a fully collaborative manner, as recommended throughout this book.

Either way, there are a number of rules that will make negotiating sponsorship a lot easier for you.

Negotiate peer to peer

Be sure you actually carry out the negotiation with someone who has the authority to negotiate and the ability to approve the expenditure. You will find that, in many companies, different levels of marketing executives will have different levels of financial authority.

Know your bottom line

In the heat of a meeting, it is easy to get caught up in the process and make a deal that you realise later does not achieve your financial objectives.

Before you go into any negotiation, be sure to do your homework. Go back to your pricing exercises and set yourself a bottom limit that you will under no circumstances fall below (e.g. 225% of your cost to deliver the program). You may also want to set yourself a limit as to how much of the fee you will accept in contra.

Keep the target markets in the picture

If the target markets—your audience, their customers, etc.—don't win, it's not going to work for anyone. Some sponsors get this and some don't. Even if you are negotiating with a sponsor who doesn't get it, it's in everyone's best interest if you keep talking about how various aspects of the sponsorship will impact (or not impact) on the target markets.

> The goal is win–win–win.

Have something up your sleeve

When you create an offer for a sponsor, always keep a couple of nice benefits up your sleeve to use during the negotiation process. If you plan from the start to negotiate by offering them more, rather than settling for less money (and calculate your costs accordingly), you will end up far better off in the end.

Don't be bullied

Some sponsors routinely offer 20–25% less than your asking price, assuming that if you are hungry enough, you will be grateful for anything. Don't fall for this ploy.

You need to approach the negotiation from a position of confidence—you are holding a negotiation, not a fire sale. You've done your research and know your value. If they have a problem with the price point, then you need to adjust your package accordingly. Do not ever simply accept a discounted offer. A sponsor worth working with will respect your need to protect the value of your property.

If you have approached the sponsorship process in a fully professional manner and taken all of the above negotiation advice, and the potential sponsor is still treating you like a second-class organisation, walk away because the relationship will never get any better.

> You are holding a negotiation, not a fire sale.

Stay composed no matter what

Negotiations can be difficult, no question about it. Even if you have created a strong offer and followed the guidelines set out here, sometimes you will work with a sponsor who is an old-style negotiator, approaching the process as adversarial rather than collaborative.

If things start heating up, call for time out. Tell the potential sponsor that it is clear you both need to give this relationship a fresh look. Tell them that you will rework the offer, taking into account their concerns, and that you will get back to them in a couple of days. Then do it. Put any defensiveness or acrimony aside and find a way. Put the new offer in writing, which allows you to think it out fully, and remember to stay focused on a solution.

Also note, there may be times when a sponsorship negotiation will turn sour even when both sides are working together, as the result of an international directive, a change in business climate or because of an internal change at the company. Don't hold this against the potential sponsor as it is out of their control. Just stay composed and stay in touch, and when everything settles back down for them, resume discussions.

Be prepared to walk away

Don't ever walk into a negotiation with the mindset that you need to close the deal. This puts you at a distinct disadvantage and will result in you giving up more than you need to cement the relationship. You may as well have a 'kick me' sign on your back!

If at some point during the negotiation you determine that the relationship is unlikely to end up a win–win situation, then it is time to thank your counterpart and graciously walk away. This is an infinitely more positive outcome than creating a bad relationship. Sponsorship is notoriously incestuous—if you burn a bridge, it stays burned.

Payment arrangements

Sometimes the payment arrangements will be as important to a sponsor as the amount of money committed, so you need to be prepared to work with them.

Spreading payments across time

Oftentimes, a sponsor will want to spread payments over time. There are several reasons for this but the two overriding reasons are:

1   Comfort level—they want some assurance that the event is actually going ahead and that the benefits promised are being delivered. Often, once you have gone through the first year of a sponsorship, the sponsor will be more comfortable paying the entire fee up-front.
2   Budgeting—if they have already budgeted for that time period, they may need to access quarterly marketing funds or some other kind of time-bound budgets.

Whatever the reason, you need to be prepared to work with the sponsor. You should endeavour to secure a substantial proportion of the fee up-front, both as a measure of good faith and to assist you in your cash flow in the lead up to your event.

It is reasonable that fees above a given amount ($15 000–$20 000) be paid in instalments. One common way of doing this is to request one-third upon signing of the agreement, another third three months later, and the final instalment two weeks before the event starts.

Ongoing contracts, such as sponsorships of cultural organisations or sporting teams, may be paid annually, semi-annually or quarterly.

Also keep in mind that if you are negotiating a small sponsorship with a company that has a major sponsorship budget, it may be more convenient for them to pay the entire amount at once. The only way to know which payment option they prefer is to ask.

Spreading payments across budgeting cycles

It may be necessary to spread payments across financial years, particularly for larger sponsorships or investments made after the current period has been budgeted. This can often make finding the money for your opportunity easier for the sponsor.

Companies' financial years vary widely, with multinationals often mirroring the financial year in their home country. Some companies have their own fiscal year. You should have found out what financial year they operate under during your initial research but, as a general guideline, here are a few typical periods:

> United States: 1 January–31 December
> Japan: 1 April–31 March
> Australia/New Zealand: 1 July–30 June
> United Kingdom: 1 April–31 March.

Case studies: Payment structures

Lincoln Center for the Performing Arts and sponsor Continental Airlines have come up with a very unusual enhancement to their cash sponsorship arrangement. Continental frequent flyers are now able to cash in points to buy seats for Lincoln Center shows, with the points being transferred to Lincoln Center instead of cash. Lincoln Center will then use the points as an added perk to lure new subscribers.

For their sponsorship of the MS Society, Sandbox.com paid nothing. That's right, nothing. The MS Society will receive all or part of its $500 000 fee only when someone wins Sandbox.com's $1 million or $100 million jackpots. With nearly 7 million members when this book went to press, it is reasonable to expect that this payment is a real possibility. In return for their commitment, Sandbox.com is receiving introductions from the MS Society to potential site advertisers and partners, as well as promotion in the MS Society's magazine.

Recruitment company, Manpower, won the Swedish Sponsor of the Year Award with their sponsorship of various causes. Manpower's main investment is expertise, providing skills such as management, consulting and bookkeeping to causes for a minimum of three months. They have provided many thousands of hours so far, and have successfully demonstrated their service not only to the causes themselves, but to their other sponsors, board members and associated organisations.

Multi-year agreements

When structuring a multi-year agreement, keep in mind the following things:

> If your event is new and will likely grow more valuable as time goes on, you should structure your fees to reflect larger payments in later years.
> If your event has a long track record of delivering the goods, you may elect a flat payment structure.

➤ If your event is new and you have one key sponsor who is the 'perceived owner' of the event, you *may* be able to get a larger fee in the first year to assist in underwriting the infrastructure but this will come at a dramatic cost in future years.

Proactively offer incentive-based fees

We are strongly in favour of fee structures that incorporate a component that is performance based. This creates an incentive for the sponsee to deliver as promised—to go that extra mile—and sponsors see this as a refreshing departure from sponsees that take the money and run.

It also means that you could make more money on the sponsorship because you are lowering the risk to the sponsor (and let's face it, sponsors still tend to think sponsorship is a risk!). The key is to tie the performance-based component to specific, quantifiable and desirable outcomes.

Instead of charging $10 000 cash for a sponsorship from a car maker, you could do this:

➤ $8000 up-front payment
➤ $2000 if more than 60 attendees test drive their car
➤ $2000 if they get more than 200 qualified prospects onto their database.

This gives you a total of $12 000, reduces the perceived risk to the sponsor and shows that you are absolutely confident that you will produce results. Of course, if you are not confident of producing results, do not do it. In fact, if you are not confident of producing results, get out of sponsorship!

Incentive-based fees lower the perceived risk to the sponsor.

Special note on sales-based incentives

When incentive-based fees are mentioned to sponsors, they will often immediately want to negotiate an incentive based upon sales. Whatever you do, don't agree to a sales-based incentive.

You can provide a lot of the ingredients to making a sale, including:

➤ promoting the product
➤ enhancing the product's image
➤ providing opportunities for sales (e.g. on-site sales or sales to your members)
➤ product demonstrations
➤ relationship-building opportunities.

What you can't deliver are actual sales, as these will be largely based upon the quality and value inherent in the product. For instance, a soft-drink manufacturer may

Never agree to a sales-based fee.

be the exclusive vendor at your summer event but if a malfunction occurs and the drinks are warm and flat, or if they price it above market value, they won't hit their sales projections no matter how many people you get through your gate. You should not be held accountable for that.

It is far better to negotiate an incentive based upon how many people come to your event and leave delivering the right product at the right price to your sponsor.

Contra sponsorship

Contra sponsorship occurs when a sponsor pays for their sponsorship with products or services instead of cash. Also known as barter, trade or in-kind sponsorship, contra sponsorship makes up at least a portion of a large number of sponsorships.

When negotiating for contra sponsorship, keep three things in mind.

1   Contra sponsorship is only of value to you if:
    (a) you have budgeted for the specific item already. In that case it is only worth as much as it is saving you in cash expenditure. For example, if a company offers to loan you $10 000 in new computer equipment when your planned expenditure was only $2000 lease payments, the offer is only worth $2000 to you.
    (b) it adds value to your other sponsorship packages. For instance, if you secure an airline sponsor, you could include air tickets to your event with your other sponsorship packages, making them more attractive for other potential sponsors.
2   If the contra sponsor is saving you cash, they are as valuable to you as a fully cash sponsor and they need to be serviced as a cash sponsor (see Part 3).
3   You still need money to run your event or property, so endeavour to negotiate sponsorships where contra sponsorship is only a component of the investment.

There's more to contra sponsorship than you think

When they hear the word 'contra', most people think only of a sponsored product such as an airline providing free travel, a high-technology company providing computers, etc.

The fact is that sponsors have access to dozens of opportunities and services that can save you a lot of money. What follows is a generic sponsor contra list. This is a great tool to use when negotiating with a sponsor, particularly one that is baulking at making the full investment in cash.

Contra sponsorship is only of value if you have budgeted for that item already.

Promotion

- Media promotion
- Promotion of sponsee through retailers
- Promotion of sponsee on pack
- Promotion in internal employee communication
- Promotion to customers (mailings, magazine, newsletter, website, database etc.)
- Sponsee signage on sponsor building

Media

- Access to heavily discounted media rates through sponsor's media buyer
- Tags on existing advertising
- New advertisements profiling sponsee
- Providing a limited media schedule (probably shared with sponsor)

Creativity

- Creative work for the sponsee done by sponsor's advertising agency or in-house graphic department

People

- Provision of sponsor-contracted celebrity for event endorsement or appearances
- Donation of employee for fixed-term assignment (full or part time for set number of weeks/months)
- Employee volunteers to augment on-site staff
- Access to in-house experts and subcontractors (public relations, printing, media planning, database development, web development and optimisation etc.)

Infrastructure

- Office space
- Office equipment or services
- Event equipment or services

Other contra products or services

- For use as prizes, incentives or giveaways
- To add value to other sponsorship packages

Travel
- Access to discounted airline or hotel deals
- Contra travel or hotel (if sponsor is in travel business)

Contracts

When entering into a sponsorship agreement, the hope is always that the sponsorship will go perfectly and the terms of the contract will never be called into play. Unfortunately, this is not always the case, so it is important to understand the issues.

Types of agreements

Always have some sort of written agreement in force. The more formal the agreement, the more likely it will be complete and legally binding. In order of desirability, these are the types of agreements you could have:

1   a legal contract drawn up by a lawyer and bearing signatures and company seals of both organisations
2   a legal contract adapted from a template drawn up by a lawyer (we have included a comprehensive pro forma which has been created for this book by Gadens Lawyers, Australia), bearing signatures and company seals of both organisations
3   a letter of agreement outlining all points of agreement, including benefits, communication and payment dates, and signed by both organisations
4   a confirmation letter from the sponsee outlining the benefits and payment dates (this is not desirable and should be avoided).

Determine at what level you need a letter of agreement or a contract. Often a letter of agreement, signed by both parties, will be used for sponsorships valued at under a certain amount, anywhere from $5000 to $20 000. Above that amount, a full contract will be required.

If you have a good **Sponsorship Agreement Pro Forma** (see page 215), it will make your job much easier when it comes to developing an appropriate agreement. This is a very useful tool that can be utilised in several ways:

- as the basis for your agreement
- as your 'first pass' at a legal contract which will then be given to a lawyer for finetuning (saving you a considerable amount in legal fees)
- as a reference, so that you are aware of possible issues and legal considerations.

We do not recommend using the pro forma as the basis for your agreement unless you have a lawyer check the agreement prior to entering into it.

Who should provide the contract

It is nearly always quicker and more straightforward for the sponsee to develop the contract, as corporate legal departments are notoriously bureaucratic and often develop contracts that are difficult to read and less than win–win.

Resolving disputes

When structuring an agreement, always try to work in a series of steps for resolving any conflicts that might arise. You only move onto the next step when what you have already tried has not worked. The four basic steps are, in order:

1 **Discussion**—This means having a meeting with the express purpose of coming to a resolution that is agreeable to both parties.

2 **Mediation**—This involves getting an independent arbiter to mediate a discussion between the parties, ensuring that they stay on track and open to solutions.

3 **Arbitration**—This is similar to mediation, except that the parties agree that the arbiter will hear both sides and make a decision. Beware, this could be almost as expensive as litigation.

4 **Litigation**—A long and usually expensive foray into the legal system, which is to be avoided if at all possible.

Exclusivity

There are three types of exclusivity:

1 Sponsorship

2 Signage (in cases where the venue may have existing conflicting signage)

3 Sales.

You can grant exclusivity across any or all of these areas, and the more you grant, the more valuable it is to the sponsor. For more on this, see 'How do we define category exclusivity?' on page 114.

Exclusive sales provisions could contravene trade practices or anti-trust laws. This is another reason why it is important for a lawyer to prepare or check your agreement.

Sponsorship agreement pro forma

Included in Appendix 3 is a **Sponsorship Agreement Pro Forma** that was developed specifically for us by Lionel Hogg, Partner of Gadens Lawyers. The full agreement can also be found on disk.

This sample agreement may be a useful starting point for a sponsorship agreement. However, it is very general because it is impossible to draft a document that accounts for all situations or for legal differences in all countries.

Ideally, it should be used as a template that is completed by the sponsee and sponsor and then given to a lawyer to check the drafting, change it to suit the law of the relevant place and better outline the rights of the parties. This will ensure that the agreement process is collaborative and will probably cost you far less than securing a lawyer to draft an agreement from scratch.

Warning

This document is provided as a sample only and is not a substitute for legal advice. You should seek the advice of a suitably qualified and experienced lawyer before using this document.

In particular, you or your lawyer should:

➤ check the law in your jurisdiction—make sure this agreement works there

➤ check for changes to the law—law and practice might have altered since this document was drafted or you last checked the situation

➤ modify wherever necessary—review this document critically and never use it without first amending it to suit your needs as every sponsorship is different

➤ beware of limits of expertise. If you are not legally qualified or are not familiar with this area of the law, do not use this document without first obtaining legal advice about it.

How this agreement works

The agreement assumes that there are standard clauses that should be in every agreement and special clauses needed for your sponsorship. The standard clauses that should apply all of the time are called the 'Standard Conditions'. The parts that relate to your specific sponsorship are the 'Schedules' and the 'Special Conditions'.

The schedules and the special conditions have precedence over the standard conditions. In other words, what you insert is more important than what is already written. This is why it is vital to use a lawyer or know about what you are doing.

Read the agreement

Before doing anything, read the agreement and see how it might apply to your situation. There might be standard conditions that are unsuitable. There might be new conditions you need to add. Do not assume that the agreement is right for you.

The sample agreement is for an *exclusive* sponsorship for the relevant sponsorship category.

Complete the schedules

You should complete each schedule following the guidance notes in that schedule.

For example, Schedule 23 is called 'Sponsor's termination events'. The guidance note tells you to see clause 9.2. You should read clause 9.2 and understand the circumstances in which the sponsor has a right to terminate the agreement. You should then insert in Schedule 23 any other circumstances peculiar to your sponsorship (e.g. the sponsor might want to terminate the agreement if the team being sponsored loses its licence to play in the major league or if the contracted lead performers for the musical withdraw their services).

Add special conditions

The special conditions (at the end of the schedules) enable you to insert other conditions that are not dealt with by this sample agreement.

Changing standard conditions

You should *not* change the standard conditions without consulting a lawyer. The agreement is drafted as a package and changing the standard conditions might have an unintended domino effect on other terms.

If you have to change the standard conditions, do so by adding a special condition, such as, 'clause 18 of the standard conditions does not apply'.

Sign the agreement

The parties sign and date the document on the last page. Make sure that the person with whom you do the deal is authorised to sign.

Finding a lawyer

You should consult a lawyer practising in your jurisdiction and experienced in sponsorship matters. If you don't have a good sponsorship lawyer, there are a number of sports law organisations around the world that can provide a referral, or you can contact Gadens Lawyers in Australia.

Although you may not be a sporting organisation, these associations will be a great source for referrals, as sponsorship law skills are quite transferable across sponsorship genres.

Full contact details for a number of these organisations can be found in Appendix 2.

If you have questions about the pro forma agreement

If you or your lawyer have questions about the **Sponsorship Agreement Pro Forma**, you are welcome to contact its author:

Lionel Hogg
Partner
Gadens Lawyers
GPO Box 129
Brisbane Qld 4001 Australia
Phone: (61-7) 3231 1518
email: lhogg@qld.gadens.com.au

Part 3

servicing

Chapter 10

Sponsorship planning and management

Sourcing and acquiring new sponsors is not the hardest part of a sponsorship manager's job. Servicing your sponsor is when the real work begins. Sponsorship is all about building and maintaining long-term relationships. The primary responsibility of organisations receiving sponsorship is to build positive relationships with their sponsors by ensuring that all agreed benefits are provided within the negotiated time frame.

It is equally important that organisations are committed to ensuring that their sponsors are provided with information, feedback and quantitative and qualitative research results that will assist their sponsors in determining if their objectives have been met. Simply providing the sponsor with the contracted benefits and a media report at the end of the event means you are only doing half the job.

Sponsors require and deserve total commitment from their sponsees. Evaluation is perhaps one of the most overlooked areas of sponsorship servicing today. The most successful sponsorship managers provide complete sponsorship service, which includes in-depth ongoing summary evaluation and assessment.

There is no secret on how to manage your sponsorships effectively. Once you have acquired your sponsorship, it comes down to three simple steps:

1 **develop** a sponsorship plan
2. **implement** the sponsorship plan
3 **evaluate** the sponsorship plan.

Develop the sponsorship plan

Once you have found a sponsor for your event you must firstly develop a sponsorship plan. The sponsorship plan defines what you and the sponsor want to achieve and how you are going to manage the sponsorship. Each sponsorship, regardless of its size or value, requires its own plan.

Every sponsorship plan should include:

- an executive summary
- a situation analysis
- a list of objectives
- strategies to meet those objectives
- performance indicators that will be used to measure the success of those strategies
- target audiences
- an action list/timeline/accountability list
- a budget
- an evaluation strategy.

A sponsorship plan states what you want to achieve, how you are going to achieve it and how you will know when you have achieved it. A **Sponsorship Implementation Plan** template can be found on page 158.

In terms of quantifying returns on a sponsorship investment, a sponsorship plan provides you with two critical strategies for measuring returns—performance indicators and evaluation. If it is in your plan, you will not forget it. You will also have agreement from within your organisation and from the sponsor as to what you are trying to achieve and how you will measure the results.

Implement the sponsorship plan

Sponsorship is about creating an effective relationship between your organisation and the sponsor. Managing the sponsorship or implementing a well-thought-out sponsorship plan is about building and maintaining that relationship.

Evaluating the sponsorship plan

If you have followed your sponsorship plan, you will have identified performance indicators and ways of measuring or evaluating whether the sponsor has successfully met their sponsorship objectives. The best sponsorship implementation and evaluation plans are drawn up in consultation with your sponsors.

Your evaluation plan should include the following, some of which you will provide and some the sponsor will carry out:

Each sponsorship, regardless of its size, requires a sponsorship plan.

> pre- and post-sponsorship surveys
> sales or visitation figures at your event
> qualitative research results
> media assessment.

Sponsorship implementation plan

 Service1.doc

You should create a sponsorship implementation plan for each of your sponsors. This should be comprehensive, providing a blueprint for the execution of the program.

Introduction

Include details on the overall aims and objectives of the sponsorship plan. Briefly outline the strategies that you will undertake to assist the sponsor in meeting the objectives.

Situational analysis

Give a brief overview of where the sponsorship is at, who the key contacts are and any major issues that might affect the sponsorship.

If the sponsorship is ongoing, outline the past history of the sponsorship, recommendations for enhancement and tactics that will be undertaken to refocus the sponsorship.

Sponsorship objectives

In dot points, detail the objectives of the sponsorship. Remember, objectives must always be SMART—specific, measurable, achievable, results oriented and time bound.

Each objective should be followed by a list of quantification mechanisms relevant to the objective. For example, one of the sponsor's objectives is to create a contact database of 5000 exhibition attendees intending to purchase a luxury car within the next 12 months, and they want to achieve that by the fourth week. Your quantification mechanisms may be:

> number of names on the database
> quality of information on the database
> timeliness of capturing the information
> timeliness of forwarding the completed database to the sponsor.

Target markets

Who are the target markets? Who else might this program affect? Your list may include staff, audiences, senior management, media and ticket holders.

Sponsorship benefits

Include a list of all benefits that have been included in the sponsorship contract as well as a list of any other benefits that may have been agreed to. A detailed list will assist both the sponsors and the sponsee in keeping tabs on the marketing opportunities available.

Evaluation

You should work with your sponsor to determine how they will measure the success of the sponsorship program. Detail how the sponsorship will be evaluated through key performance indicators.

Action list

Detail every marketing activity, event, media launch, report, meeting and every aspect of the provision of benefits and information you have promised the sponsor. Next to the item, indicate the time frame and person responsible.

Budget

Detail all costs that are required to make this sponsorship plan happen. Ensure you have accurately costed support and management of the sponsorship. Use your organisation's formula for calculating real staff and administration costs of employment (including overheads). See 'Calculating overheads' on page 57 for more information.

Objective-based measurement

In the past, sponsors and sponsees have often tried to put dollar figures on the value of everything delivered and then crossed their fingers that this figure came up to something more than what was paid. If their estimates fell short, the sponsorship manager would often whack some arbitrarily large dollar amount on the bottom and call it 'good corporate citizenship'. There is no question that many sponsorship managers have covered their behinds with that old gem.

What good sponsorship practitioners have come to realise is that, although there are some objectives that can be quantified in dollars, such as incremental or on-site

---

Double check your costs

When calculating costs, be sure to look at every benefit promised and every objective to be met. These costs will vary widely depending upon the type of event and benefits offered. Listed below are some of the more common costs encountered to get you started:

- VIP hospitality—tickets, invitations, catering, parking, gifts, security, travel/transport and accommodation
- signage—production, maintenance, construction, storage, backdrops, transport
- advertising—design, production, media time/space, agency advice
- endorsement or appearance fees
- promotional material—design, printing, shipping
- prize money, competition prizes
- product samples and discounts
- legal fees
- media/public relations support— media kits (design and production), media training, photographers, launch venue
- evaluation—research fees, media monitoring, compilation of data
- servicing costs—staff costs (remember to calculate the real cost of employment), consultants, travel.

Measuring
sponsorship in
terms of dollars
doesn't work.

sales, it is impossible to put an accurate dollar figure on many very important aspects of sponsorship, including the:

- shifts in consumer perception of the sponsor
- shifts in consumer behaviour
- underpinning of core brand values and attributes
- understanding and alignment with key sponsor messages (e.g. 'if you drink and drive, you're a bloody idiot' or 'just do it')
- increasing the loyalty or advocacy of key target markets
- deepening of relationships with major clients
- introduction to new potential clients
- launch, demonstration or trial of a new product
- networking with corporate and/or government decisionmakers
- increased retail support or preference by a sponsor's intermediary market.

The second thing you should realise, after reading that list, is that the sponsee will not be able to measure most of these very important objectives. Objective-based measurement is the most recent and useful trend for measurement since sponsorship began. It brings the results of sponsorship right back to what the sponsor is trying to achieve in their marketing program. It also puts the responsibility in the right place. Sponsors set the objectives, will leverage the sponsorship to meet those objectives, and have the experts on staff who measure all of these areas and many more every day.

The other argument against measuring sponsorship in terms of dollars is that this creates an unnatural preoccupation on the sponsor's part with 'getting their money's worth'. If we equate this with above the line advertising, it would be like a sponsorship manager patting him or herself on the back and calling it a day because s/he paid \$200 000 and got \$220 000 worth of television advertising. Whether the advertisements actually achieved anything has not been quantified at all. It is exactly the same with measuring sponsorship. Whichever way you look at it, if you are measuring an entire sponsorship program in terms of dollars, you are measuring the process, not the results, and that's just plain silly.

Determine
measurement
mechanisms with
your sponsor as
you work with
them to develop
your sponsorship
objectives.

Making the sponsor's investment measurable

As previously noted, measurement is another one of those areas that is primarily the sponsor's responsibility but with which you should be involved from the outset. And if your sponsor is not thinking in terms of measurement at all, you may need to do some gentle education. In any case, if you can assist the sponsor to see the full value of their investment in terms of objective-based outcomes, you will already have made your case for renewal of sponsorship.

Before developing measurement mechanisms, you must keep in mind the following rules:

➤ Benchmarking is a must. A sponsor can't know what you have achieved if you don't know where you started.
➤ Specify measurement mechanisms from the outset.
➤ Don't try to change everything into a dollar value because it really doesn't work.

The basis of this type of measurement is that it's all about objectives and, if objectives are SMART, they should be measurable.

Each objective should be made as clear and specific as possible. Generalisations and ambiguity virtually guarantee that a sponsorship will be unmeasurable. Even if your organisation has given a stellar performance on the sponsorship, it will be impossible to prove that the sponsorship has delivered on the objectives. And we hate to break it to you but, as a sponsorship seeker, the assumption by sponsors (and particularly their boards) is that if you can't prove it, you haven't done it.

More importantly to you, if you don't know exactly what the sponsor is trying to achieve, you will not be able to deliver it.

We often see sponsors specify their objectives in a series of two-word phrases, such as 'increase sales'. While this is certainly a worthwhile pursuit, neither you nor the sponsor will be able to determine the extent to which this objective has been met because it is too vague. When faced with vague objectives such as this, you need to keep asking questions until you have agreed upon a SMART objective.

For example, if you have developed an initial objective of 'increasing sales', you could ask the following types of questions:

➤ What type of sales (new customer, incremental, loyalty or up-selling)?
➤ Through what distribution channel (retail, catalogue, hotline, etc.)?
➤ To which target market(s)?
➤ During what time frame?
➤ From what benchmark?
➤ Determined how?

If you ask these questions, your sponsor will also most likely realise that they need to get their own sales department involved to define, benchmark and measure this aspect of the sponsorship. That realisation is a big win for a sponsee.

The table overleaf provides some examples of typical short, snappy (but non-quantifiable) objectives and how they might be turned into SMART objectives.

> Beware of two-word objectives.

Not	Instead
Increase sales	Create incremental sales of 10% over the benchmark of $240 000 per week during the six-week promotional period, as determined by retailer case commitments in the Tri-State region.
Develop database	Develop a database of no less than 2500 qualified prospects, as determined by salary level, age range, professional and family status, investment risk profile, and current insurance products owned. A profile of acceptable ranges is attached.
Gain publicity	Raise the understanding of the legal blood alcohol limit for drivers from 64% to 85%, and raise the proportion of our target market that 'strongly agrees' with the statement, 'I would never consider drinking and driving', from 34% to 55% over the 12-month sponsorship term.
Demonstrate 'good corporate citizenship'	Increase positive responses within our target market about our firm's professionalism (from 45% to 64%), commitment to representing New Zealand positively overseas (from 12% to 35%) and intention to expand their business with us (from 42% to 66%) over the six-month promotional period, as determined by responses to our annual client survey. A profile of the target markets is attached.

After looking at the examples in the above table you may be thinking to yourself, 'these objectives are so specific, they can't possibly encompass the entire value of the sponsorship'. You're right, there are a number of areas that are very difficult to quantify directly. What you should try to do is to develop with your sponsor not one but several SMART objectives that will quantify key aspects of the sponsorship and be indicative of the overall success of their investment.

Once the objectives have been fully developed, the big question for the sponsor is 'If these objectives are achieved, will you consider this sponsorship to have been a success?' If the answer is no, then the objectives need to be developed or extended further. If the answer is yes, you know exactly what you are working towards.

Measurement mechanisms

The most vexing part of creating SMART objectives is the 'M' part, that is, making them measurable. Do not despair, however, as there are many more ways to measure sponsorship results than you realise.

Depending upon what objectives the sponsor is trying to achieve, you can work with them to ensure that one or more mechanisms are in place for each objective. Some suggestions on measurement mechanisms for different categories of objectives can be found below.

Sales—new customer, incremental, up-selling or loyalty sales

➤ Retail figures
➤ Scanner data

What are all those kinds of sales?

Just as there are different kinds of customers, there are also different kinds of sales. To demonstrate the differences between the four main types of sales, let's think about them in terms of a fast-food chain:

- *New customer.* Someone who has never been to the fast-food chain comes in for the first time.
- *Loyalty.* An existing customer starts coming in for lunch more often or starts coming in for other meals as well.
- *Incremental sales.* 'Do you want fries with that?' In other words, when someone buys more items of food than they were planning (or than they usually do) on any given visit.
- *Up-selling.* 'For just 50 cents you can upgrade to a Great Big Meal.' In other words, buying an item that is bigger or more expensive than originally planned.

➤ Case commitments

➤ Sales promotion participation

➤ On-site or direct sales (sales at or as a direct result of your event)

➤ Coupon redemptions

➤ Profit margins

Customer or general public perceptions/behaviour

➤ Quantitative research (against benchmark)

➤ Qualitative research (against benchmark)

Database/loyalty marketing

➤ Number and quality of people joining the database

➤ Loyalty activity

➤ Sales or media promotion participation

➤ Merchandising (members/customers buying brand event merchandise through your sponsor)

Media promotion

➤ Number and quality of media placements

➤ Media exposure of marketing message

➤ Media exposure of logo (not a strategic objective, so not recommended)

Product/attribute awareness

➤ Entrance/exit surveys (i.e. people who have actually been to your event)

➤ Target market surveys (i.e. people who are in the target market group and have probably heard about the event, but may or may not have attended)

➤ General public surveys (not a strategic objective, so not recommended)

Employees

➤ Product knowledge contest results (i.e. if you launch a range of new products and use a sponsorship to drive an understanding of all of the new features)

➤ Incentive program results

➤ Surveys—attitude about the sponsorship, morale and job satisfaction, preferred place to work etc.

➤ Merchandise program sales

Key customers

➤ Incentive program results—long and short term

➤ Relationship-building opportunities

Retailers

- Number and quality of retail displays
- Number of newspaper specials
- Preference/attitude surveys
- Relationship-building opportunities

Measuring media

If you have ever been guilty of handing a sponsor a stack of media clippings at the end of an event, whether they have anything to do with the sponsorship or not (and most of us have at one time or another!), now is the time to clean up your act.

That approach to measuring media is called media monitoring—literally providing copies of all media clippings, television and radio interview transcripts and tapes without any analysis of their value. Unfortunately, a folder of articles and clippings provides the sponsor with few tangible results. Your media monitoring activities will be greatly enhanced if you provide your sponsors with a media assessment report. This is also one of the only aspects of measurement that you can do as well as the sponsor.

Media assessment report

There is no question that it is difficult to assess the monetary value of a newspaper article or a television interview. There are a number of methods available but results of these evaluation methods vary widely. Instead of trying to quantify a highly nebulous aspect of sponsorship in terms of hard and fast dollars, we strongly advocate a more objective-oriented approach. Not only does this bring media evaluation into line with the measurement of the entire sponsorship but it also removes all question as to what the sponsor is trying to achieve through media coverage.

In preparing your sponsorship plan and evaluation strategies, work with the corporate sponsorship manager to determine the specific kinds of results they are seeking. How do they evaluate their media placements? By working closely with the sponsorship manager, you will ensure that both organisations understand how you will evaluate the media gained and what specific results you are seeking.

A media assessment report might include the following:

- determination of the quality of the placement
- audience profile (who watches or reads the media or visits that website)
- type of coverage
- key messages communicated

- prominence and position
- theme of articles and interviews
- reach of media geographic, size of audience, range of media
- sponsorship acknowledgment by number of articles and interviews.

Managing the sponsor

Although sponsors are generally becoming much more professional in the way that they do business, as a major stakeholder you will probably still find yourself managing the process at one time or another. The following information should help.

Sponsee information kit

In your first meeting with the sponsor once the contract is signed, we suggest providing the sponsor with an information kit that contains the following items:

- details and an overview of responsibilities for all key contacts on your side
- a copy of your sponsorship plan
- media/marketing matrix, showing dates for all marketing activities, preferably including the promotional activities of all sponsors as well
- key dates and deadlines
- artwork, including any guidelines, PMS colours etc. in a range of electronic formats
- logo approval process (for sponsor using your logo)
- any other information or materials that will streamline the sponsorship process.

Sponsor information kit

At that same meeting, we suggest you also request an information kit from your sponsor that contains the following items:

- details and an overview of responsibilities for all key contacts on the sponsor's side
- a restatement of their objectives for this sponsorship, your target markets, core brand values etc.
- how the sponsorship and sponsee performance will be evaluated (key performance indicators)
- a template for written reports created by the sponsor in the format they need
- artwork, including any guidelines, PMS colours and so on, both as bromides and on disk
- any other information or materials that will streamline the sponsorship process.

> Providing an information kit will start the relationship on the right foot.

Regular meetings

No, having a beer with them in the sky box does not count. You need to hold regular meetings with the sponsor from inception of the contract right through to the conclusion. This will ensure that you are aware of their situation and goals at all times and will ensure you keep on top of all developments, opportunities and potential trouble spots.

As for timing, we find bi-weekly meetings to be very beneficial. Under no circumstances should you go longer than a month between meetings.

Written updates

If you only have time to meet monthly, then you should definitely be providing a mid-month written update to your sponsor. This only needs to be a concise report of where the sponsorship is, noting anything that is currently outstanding. Ask the sponsor from the outset what information they will need so there is no confusion. Below, you will find a short reporting template that should be very useful.

Reporting template

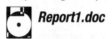

[SPONSORSHIP NAME]

Report date:

Report period:

Report prepared by:

Contracted benefits provided to [*sponsor*] during the month of [*previous month*]:

Added-value benefits provided to [*sponsor*] during the month of [*previous month*]:

Overview of activities to be undertaken by [*sponsee*] during the month of [*next month*]:

Cash payments or contra to be provided during the month of [*next month*]:

Key dates, meetings, and activities for upcoming month(s):

Opportunities/issues to address:

Put everything in writing

It is important to put everything in writing. This way, you have some recourse if something does not get done, addressed or checked. Every time you meet, someone needs to take notes and confirm all action items, including responsibilities and timelines, in writing.

Also, if something needs doing between meetings (and it always does), be sure to put that in writing as well. It does not need to be formal, just a quick email will be sufficient.

Another option is to use an online project management website, which both parties can log onto at anytime. New action items, deadlines, meetings, changes and more can be documented at any time, with reminders sent. There are a number of companies that offer this service. A good starting place might be Basecamp (www.basecamphq.com).

Chapter 11

Leverage

Leverage, to a sponsor, means getting the greatest possible benefit from an investment of money, time or other resources. You may be thinking to yourself, 'What does this have to do with me?' Although maximising a sponsorship is primarily the sponsor's responsibility, you are not completely off the hook.

Even as sponsorship has become more sophisticated, there are still companies that believe that simply becoming a sponsor will achieve their objectives so they don't need to support it. This type of investment is destined to under perform. When they invest in sponsorship, they are investing in opportunity. Leverage is what will reap them results.

Understanding some of the options for leveraging a sponsorship will allow you to educate your sponsor gently and encourage them to utilise their partnership with your organisation fully. We all know that a happy sponsor is a good sponsor, so helping them to achieve their goals is always in your best interest.

There is a rule of thumb that states that for every dollar a sponsor spends on a sponsorship fee, they need to spend another dollar to leverage the sponsorship. This rule is useful if you are working with a sponsor who really does not understand that the sponsorship must be supported, but is not in line with current thinking on sponsorship.

Switched-on sponsors have moved from supporting their sponsorships with other activities, like promotions or public relations, to using sponsorship as a catalyst to improve the results they are getting from other marketing media. They have realised that sponsorship can provide more relevance and excitement around things on which they are already spending money, such as advertising, promotions, e-commerce, loyalty marketing and employee programs. The net effect is that sponsorship is supporting the overall marketing program, not the other way around.

You are probably also wondering what to do with that 10–15% of the sponsorship fee that we have told you to hold aside for servicing the sponsor. Again, that money is not to be used for taking them to lunch or for providing benefits that you have already promised in your agreement. It is for providing additional benefits that will assist your sponsor in achieving their objectives—*leveraging* their sponsorship.

> Although leveraging is not your responsibility, encouraging it is always in your best interests.

Integration

The primary mechanism for any sponsor to leverage their investment is to ensure that it is integrated. Companies around the world are spending billions of dollars on sponsorship. Unfortunately many of those sponsorships are running as self-contained units, having little if anything to do with their greater marketing program or objectives, and they are certainly not performing as well as they could.

Sponsors often think that leverage will cost a large amount of money. In fact, integrating sponsorship with the existing media integration can ease the burden of additional costs by fully utilising all of the marketing vehicles that the sponsor is already paying for. They can drop their costs dramatically, making their whole sponsorship program more cost effective and making it easier to say yes to your offer.

Helping your sponsor to integrate in two ways

Again, integration is not primarily your responsibility. In fact, you will probably shock your sponsor if you take a proactive stance in leveraging their sponsorship. Don't let this unfortunate lack of precedent deter you, however, because sponsors will generally be very happy that you are taking an interest in their success.

The two ideal times to discuss how the sponsorship will be integrated into the sponsor's marketing program are:

1   during your initial sponsor research, when you will ascertain how the sponsor *usually* leverages a sponsorship
2   during the negotiation phase, when you will discuss the specifics of how they will be using—leveraging—this sponsorship, so you can determine the best set of benefits for the job.

Not only will this add value to their sponsorship of your organisation but also to their greater sponsorship program, showing your total dedication to understanding and helping them to achieve their goals.

Although there are several ways for a sponsor to integrate their sponsorship program, the two ways that are appropriate for you to encourage are integrating their team and integrating their marketing media.

Integrating their team

Encouraging your sponsor to create a team of decisionmakers from across departments and outside resources is a great first step. If they hold regular meetings with this team, it will provide them with additional opportunities for leveraging their sponsorships, as well as pointing out potential trouble spots.

Integration can make it easier for a sponsor to say yes to your offer.

Approach integration early in your discussions.

Encourage the sponsor not to overwhelm the group with 'marketing people'. You want to create a multifaceted think tank. Ask them to consider including representatives from the following areas:

➤ advertising agency
➤ corporate communications
➤ customer service
➤ information technology (the people creating website, mobile phone or other electronic content)
➤ distribution
➤ employee representation
➤ key retailers
➤ market research
➤ merchandising
➤ packaging/production
➤ product management
➤ public relations
➤ relationship/loyalty marketing
➤ sales
➤ sales development
➤ sales promotion
➤ sponsorship consultant.

As their sponsorship partner, you should also be involved in all meetings around the planning and implementation of your sponsorship.

If your sponsor seems reluctant to create and administer a team like this, our suggestion is to ask permission from your sponsor to hold a meeting at your premises for representatives of the above departments/subcontractors. Position it as a one-off brainstorming session, which will be followed after the event by a debriefing session. This makes it easy for the sponsor to say yes to this valuable activity and, in many cases, the sponsor will see the value and continue the meetings internally.

Integrating their marketing media

Sponsorship is probably the easiest marketing activity to integrate across marketing media and there is no question that the results are the most dramatic. One needs to look no further than Pepsi or Nike to see that sponsorship really lends itself to this type of activity. Their sponsorships of people and events appear on everything from television commercials to product packaging.

Figure 11.1

Integration has
real commercial
value to *your*
organisation.

This type of integration leverages the sponsor's program by marrying the power of sponsorship to the myriad marketing vehicles that they already have in place. Although there are still costs associated with integration, the cost is generally lower than creating separate supporting programs from scratch.

During the meeting with the sponsor's team, as outlined above, one of the primary questions should be, 'What are all the ways we can use this sponsorship across our existing marketing and communications programs?' Some of the concepts will be great and some won't, but it takes a free flow of ideas in order to find the ones of value.

The good news for you as the sponsee is that every time the sponsor promotes the sponsorship through their various marketing channels, they are also promoting your event. Encouraging this type of integration can greatly extend your marketing reach and has real commercial value to your organisation.

If you can't convince the sponsor of the value of convening a sponsorship team, you can still help your sponsor get buy-in from their various business units, such as sales, loyalty marketing, public relations, information technology or human resources. Work with your key contact to engender their participation through any or all of the following methods:

➤ Meet with business unit decisionmakers to determine their sponsorship needs and discuss how your organisation can help them achieve those objectives.

➢ Provide decisionmakers with a written overview of the sponsorship benefits, target markets reached and some ideas as to how they could use the sponsorship.

➢ Provide a couple of case studies of how other sponsors of your event have achieved tangible results in each of their areas of operation.

➢ Invite decisionmakers to your event so they get a feel for it and so you can start building a relationship.

➢ As business units do start using the sponsorship, keep other decisionmakers informed about how it's going.

This can be done in a subtle or straightforward manner. You will need to work with your key contact to determine which method will get the best response within their company.

> You need to know what a sponsor goes through to leverage a sponsorship.

Leverage options

There are dozens, if not hundreds, of ways to leverage a sponsorship. If you are going to assist your sponsor in achieving a fully leveraged program, you should have at least a working knowledge of their options.

This section is also meant to give you an understanding of what the sponsor will go through in order to make their sponsorship of your organisation work. We are not suggesting that you do this for them but you should assist the sponsor in any way that you can. Don't fall into the trap of thinking that the sponsor has the easy job, because making a sponsorship really deliver on objectives is hard work.

This is not an exhaustive study of the subject but outlines some of the more common ways of leveraging a sponsorship.

Promotions

Promotion is the general term for a sponsor creating a sponsorship-driven activity in partnership with one or more other organisations that benefits all involved. These could include:

➢ media promotion

➢ sponsor cross-promotion

➢ non-sponsor cross-promotion

➢ retail promotion

➢ internal promotion.

The different types of promotions are defined below.

Media promotion

Media promotion is when a sponsor develops a cross-promotion with one or more media organisations. This is very common and can be extremely powerful—the more creative the execution the better.

EXAMPLE

A frozen pizza company is a sponsor of the local baseball team, along with a lot of other companies. It decides to stand out from the crowd by creating a promotion with one of the top radio stations in town, with winners attending spring training with the team in Florida, all expenses paid. The hook—contestants have to rewrite the words to the classic baseball anthem, 'Take me out to the ballgame', using the sponsor's name and pleading its case as to why it should be chosen. Entries, along with proofs of purchase of its pizzas, were sent to the radio station, with the best entries chosen to sing their songs on air. The result was a terrific breakthrough and exceptionally strong linkages between the pizza company and the team.

Sponsor cross-promotion

This is when two or more sponsors work together to create a promotion that achieves objectives for each of them.

EXAMPLE

A surf clothing manufacturer and music retailer are both sponsors of a surf and skate festival. They are both targeting the same audience. Using the event as the focal point of the promotion, they decide to work together to double the effectiveness of their support spend by structuring the following deal:

➤ *With every two CDs purchased from the music retailer, the customer receives a coupon redeemable for $10 off the purchase of two items of the sponsor's surf clothing. This creates a point of difference for the highly value-oriented customers of the music retailer, while driving people to retailers of surf clothing to redeem their coupons.*

➤ *With every $100 spent on the sponsor's surf clothing, the customer receives a voucher for a free CD from a selected range at the music sponsor's stores, offering a strong incentive for people to purchase that brand of surf clothing rather than any other brand carried by surf retailers. The surf clothing manufacturer then agreed to pay the music retailer a heavily discounted rate for each CD redeemed, and the music retailer further benefited because research has shown that most people buy more than one CD at a time.*

> You should be
> proactive in
> getting your
> sponsors together.

As sponsors of the same property, they already have something in common. They are also probably interested in the same marketplace (or at least segments of the same marketplace). It makes perfect sense that sponsors can get together to create cross-promotions that support both sponsorships—saving both parties money while doubling the communication base.

Some sponsees go to great lengths to keep their sponsors apart, afraid that they will compare notes on benefits and costs. We do not recommend this strategy and, instead, recommend that you facilitate sponsor cooperation. After all, if your sponsorships work better, you are more likely to have happy, productive sponsors that you will retain year after year.

Cross-promoting with non-sponsors

Sometimes it makes sense for sponsors to develop cross-promotions with companies outside of the circle of event sponsors.

EXAMPLE

A web-based travel agency is a major sponsor of a large consumer travel expo. It is targeting the savvy vacation traveller with a new service set to revolutionise how computer users travel. As there is a necessary correlation between using the service and having access to a computer, they decided to create a promotion with a non-sponsor computer manufacturer. The computer company was interested because there is a strong correlation between savvy vacation travellers and home computer owners and they also wanted an opportunity to showcase the exceptional multimedia and Internet capabilities of their machine.

At the event, the travel agency and computer company set up a large number of top-quality home computing machines, allowing the consumer to test drive both the service and the computer's capabilities. When a person logged on for a demonstration, they filled in a comprehensive, computer-based questionnaire, building a database and capturing information about both their travel habits and computer use. This also entered the consumer into a draw to win the vacation they requested using the service (further encouraging them to test the service to the fullest) and a home computer.

Cross-promoting with non-sponsors can provide a lot of freedom in selecting cross-promotional partners and, hence, excellent results can be gained. You must, however, be aware of some potential areas for conflict:

➤ Cross-promotions can be used by non-sponsors as a means for ambushing their competition, for example, if the event sponsor, Gatorade, created a promotion

Warning: non-sponsor cross-promotions can be very problematic.

with non-sponsor Reebok, when Nike is among the other event sponsors. The deal may be great and their intentions may be honourable but you could be caught up in controversy. If you want to be seen as protecting your sponsors from ambush, you must ensure that no promotional partners are seen as competing, directly or indirectly, with your current sponsors.

➤ Even if there isn't a potential conflict involved, sponsees need to be careful about cross-promotions with non-sponsors. If you are not careful about limiting the benefits provided (through the sponsor) to their partner, you may end up with a situation where the non-sponsor is getting the benefits of sponsorship without paying a fee. Do two things: ensure your contract employs ample controls for passing on benefits to a partner; and be sure that the benefits delivered to your own organisation through the cross-promotion are greater than the perceived loss.

➤ Media can also be a problem. If an event has an official media partner and one of your sponsors does a media promotion with a competitor, there are likely to be some noses out of joint, although that rarely stops it from happening.

Retail cross-promotion

Retail cross-promotion involves the sponsor's retailers and/or distribution system and is often a key element in fully leveraged sponsorship programs. Retail cross-promotion can add weight to other sales promotional activities and can serve to communicate the marketing message powerfully at the point of purchase.

EXAMPLE

A prestige car manufacturer took out the presenting sponsorship of a major national tour by a high-profile symphony orchestra. The car manufacturer was about to introduce a new roadster and decided to use the tour to launch the new car to their most influential customers.

The car manufacturer worked closely with their top dealers in each city to develop launch receptions for current owners of their marque. These receptions were held on opening night and featured the unveiling of the new car. Everything about the launch reeked of quality and prestige and, after the event, guests were treated to the opening night performance in the best seats in the house.

The dealers used the event to add value to their relationships with their top customers, underscoring not only the quality of the vehicles but the esteem in which the dealers hold their clients. To extend the relationship even further, after the event the dealer sent a thank you card to each client, along with a special-edition branded CD of the symphony orchestra.

Although the above example deals with a very targeted customer group, retail sponsorship can work just as well with a wide variety of retail outlets, such as grocery stores, specialty retailers or petrol stations.

On the side of the retailer, a powerful cross-promotion can serve to increase store traffic and sales, as well as to create a point of difference from the competition. In order to achieve this for the retailer, the sponsor must be willing to share perceived ownership of all or part of their sponsorship of your organisation.

As the sponsee, a major retail promotion driven by one of your sponsors can be an extraordinarily effective way to communicate your marketing message. So if it is not conflicting with other paying sponsors, we wholeheartedly recommend that you are proactive on this point.

> We strongly recommend retail cross-promotions.

Internal promotion

As powerful as sponsorship can be for communicating with a sponsor's customers, it can be just as powerful for communicating with their employees and shareholders. It can help them to increase their knowledge base, boost morale, increase productivity or simply give something back to the people who make their company what it is.

Within a larger sponsorship portfolio, it is not above the realm of possibility that a sponsor could select a sponsorship specifically to achieve employee-based objectives.

When looking at promoting sponsorships internally, be sure to think about what is important to the sponsor's employees. There are no hard and fast rules but here are some suggestions:

- merchandising, usually done to employees or shareholders at cost
- employee perks (merchandise, tickets, celebrity appearances etc.)
- product knowledge programs
- incentive programs
- volunteer programs, creating fun ways for the sponsor's employees to become materially involved in the sponsorship
- contests for an employee to travel to a major event to be the company 'representative'
- 'family day at . . .' where employees and their families go for free.

Loyalty marketing

Once the bastion of airlines and hotel groups, loyalty marketing has now become a huge and growing area for a whole range of sponsors. From breweries to shampoos to cars to software, they are realising that keeping customers and encouraging them to

Case studies: Employee programs

Northern Ireland has the highest incidence of breast cancer in the world and there is a crying need for both education and fundraising. Action Cancer worked with the Nambarrie Tea Company to create an award-winning cause-related marketing program that accomplished both. The key to their success was staff involvement. Nambarrie actually shut down production for a day so that staff could create boxes of 'Breast Cancer Awareness' ribbons instead, which Nambarrie's route drivers then delivered to stores around Northern Ireland. Not only were the staff involved in the creation of an on-pack promotion that raised over £200 000 for the charity, they also helped educate the community about breast cancer, and calls to Action Cancer's help line increased dramatically.

Australia Post was a sponsor of the 1996 Australian Olympic Team that competed in Atlanta and, in addition to numerous consumer and business activities, used this sponsorship to anchor a number of staff initiatives, including:

- Product knowledge competition—Australia Post had introduced a number of products to compete with new expedited delivery entrants to the marketplace, but soon realised that a lot of their employees didn't fully understand the new products. This competition raised the level of product understanding, requiring a perfect score for an entry to go into a draw for a trip to the Atlanta Games. Product knowledge rose by more than 60% as a direct result of this promotion.
- Olympic Postie competition—with hundreds of athletes at the games, there would be a lot of fan mail to deliver to them. Australia Post held a competition to search for the ultimate postie, who would have the

honour of representing the company in Atlanta. Entrants had to demonstrate both outstanding knowledge of and patriotism for both Australia and Australia Post.

- Merchandise—Australia Post partnered with Australian team sponsor Adidas to produce a line of authentic athletic wear—much of it the same as the team would wear—that carried the Australia Post logo along with the Australian flag and the Olympic rings. This merchandise was offered at wholesale price to Australia Post employees, who purchased hundreds of thousands of dollars' worth in the lead-up to the games.
- Olympic Job Opportunity Program—in addition to sponsoring the Australian team, Australia Post also employed twelve high-profile team members, providing them with an income and flexible hours in the lead-up to Atlanta. They had all kinds of jobs. Some even delivered mail! In addition to the promotional opportunities created by this program, having these athletes employed alongside the regular workforce was a real morale builder. They also won six medals—two gold, two silver and two bronze.

An employee survey showed that the impact of this sponsorship on their performance and commitment to their jobs was at least 15 points higher on every aspect than for Australia Post's sponsorship of the 1992 Olympic team. The Olympic Postie delivered 200 000 pieces of mail to Australian athletes in Atlanta.

Some sponsors even take on sponsorship to *attract* employees. Taste of the Nation worked with aeronautics company Lockheed Martin to promote employment opportunities to the event's affluent, ambitious 25–35 year old target market.

be more loyal and involved with the product are more cost effective than chasing new customers. They are constantly trying to move their customers through the relationship continuum and are realising that sponsorship is one of the most effective and powerful ways to do this.

Figure 11.2

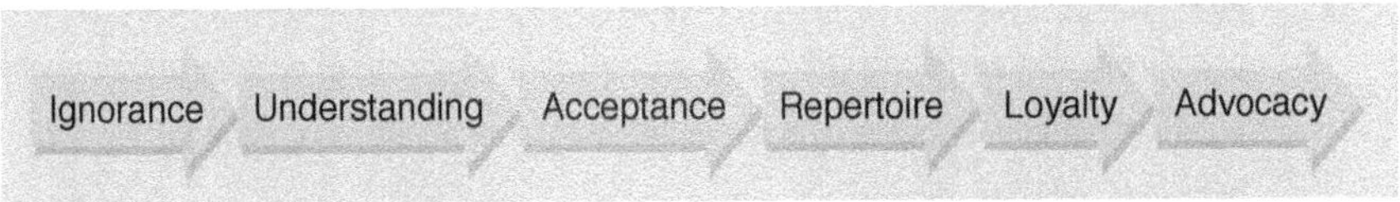

Ignorance | Understanding | Acceptance | Repertoire | Loyalty | Advocacy

> Ignorance—Have heard of the sponsor's brand, but don't understand it
> Understanding—understand the sponsor's brand, but haven't determined its relevance to them
> Acceptance—accept the sponsor's brand, but don't regularly use it
> Repertoire—sponsor's brand is part of the repertoire of brands in the category (e.g. soft drink, airline) that the consumer uses regularly
> Loyalty—only use the sponsor's brand
> Advocacy—only use the sponsor's brand and advocate it to others

There are two main ways of developing loyalty: increasing relevance, and adding value to the relationship.

Increasing relevance

In basic terms, this is about communicating or demonstrating why a brand or product should be important to someone—increasing the relevance of that brand or product in that person's life.

As a sponsee, you are well placed to do this. The sponsor's target market already sees your event as being relevant to them—they care about it and are spending their money and/or time being involved. If you can help the sponsor showcase the product in a way that aligns it with the target market interests, needs or desires, you are providing huge value to the sponsor.

EXAMPLE

An environmental cause takes up a sponsorship from a laundry powder manufacturer. The powder is very environmentally friendly, but this has never been a major part of their marketing campaigns. In the face of increasing competition from other mainstream laundry powders, the manufactuer has now decided to highlight their environmental point of difference and is looking for a credible platform for their new marketing plan.

The environmental cause assists the sponsor in creating this relevant point of difference in a number of ways, including focusing communication on the damage to waterways of using many mainstream soap products. It promotes the sponsor's powder as a responsible household product. They also puts an endorsement on the laundry powder packaging and provides information on waterway conservation for use on the box. Finally, the environmental cause works with the sponsor to develop and promote a cause-related marketing program whereby a small donation is made for every box of laundry powder sold.

Adding value

In the old days, this was referred to as 'giving perks', but back then perks were usually reserved for important clients and, sometimes, employees.

When frequent flyer programs came on the scene, they changed the way companies did business forever. As soon as airlines started telling people that their loyalty was important enough for them to reward, consumers started expecting their loyalty to be valued by other companies as well.

The past few years have seen sponsorship used as a big source of perks for loyal customers. Because of the personal, and often emotional, nature of people's relationships with events, offering event-related benefits to these customers carries a lot more weight than more standard rewards.

Your job as a sponsorship seeker is one of working with the sponsor to provide benefits or create opportunities that make your sponsor's customers feel valued, because they aren't available to just anyone.

> It is usually better to provide a small benefit to a lot of customers than a big prize to just one.

While it is often easier to create a customer-only promotion offering prizes to a few winners, it is usually far more effective to offer a small benefit that is available to everyone in the target group. These could include:

- discounts to the event (or some related aspect, like parking)
- an exclusive event just for customers
- a service that is available only to customers. Orange offering their mobile phone customers a place to charge up their phones at music festivals is a good example
- early access to event tickets
- exclusive access to special online events, like chats with celebrities or event videos
- access to exclusive merchandise
- a special area of the event dedicated to customers.

Case studies: Driving brand loyalty

In 2002, an IEG/Performance Research survey indicated that 'increasing consumer loyalty' was the top priority of corporate sponsors, with 62% rating it a 9 or 10 out of 10 in terms of importance. Translate this to sponsorship seekers, and it means that your sponsor benefits packages will need to reflect a bigger emphasis on increasing loyalty. Here are a few ways that sponsors and sponsorship seekers are working together to engender loyalty.

In 2000, American Express launched the Blue Card in the United States. The Blue Card is a 'smart' credit card aimed at the younger, technology savvy consumer. American Express chose a Sheryl Crow concert in Central Park, New York City, for the launch of the new card, selling advance tickets exclusively to new Blue Card holders. The concert sold out in three hours. Blue was launched as the hip, must-have credit card.

Diet Coke provided UK drinkers with an extra chapter of *Bridget Jones's Diary*, available only with the purchase of a Diet Coke multi-pack.

The Radio City Christmas Spectacular provided sponsor Chase Manhattan Bank with the opportunity to offer employees and customers $10 discounts on tickets.

The Rolling Stones' 1997 US tour was sponsored by telecommunications company Sprint, who provided customers with the unique opportunity to purchase tickets before they went on sale to the general public.

Through a partnership with the exhibition 'Paul Cezanne, the father of modern painters', Italy's Omnitel Vodafone offered their mobile phone customers a 50% discount on the admission price.

| Web-based activities

Putting your sponsor's logo and a link on your website is old news. The new wave in sponsorship and the Internet is for the sponsor to increase interest in the website by using sponsorship-driven content as the drawcard.

The ways that your event can enhance a sponsor's website and the result the sponsor gets from that website are limited only by imagination. They could include:

➤ webcasting all or part of the event

➤ videos

➤ online chats with event-related celebrities

➤ provision of event programs, maps and coupons

➤ event-driven promotions

➤ event-oriented games or chat rooms

➤ event-oriented wallpaper

➤ creating forums for people to participate in the event in some way. Sponsors have used comedy festival sponsorships to host online joke contests, sport sponsorships

to provide a 'coaching suggestion box' and food festival sponsorships to host online recipe contests (using their product, of course).

Whatever you do, work with your sponsor to create something that will really grab the audience. And remember, anything a sponsor does with a sponsorship on their website can be very beneficial to your event as well.

Some of our favourite examples of using a sponsorship to create a great destination website are:

- www.pepsi.com
- www.skichevy.com
- www.savethejaguar.com
- www.xxxx.com.au (and no, it's not an x-rated site—XXXX is a beer!)
- www.budweiser.com
- www.millerbeer.com

We know, there are a lot of breweries on the list. They just happen to be really good at using sponsorship and the Internet. Use all of these sites for inspiration. Show them to your sponsors and suggest ways that you can help them to create a more interesting, relevant site for their customers and potential customers.

Finally, don't limit yourself to Internet activity. SMS, MMS and 3G technology is increasingly being used by telecommunications sponsors to leverage their sponsorships. Banks are starting to put sponsorship-driven communications and promotions on their ATMs. As technology increases in penetration and sophistication, the opportunities for enhancing marketing efforts through that technology will increase as well.

Case studies: Web-based activities

Pepsi has used their major sponsorships of properties as diverse as motor sport, music, baseball and big budget movies to create a content-driven destination site that appeals to several key target markets. This is one of the very best in the business: www.pepsi.com

Miller Beer has another terrific sponsorship-driven website. They provide a variety of interactive games online, including a game called 'Digital Crew Chief' where you are in charge of the Miller Racing Team's pit crew. Miller also has a great music section for their

brand, Rellim, complete with video footage and an interactive 'Backstage Experience' (www.millerbeer.com).

The National Space Centre in the UK provided telecommunications giant BT with the opportunity for children to have their digital photo taken with ET. All of the photos were then posted to the BT website, driving traffic and providing an added-value experience for BT's target market of kids 10–13 and their families. In the first four months of operation, almost 70 000 children participated.

Subaru uses its sponsorships of various outdoorsy events and associations to generate content for the Outdoor Life section its website. Content includes event information, training tips and even a gardening section, all tailored to appeal to the Subaru target market: www.subaru.com

Madonna's 2001 Drowned World Tour provided America Online with a huge variety of content for their website. Online activities included the creation of a 'virtual backstage pass', with videos, chat rooms, tour news and exclusive photos. AOL also included online access to concerts through online promotions for tickets and early ticket sales to new members.

Wireless sponsors or major sport teams around the world are now using that sponsorship to bolster their WAP offering, providing up-to-the-minute team news to subscribers.

People attend parades for the atmosphere, and Santa.com made the crowd an even bigger part of the atmosphere at the Santa.com Holiday Parade. They filled the streets with camera-wielding elves who snapped hundreds of digital photos of attendees, which were then shown on parade floats for everyone to see—instant holiday stardom!

Database generation and research

Many sponsors have a component of database marketing to their businesses. If they do any kind of mailings or billings, or have a loyalty program (e.g. frequent flyer points), they will probably be very interested in database development.

Even if actually generating a database is not a big priority, they may be very interested in using the sponsorship as a catalyst to poll their target market, gaining research on their opinions and purchasing habits. There are literally dozens of ways to generate database information around a sponsorship, including:

➤ ticket sales
➤ contests
➤ competitions
➤ toll-free numbers
➤ trial offers
➤ discount offers
➤ test drives
➤ coupons
➤ registrations
➤ point of sale material
➤ kids' pages
➤ fan clubs
➤ Internet sites
➤ sales receipts

➤ information inquiries

➤ membership programs

➤ warranties

➤ welcome cards

➤ exit/entrance surveys

➤ post-event research

➤ product registration.

Once your sponsor has chosen one or more mechanisms for capturing data, they will need to decide what kind of information to ask. You need to keep it short and simple, but should capture:

➤ name

➤ email

➤ telephone number

➤ age range

➤ date and product or brand last purchased

➤ why they chose that product or brand.

It can also be very useful to capture the following types of information, which serve the dual purpose of providing customer and potential customer research:

➤ income level

➤ what other brands they have tried

➤ their three most important product characteristics (e.g. quality, price, warranty, location of retailer)

➤ how often they purchase the product

➤ where they purchase the product (e.g. grocery store, petrol station)

➤ when they plan to make their next purchase of . . . (e.g. car, home loan, holiday, computer).

As you are reading through this, you should be thinking to yourself that these activities parallel nicely with the kind of research you want to be doing for your organisation or event. Working together with your sponsor can generate a lot of information very cost effectively for both of you.

| Hospitality

Many sponsors have realised that standard VIP hospitality programs—sky boxes, tickets to the opera etc.—are no longer cutting it. Their customers were receiving too many invitations from too many companies and they were all virtually identical. Many

Database generation will often work well in concert with your event research.

sponsees have responded by developing much more creative hospitality opportunities that allow their sponsors to stand apart from the crowd and appeal to their customers in a far more personal way.

Work with your sponsors to determine who their key customers are and what will appeal to them. If they are family oriented, create something that lets them spend quality time with their kids. If they are young and sporty, create something that appeals to their sense of competition or adventure. If they are status oriented, create something that stands out as an exclusive, must-attend event. Whatever you do, try to encourage the sponsor to think outside the square and do something that has real meaning to their key customers.

Case studies: Hospitality

Habitat for Humanity encourages their sponsors to invite their key customers to build days, and sponsors are seeing big uptake. They are finding that the idea of picking up a hammer to help build a house for an underprivileged family has a lot of appeal to key customers, and the demonstration of shared values creates bonds on a whole different level.

Several Ryder Cup golf matches feature high-tech business centres created by telecommunications company Sprint. They allow businesspeople attending the all-day event to keep in touch with the office by email, phone and even videoconferencing, showcasing Sprint's products while providing a truly valuable service to clients and potential clients alike.

One major investment bank found their hospitality package at the symphony was losing its appeal to clients. The symphony worked closely with the bank to create a series of exclusive, top quality, one-of-a-kind events, often in off-beat locations. The clients loved it from the start and it quickly became the place to be for major decisionmakers and an unbeatable relationship-building opportunity.

Many sponsees are starting to cater for family hospitality by creating events for the children and grandchildren of VIPs, such as sports clinics, behind-the-scenes tours and family days in hospitality suites (often complete with personalised merchandise and autograph sessions). Some sponsees even use children of VIPs in or around the event itself, often as extras in event advertising and public relations.

Publicity

Publicity is often an important part of sponsorship programs. There is plenty written about publicity and we are not pretending to be experts in this area but we offer the following general advice.

You can do several very simple things to help your sponsor leverage public relations around their investment:

➤ Work closely with your sponsor's public relations department or agency so that you are involved in any publicity activities they may undertake around the sponsorship.

> Include the sponsor's marketing message in all of your publicity activities and endeavour to weave that message into newsworthy angles.

> Ensure that your organisation's publicity activities include the sponsor's target marketplaces, even if they may not be your core markets (e.g. if your sponsor is an automobile manufacturer, ensure that the motoring press are included). Ask your sponsor who their specific targets are, including both consumer and intermediate customers.

One other thing to remember about publicity: of all the ways that a sponsor can leverage their sponsorship, publicity is the one over which they have the least control. They can't make someone cover the event, much less say what they want them to say about their brand or the sponsorship. If a sponsor is overly fixated on publicity as the goal of sponsorship, it might be prudent to point this out before outlining the myriad of ways that you can work together on more controllable leverage options.

Ambush protection

No other aspect of sponsorship has received as much attention in recent years as ambush marketing. Ambush marketing is, very simply, when a non-sponsor undertakes activities that do one or both of the following:

> Create confusion in the marketplace as to who the rightful sponsor is. This is often accomplished through the creation of promotions that have the look and feel of the event, or use similar or leading words, without actually saying they are a sponsor. The result is that the non-sponsor receives much of the benefit of being a sponsor without paying the fee.

> Undermine a rightful sponsor. Even if a company does not engage in the more obvious type of ambush outlined above, they can still cause problems for a rightful sponsor. A classic example is the major football event that was sponsored by a brewer. A rival brewer paid a stripper a few hundred dollars to streak across the field at an appropriate moment. The result was that virtually every newspaper in the country ran a photo of the streaker instead of the game on the front page of the sports section.

There are two ways for a sponsor to be protected against ambush, and even then it can happen.

Legal

The main problem with preventing ambush marketing is that most of the time it is perfectly legal. The only time that it is not legal is if the ambushing company falsely represents that it is a sponsor, claims endorsement by the sponsee or blatantly misleads the public into believing these things to be true.

The best way to protect your sponsors through legal channels is to ensure that ambush protection is written into the contract. This will demonstrate that you will not under any circumstances sell sponsorship, vending rights or signage to any of the sponsor's competitors and will compel you to protect their rights within the scope of any media or subcontractor deals. But this is still only a partial measure because most ambushes have nothing directly to do with the sponsee.

Strategic

The best ambush protection a sponsor can possibly have is to leverage their sponsorship fully. If they have created a strong program of support for their investment, any activities mounted by their competition will look weak and stupid by comparison.

If you want to assist the sponsor in checking their vulnerability, work closely with them to assess potential risk areas and assist in any way you can to minimise those risks.

Chapter 12

Renewals and exits

All good things must come to an end, and sponsorship is no exception. Whether the sponsorship has been short or long term, the time will eventually come when it will either be renewed or exited.

This scenario causes a lot of angst among some sponsorship seekers, particularly those who think themselves lucky for having signed up a sponsor in the first place, but it really doesn't need to. Like death and taxes, it is just part of the process.

Renewals

It is usually far easier to renew an existing sponsor than it is to find a new one, so taking the right approach to renewals will save you a lot of time, money and angst.

Start early

Many contracts have a specific time by which the renewal process will start, but our advice is to ignore it. Start the renewal process as early as you can, making it essentially an extension of your servicing activities. Throughout the sponsorship, you should be working with the sponsor to understand and meet their needs. As you get closer to the end of the contract, your vocabulary should shift from focusing on the coming year to a focus on the bigger picture and how you can continue to develop your relationship through coming years and events.

The timing of when you will want to start discussing renewal in earnest will vary from one event to another, but you will need to keep the following well in mind:

➤ It takes most sponsors at least 4–6 months to create and implement a leverage program for a sponsorship. If their needs, and the benefits package you are offering to meet them, have changed significantly, you need to give them enough time to get a new leverage program together.

➤ Give yourself enough leeway so that, just in case the sponsor doesn't renew, you have plenty of time to re-sell the sponsorship.

> If you have been servicing your sponsor well, there will be no surprises.

Start fresh

Many sponsorship seekers make the mistake of offering a sponsor the same benefits package again at renewal. This may be easy, but you will be missing out on a great opportunity to improve your relationship and their results.

The beginning of the renewal process is the ideal time to sit down with your sponsor to discuss their current needs, objectives, target markets and any new initiatives so that a new package can be developed that really does the job for them.

➤ Go through the same information gathering process that you would if they were a new sponsor. You may even want to use the **Sponsor Information Checklist** as a guide.

➤ Speak with decisionmakers across the sponsor's business units. You may be able to create a package that meets more of their needs.

➤ Be open with the sponsor regarding your organisation's marketing needs and challenges. This is a golden opportunity to re-create a relationship that achieves *mutual* marketing objectives.

➤ Don't be constrained by set benefits packages. Be flexible and creative in your response to the sponsor's needs. Use your inventory!

> If your sponsor doesn't renew, don't lose your cool.

Exits

When a sponsor doesn't renew, it can be very stressful on an entire organisation and it can be very tempting to start apportioning blame. This is always counterproductive. Most sponsorships are exited for strategic reasons, not because your organisation has done anything wrong or because the sponsor is being unfair or arbitrary.

There are a number of reasons why a sponsor may want to exit a sponsorship, including:

➤ a major shift in objectives or target markets

➤ the sponsorship was entered into for the wrong reasons or it wasn't a good match from the start

➤ lack of interest, and therefore integration, across the business units

➤ consolidation of the sponsorship portfolio into fewer, larger investments

➤ a new sponsorship or brand manager who wants to overhaul the sponsorship portfolio whether it needs it or not

➤ budget cutbacks

➤ a global directive to concentrate on a specific sponsorship or type of sponsorship (e.g. the Olympics)

➤ a corporate merger resulting in the duplication of some sponsorship investments

➤ a major change in the type of event and/or its audience (e.g. your organisation has shifted from presenting a consumer travel show to a travel trade show).

Then again, the sponsorship may have simply passed its prime and it's just time to do something else. It is widely accepted that the lifespan of a fully leveraged sponsorship averages around seven years. Even if the sponsorship has been livened up every year, at some point the returns gained by the sponsor are going to start diminishing and it will be time to move on.

Again, if you have been doing a good job at servicing your sponsor, the fact that they don't plan to renew should not come as any surprise. In most cases, you should know far enough ahead of time to find another sponsor to take their place.

Even if it does come as a surprise, try to take it in your stride. There have been many cases where sponsorship seekers have thrown the equivalent of a tantrum—going to the media, badmouthing the sponsor—and all they ever accomplished was looking like a bunch of idiots and scaring off potential new sponsors. After all, what sponsor would want to work with a sponsee who may try to damage the brand if the relationship doesn't go on forever?

Next steps

As soon as you find out that your sponsor is not renewing, there are a few things you need to do:

1 Debrief the sponsor so you can understand exactly why they aren't renewing.

2 If your organisation is at fault in any way, accept responsibility and go about fixing the problem. You should also discuss the problem with your other sponsors to let them know it is being addressed.

3 If your organisation wasn't at fault, ask the sponsor for referrals to other sponsors who may be a better fit. You should also ask the sponsor if you can use them as a reference.

4 Ask your other sponsors for referrals.

5 Look at the benefits package you have been providing the sponsor. Is there an opportunity to use those benefits to increase your other existing sponsorships?

6 Take the opportunity to update your inventory and proposal template.

7 Get out there and find another sponsor.

What if it's *your* organisation that doesn't want to renew?

It happens. Sometimes a sponsor is unresponsive. Sometimes they are painful to work with. Sometimes they just don't fit well with your image or audience. Sometimes there is a better, more profitable, more active and more partnership-oriented sponsor waiting in the wings. (If that is the case, count yourself lucky.)

Before you write off a sponsor, be sure you have done everything you can to get the relationship on track. If it's just not happening, try to afford the sponsor the same courtesy you would expect from them. Give them plenty of notice that you are not intending to go forward with the sponsorship and, without vilifying them, tell them why.

Conclusion

That's it . . . the 3rd edition of *The Sponsorship Seeker's Toolkit*. If your head is spinning and you're wondering if sponsorship is really worth all the effort, don't worry, that's normal. On the other hand, you may be so excited about the possibilities that you can't wait to put these systems into place in your organisation tomorrow. That's normal too. In fact, we wouldn't be surprised if you were feeling both ways!

There is no doubt that sponsorship is a sophisticated, demanding pursuit, and one that is easier to get wrong than right. Our aim in putting this book together is to provide you with a system for selling and servicing sponsorships, as well as the street smarts that will make operating in this complicated field much easier.

We have developed and refined our approach over our combined 40-odd years in sponsorship. The results enjoyed by the hundreds of participants in our workshops, and readers of previous editions who have raved non-stop since the book was first published in 1999, prove without a shadow of doubt that this approach works exceedingly well across a wide range of sponsorship seekers—from sport to culture to government, large organisations to small, beginners to seasoned professionals.

Asking for money is never easy. What we have provided you with are the theory and tools for creating successful partnerships. Our premise is simple and based on three key principles:

1 Ensure you fully understand your audience, values and attributes, and what you have to offer a sponsor.
2 Create a customised proposal that meets the marketing and business objectives of your potential sponsor.
3 Undersell and over-deliver.

There is no magic wand for sponsorship. Success revolves around good research and hard work. Consider the sales process as 75% preparation, 10% sales and 15% follow through, and you will be pretty close to the mark. Most organisations barely prepare, approach sales as a simple transaction and don't follow up at all. It's no wonder that most sponsorship efforts fail.

No one can guarantee that every proposal you create will be successful. What we can guarantee you is that if you follow the process we've outlined in this book, your offers will have a much greater rate of success.

It is important that all of us as practitioners recognise that sponsorship marketing is a rapidly evolving marketing tool. We need to work together—sharing ideas, evaluation techniques and case studies—if we are to continue to succeed in creating win–win–win partnerships. Don't be afraid to share information, pricing and evaluation strategies and networks. Remember, what goes around comes around.

In the same vein, we would love to hear how this approach to sponsorship works for you and welcome your feedback. Our contact details can be found at the back of the book.

We have greatly enjoyed creating both *The Sponsorship Seeker's Toolkit* and its third edition for you and look forward to meeting many of you as we travel around the world doing workshops.

Wishing you successful sponsorships!

Kim and Anne-Marie

Part 4

appendices

Glossary

Above-the-line advertising
Traditional advertising venues—television, radio, newspaper, magazine and outdoor advertising. Also known as 'main media'.

Activation
The sponsor-generated activities that take place around a sponsorship and deliver most of the value of a sponsorship investment. Also called 'maximisation' or 'leverage'.

Added value
The provision of an unexpected, meaningful benefit to a customer or sponsor, primarily done to strengthen the relationship with them.

Advertising
Placing a commercial message in above-the-line media.

Advertorial
When a company purchases the right to place favourable editorial material or editorial material with a distinctly commercial slant in a publication or on a program for a fee. Generally, it must carry wording that clearly states that it is a paid advertisement.

Agent
An individual or organisation that sells sponsorship properties on a commission or fee basis. Also known as a 'broker'.

Ambush marketing
An organisation creating the perception that they are a sponsor of a property, or somehow involved with the event experience, when they have not purchased the rights to that property.

Below-the-line advertising
Non-traditional advertising avenues (anything that is not 'above the line'), such as sponsorship, publicity, sales promotion, online activities, relationship or loyalty marketing, coupons, database marketing, direct response and retail promotions.

Brand marketing
Marketing activities with the primary goal of communicating the positioning, personality and non-functional attributes of a brand.

Broker
An individual or organisation that sells sponsorship properties on a commission or fee basis. Also known as an 'agent'.

Cause-related marketing
Cause-related marketing is an investment that strategically links a product, a service or company with a cause or an issue and yields a return for the corporate partner, the non-profit organisation and

the community. Cause-related marketing may include licensing, sponsorship, joint ventures, underwriting and sales promotion.

Clutter

A term used to describe an overload of sponsor messages around one event. It is also used more generally to describe the massive amount of advertising and other marketing messages ever present in developed society today.

Contra

Term to describe products or services that are provided in lieu of cash in exchange for sponsorship rights. Also known as 'in-kind'.

Coverage

Media term referring to the proportion of the target market that has the opportunity to see or hear any one advertisement. It is expressed as a percentage of the total target market. Also known as 'reach'.

Critical success factor

This refers to something you or your sponsor must do right for the sponsorship or event to be a success. Often there are a number of critical success factors for any given activity.

Cross-promotion

When two or more organisations create promotional opportunities that benefit all partners.

CRM

Customer relationship management. The area that controls and manages loyalty and database marketing activity. CRM can also stand for 'cause-related marketing'.

Donation

An offering of product or cash that is given by a company without any anticipated commercial return.

Early adopter(s)

A person or group of people who tend to try new things earlier than others and spread opinions about them. These people are very important to new products and brands and often attract a large percentage of early marketing budgets. Also known as 'trend setters' or 'opinion leaders'.

Exclusivity

Exclusive rights to sponsorship or on-site sales. Typically defined by the sponsor's category of business (e.g. 'exclusive automobile sponsor' or 'exclusive beer vendor').

Fit

The degree to which a sponsorship opportunity matches a brand's objectives, attributes and target markets.

Frequency

Media term referring to the average number of times each member of your target audience receives an advertising message over the course of the advertising campaign.

Grant

The provision of funds or material for a specific project generally not linked to a company's core business. The grant must usually be acknowledged by the recipient and generally must be accounted for. A grant is given on the basis of the

need for the project rather than the promotional and marketing opportunities it may provide.

Image transfer
The process by which a sponsor associates itself with the core values and attributes of a sponsee, with the goal being to introduce or reinforce those attributes within their company or product.

In-kind
Term to describe products or services that are provided in lieu of cash in exchange for sponsorship rights. Also known as 'contra'.

In-pack
The promotion of a sponsorship in the sponsor's actual product packaging. Often done in conjunction with 'on-pack' promotion.

Launch
A public unveiling or announcement of the details of an event, program or sponsorship, which is specifically designed to gain publicity. The launch often marks the start of the marketing program.

Leverage
The sponsor-generated activities that take place around a sponsorship and deliver most of the value of a sponsorship investment. Also called 'maximisation' or 'activation'.

Main media
Traditional advertising venues—television, radio, newspaper, magazine and outdoor advertising. Also known as 'above-the-line advertising'.

Marketing message
The key message that an organisation wants to convey about their product or service through a sponsorship.

Marketing mix
A company's entire marketing program, made up of a mix of marketing activities.

Maximisation
The sponsor-generated activities that take place around a sponsorship and deliver most of the value of a sponsorship investment. Also called 'leverage' or 'activation'.

Measurement
Evaluation of the results of the sponsorship program. Also called 'quantification'

Media sponsorship
An advertising package generally consisting of paid and/or contra advertising, unpaid promotion and/or editorial support and exclusivity.

Merchandising
The creation of promotional items around an event that will then be sold or given away. Merchandise can be produced and distributed by either the event, the sponsor or both.

Naming rights sponsorship
This is basically the same as a principal sponsorship with the added benefit of the sponsor having their name added to

the event name (e.g. the Blockbuster Bowl or the Emirates Melbourne Cup). Also known as 'title sponsorship'.

Narrowcasting

This is the opposite of broadcasting, that is, marketing to a tightly defined group. Also known as 'niche marketing'.

Niche marketing

Targeting a group of people with a very tightly defined set of demographic and/or psychographic characteristics. Also known as 'narrowcasting'.

Offer

The proposal offered to a potential sponsor. Also known as the 'package'.

Official supplier

A (usually) low-level sponsorship in which the sponsor either provides a product or services to the event free or at a substantial discount, often not paying any additional sponsorship fee; or pays a sponsorship fee to secure a guarantee from the sponsee that they will purchase the sponsor's product or service exclusively.

On-pack

The promotion of a sponsorship on the sponsor's actual product packaging. Often done in conjunction with 'in-pack' promotion.

On-selling

A sponsor re-selling portions of the purchased sponsor benefits to one or more other companies. This is usually done with the full knowledge and approval of the sponsee.

Outdoor

Above-the-line advertising that takes place outdoors, such as billboards, posters and taxi or bus signage.

Package

The proposal offered to a potential sponsor. Also known as the 'offer'.

Packaging

Structuring the sponsoring benefits and their relationship to the event and the sponsee.

Pass-through rights

The right for a sponsor to on-sell or give some of the sponsorship benefits to another company.

Perimeter signage

Banners and/or signs that are located near an event but not inside the boundaries of the event itself.

Philanthropy

The voluntary giving of funds by foundations, trusts, bequests, corporations or individuals to support human welfare in its broadest sense.

POD

Point of difference. An attribute that differentiates a product from its competitors. Sponsorship can often be a powerful point of difference.

Point of difference

An attribute that differentiates a product from its competitors. Sponsorship can often be a powerful point of difference.

POS	Point of sale. A display, signage or promotional item produced for display with a product in the store and designed to create excitement and differentiate the product from its competitors.
Point of sale (POS) material	A display, signage or promotional item produced for display with a product in the store and designed to create excitement and differentiate the product from its competitors.
Positioning	The personality of a brand, company or event. Strong brand marketing is often focused on positioning.
Principal sponsor	This is the pre-eminent sponsor of any event or property, receiving the highest level of benefits and promotion.
Promoter	An individual or company who takes on some of the financial risk as well as responsibility for the marketing and promotion of the event in exchange for a portion of the profits.
Property	This term is used as a generic term for 'sponsee'. Also known as 'sponsorship seeker' or 'rights holder'.
Proposal	The sponsorship offer in written form.
Public relations	Editorial media coverage (i.e. newspaper and magazine articles, television and radio coverage) generally in news, current affairs or lifestyle programming. Also known as 'publicity'.
Publicist	A specialist in gaining editorial media coverage.
Publicity	Editorial media coverage (i.e. newspaper and magazine articles, television and radio coverage) generally in news, current affairs or lifestyle programming. Also known as 'public relations'.
Quantification	Evaluation of the results of the sponsorship program. Also known as 'measurement'.
Reach	Media term referring to the proportion of the target market that has the opportunity to see or hear any one advertisement. It is expressed as a percentage of the total target market. Also known as 'coverage'.
Reporting	The ongoing process of providing a sponsor with information regarding the performance of their sponsorship against agreed marketing objectives.
Rights holder	This term is used as a genetic term for 'sponsee'. Also known as 'sponsorship seeker' or 'property'.
Sales promotion	Activities employed to encourage customers to buy a product or differentiate a product from the competition at the point of sale.

Sales sponsorship
A sponsorship that is entered into primarily to gain direct sales (e.g. a brewer sponsoring a festival in order to secure exclusive pouring rights or a hotel chain sponsoring a touring stage show to guarantee all of those room bookings).

Segmentation
Defining different segments of a marketplace based upon demographics, psychographics, perceptions and buying patterns.

Servicing
The process of providing benefits to a sponsor, both what is agreed and additional benefits to assist them in achieving their objectives. Servicing also encompasses strong two-way communication between the sponsor and sponsee, as well as reporting.

Signage
Signs that are specific to an event, such as banners, A-frames, scoreboards etc. These can feature the marketing message of the sponsor, the event or both.

Sponsee
The recipient of the sponsor's primary sponsorship investment (the fee). Typically, sponsees will fall into the categories of arts, cause, education, community service, event, individual, Internet site, sport or venue.

Sponsor
The organisation that buys sponsorship rights, packaged and granted by the sponsee.

Sponsorship
An investment in sport, community or government activities, the arts, a cause, individual or broadcast which yields a commercial return for the sponsor. The investment can be made in financial, material or human terms.

Sponsorship audit
The assessment of each component of a sponsor's sponsorship portfolio against stringent selection criteria, usually leading to a readjustment of the portfolio.

Sponsorship guidelines
A document produced by sponsors that provides potential sponsees with information on the objectives, target markets, parameters, scope and categories of sponsorship investments made by a company.

Sponsorship plan
A detailed plan that documents how a sponsorship will be serviced and implemented by the sponsee.

Sponsorship policy
A document that indicates an organisation's philosophy and approach to sponsorship, including why they are involved, key influences on the sponsorship process and any sponsorship exclusions or limitations.

Sponsorship strategy
A formal document produced by a company or organisation that outlines the target markets, objectives for sponsorship and specific strategies to achieve these goals. This document

is usually closely linked to an organisation's marketing and/or revenue raising strategies. Generally, both sponsors and sponsees will have sponsorship strategies in place.

Sticky marketing
A marketing activity that 'sticks', creating lasting changes in a market's perceptions or behaviours.

Target audience
The most appropriate audience for a particular product, service or event. The audience can be made up of one or several target markets, which can sometimes be quite diverse.

Target market
A group of people who are likely purchasers of a product or service, or who are strong candidates for attending an event, and who share a similar demographic and/or psychographic profile.

TARP (Target Audience Rating Point)
Media term referring to the percentage of the target market reached over the course of an advertising campaign. It is a gross measure, taking into account both reach (the number of people that your message reaches) and frequency.

Title sponsor
This is basically the same as a principal sponsorship with the added benefit of the sponsor having its name added to the event name (e.g. the Blockbuster Bowl or the Emirates Melbourne Cup). Also known as 'naming rights sponsor'.

USP
Unique selling point. The unique attribute(s) of a product or brand that often forms the basis of marketing activities.

Vendor
An organisation or company that sells a product or service at an event. This term is also used to describe a company that supplies a product to a retailer to sell (e.g. Kmart's vendors would include Black & Decker, Unilever, Coca-Cola etc.).

Resources

| Associations

We have put together this list of resources to assist you with skill building, research and developing your networks. This is by no means an exhaustive list but should provide a strong base to get you started. Please note, we have not accepted any fees or special consideration from any of these organisations.

International

International Festivals & Events Association (IFEA)

The IFEA is aimed at events and festival organisers, although it does have some good resources for sponsors of these types of events. There are chapters in 36 countries. IFEA has conferences, publications and even a certificate program. For details, see www.ifea.com.

North America

American Marketing Association

This large association has a wide variety of publications, conferences, workshops and symposiums available across the United States, although sponsorship does not feature heavily in its education program at present. For more information, see the AMA website at www.ama.org, or contact the chapter in your area. A full list is available at www.ama.org.

Canadian Institute of Marketing

This association is well respected across Canada, with chapters and activities in major cities. Its quarterly publication, *The Marketing Challenge*, regularly covers sponsorship. Current and back issues are available free of charge to both members and non-members on the CIM website. For details, see www.cinstmarketing.ca.

Society for Nonprofit Organizations
With more than 6000 members in the US, this association provides a wealth of information, training and other resources to the sector. For more information, see www.snpo.org.

Europe
Chartered Institute of Marketing (UK)
The CIM is the largest marketing association in the world, with branches across the UK and Ireland. Its sponsorship resources are limited, but broader marketing and networking resources are outstanding. For more information, contact the CIM, www.cim.co.uk.

European Sponsorship Association
ESA is the result of a merger between the Institute of Sports Sponsorship and the European Sponsorship Consultants Association. For more information, see www.sponsorship.org.

German Sponsorship Association
Fachverband für Sponsoring und Sonderwerbeformen (FASPO)
A big, active sponsorship association, hosting an annual sponsorship summit and awards, as well as providing other good resources to industry professionals. For more information, see www.faspo.de.

International Festivals and Events Association (Europe)
As the name states, this is the European arm of IFEA, providing a wealth of resources to a brad range of events. For more information, see www.ifeaeurope.com.

The Marketing Society (UK)
This association holds numerous events around the country, as well as a star-studded annual conference. Members also get free access to magazines *Market Leader* and *Marketing Magazine*. For details, see www.marketing-society.org.uk.

Marketing Institute of Ireland
The MII offers lots of marketing resources, news, and networking opportunities. For details, see www.mii.ie.

Norwegian Sponsor & Event Association
Sponsor- og Eventforeningen
With many educational events and resources, this association is a big part of the sophisticated Scandinavian sponsorship industry. For more information, see www.sponsorforeningen.no.

Swedish Sponsorship Association

Sponsrings & Eventföreningen

This very active sponsorship association has many great activities and resources, as well as holding the annual Scandinavian Sponsorship conference. For more information, see www.sefs.se.

Australia/New Zealand

Australasian Sponsorship Marketing Association, Inc. (ASMA)

ASMA is the sponsorship industry association for Australia, reaching into New Zealand as well. They host an annual conference. Members receive a monthly electronic newsletter and discounts to a range of networking and educational activities. For details, see www.asma.com.au.

Australian Marketing Institute

The AMI regularly holds sponsorship-oriented functions and workshops and is a good source of general marketing information. For details, see www.ami.org.au.

Australian Institute of Management

Although not specifically about marketing or sponsorship, this organisation has a good reputation for providing high-quality education to its membership. Great bookshop. For details, see www.aim.com.au.

New Zealand Institute of Management

The NZIM is a very well-respected organisation with a wide variety of marketing courses, including the occasional sponsorship event. Excellent online bookstore. Chapters across New Zealand. For details, see www.nzim.co.nz.

Africa

Institute of Marketing Management (South Africa)

The IMM is primarily a graduate school for marketing, but does hold a wide variety of marketing training sessions for professionals. For details, see www.imm.coza.

More associations

Almost every country has a marketing association, providing support, training and networking to marketing professionals. If you don't know who serves your area, or if you are starting operations in a new country, the following links may be of assistance:

Asia Pacific Marketing Federation

Provides links to marketing associations around the Asia-Pacific region. For details, see www.apmf.org.sg.

European Marketing Confederation

A good resource for European marketers in its own right, this website also links to all of Europe's country marketing associations that make up the confederation. For details, see www.emc.be/associations.cfm.

Publications

North America

Ad Age

Ad Age is very advertising-oriented, but very complete in this regard. It has an excellent website with full articles available free. For details, see www.adage.com.

Brandweek

Although similar in format to its sister publication, *Adweek*, *Brandweek's* focus is squarely on brand marketing, with a big emphasis on below-the-line marketing activities. Sponsorship, sales promotion, relationship marketing, co-promotions—you name it, the magazine covers it and does it well. See www.brandweek.com for more information.

Marketing Magazine (Canada)

This is a well-respected marketing publication with strong marketing information for both Canadians and others. For details, see www.marketingmag.ca.

PROMO

This publication bills itself as 'The Magazine of Promotional Marketing', and is very good. It also has a very complete website and a searchable archive of articles. For details, see www.promomagazine.com.

The Sponsorship Report

This monthly publication has been covering Canada's sponsorship industry for some time and is worth a look. For details, see www.sponsorship.ca.

Sports Business Daily

This is probably the pre-eminent North American publication on the business of sports. The coverage of sponsorship news is plentiful and it will point you in the right direction to get more in-depth information. It is available online at www.sportsbusinessdaily.com.

Europe

Marketing (Ireland)

This monthly consists mainly of snippets of news from around the region. While you are unlikely to get any in-depth coverage of sponsorship issues, it is certainly a good resource to keep you on top of the Irish marketing industry. For more information, see www.marketing.ie.

Marketing (UK)

This is one of the UK's pre-eminent marketing publications. It comes out weekly and has a money-back guarantee. Its website is excellent and very complete. For more information, see www.brandrepublic.com/marketing.

Marketing Week (UK)

This is another top publication in the UK market. It is very comprehensive and covers sponsorship well. It has an excellent website. For details, see www.marketingweek.co.uk.

Sport Business

This large format publication is so slick it would be easy to jump to the conclusion that it is all flash and no substance. Fortunately, that is not the case. It is a very good resource with strong international coverage. Its website is excellent. For details, see www.sportbusiness.com.

Asia

Media Asia

The name of this comprehensive, Asia-wide magazine is a bit of a misnomer, as it covers much more than just media news. The website features current articles only, so check back often. For details, see www.brandrepublic.com/mediaasia.

Australia/New Zealand

B&T/Professional Marketing

B&T is a weekly, advertising-oriented publication, although it does cover marketing in a larger sense as well. *Professional Marketing* is its monthly sister publication, and is more in-depth. *B&T* subscribers receive it for free. *B&T* has a good website. For details, see www.bandt.com.au.

Marketing Magazine

This marketing monthly focuses more on strategy and less on news than other Australian marketing publications. For details, see www.marketingmag.com.au.

NZ Marketing Magazine

This is New Zealand's top marketing magazine with an excellent website. For more information see www.marketingmag.co.nz.

New Zealand Events Update

This monthly publication does a very good job of covering the events and sponsorship industry in New Zealand. Articles tend to be aimed more at sponsees, but the information is great for sponsors as well. For details, see www.insidetourism.com and follow the link to *New Zealand Events Update*.

Sport & Sponsorship News Australia

The content of SSA is news-oriented but quite comprehensive in coverage. For details, see www.pando.com.au/sponsorshipnews.

The Sports Vine

This weekly publication is news oriented and its coverage of sports business in Australia is very complete. For details, see www.thesportsvine.com.

Conferences/seminars

IEG Sponsorship Seminar

This huge conference is held every March in Chicago. It brings together 1500 sponsors and sponsees from around the world for three intense days of education and networking. For more information, see www.sponsorship.com.

International Festivals & Events Association Conferences

IFEA holds conferences and seminars around the world and on a number of different themes, usually very well attended by a great cross-section of festival and event organisers. For details, see www.ifea.com.

UK Sponsorship Summit

A big conference organised by the publishers of *MarketingWeek*. For more information, see www.marketingweek.co.uk.

Research

Research is a large part of preparing any sponsorship document. Below you will find a number of excellent resources for background research.

General

ABI/Inform Full Text Online

Provides the full text of articles from hundreds of publications worldwide. You can print them out or download articles onto your own disk. This service is typically found at universities and business reference libraries.

International Events Group (IEG)

US-based IEG probably does more in the area of sponsorship research than any other organisation. Its databases of sponsor and sponsee information are vast, up to date and very useful. For more information on what is available, see www.sponsorship.com.

Sweeney Research

This organisation does an annual survey of Australians, determining their interest and participation in sports and cultural activities, their attitudes about sponsorship and their recall of specific sponsors. For more information, see www.sweeneyresearch.com.au.

US government sources

➤ American Statistics Index
➤ ASI Abstracts
➤ US Census

General business sources

- Encyclopedia of Business Information Sources
- Gale Research
- Business Information Sources
- Standard and Poor's Industry Surveys
- Predicasts F & S Index—United States
- Predicasts F & S Index—Europe
- Business Periodicals Index
- Thomas Register
- Statistical Reference Index

Corporate profiles

Hoover's online

www.hoovers.com

This is a great resource for finding profiles of companies and industries from the US, UK, Germany and many other countries. This is not a free service, but they do let you try it out before committing.

Prospect Research Online

www.rpbooks.com

A subscription service with more than 1000 US and 300 Canadian corporate profiles that will assist non-profit organisations in gaining sponsorship. Also provides biographies, major gift announcements and special interest group articles. Ask for the online ten-minute tour.

Websites

Sponsorship, marketing and media sites

Advertising Media Internet Centre

www.amic.com

Most features cost dollars to use, but the Centre does have some free benefits.

Advertising World

http://advertising.utexas.edu/world

This site has serious links, probably one of the most complete lists on the Internet. It is very focused on the United States but international sites are welcome and listings are free to appropriate companies.

Advertising Age

http://www.adage.com

A lot of good information, including up to a dozen articles from each weekly publication and it's available free. The list of articles goes back about two months and features a lot of useful stuff.

Adworld

www.adworld.ie

This site bills itself as 'The No. 1 online information resource for the Irish marketing, advertising, and media business'. It delivers.

Brandweek

www.brandweek.com

This is the electronic version of the excellent publication, *Brandweek*. It includes a lot of articles, as well as links to sister publications, *Adweek* and *Mediaweek*.

Brand Republic

www.brandrepublic.com

Brand Republic brings together the best of a variety of marketing and related publications and is a wealth of information and inspiration.

Event Management UK

www.event-management-uk.co.uk

This site features articles, forums and links galore covering all facets of event management, including sponsorship.

International Festivals and Events Association (IFEA)

http://www.ifea.com

This is a comprehensive site, listing all of the activities and publications for this international organisation.

Power Sponsorship

Headed by Kim Skildum-Reid (co-author of this book), Power Sponsorship provides in-house training, public workshops, webinars, workshops tailored for government and industry groups, and expert sponsorship coaching. For more information, see www.powersponsorship.com.

PR Newswire

www.prnewswire.com

This website provides up-to-the-minute news releases from major US corporations and events. It allows you to search all press releases, by company, for the last several years.

Sponsorship Insights LinkedIn Group

www.linkedin.com

Search for the 'Sponsorship Insights' group. Sponsorship Insights has a very good and substantial LinkedIn networking group that we highly recommend. The discussions are pertinent and lively and it is refreshingly free of spam.

The Strategist (India)

www.bsstrategist.com

This is an excellent resource from the publishers of the *Business Standard*. Outstanding search engine, book reviews and excerpts.

Arts and non-profit sites

Although most of these sites are specific to one country or another, don't limit yourself geographically. Many of them feature good advice and links that will be useful to a wide range of cultural and non-profit organisations.

Arts Management Network

www.artsmanagement.net

This is a very complete site, with articles, links, books and more for the cultural and broader non-profit sector.

ArtsMarketing.org

www.artsmarketing.org

This is a very interesting and very complete site run by the Arts & Business Council. It includes a lot of information on programs, education and policy, and has some excellent links.

ArtsUSA

www.artsusa.org

This is a very interesting and very complete site run by Americans for the Arts. It includes a lot of information on programs, education and policy, and has some excellent links.

The Corporate Citizenship Company

www.corporate-citizenship.com

A terrific site with links to many organisations working in the areas of corporate social responsibility and corporate citizenship. Check out the 'Resources' section.

Fuel 4 Arts

www.fuel4arts.com

This website is an initiative of the Australia Council for the Arts, but is really aimed at providing resources for and by the global arts marketing community.

The Non-Profit Times

www.nptimes.com

In the online version of a real life magazine out of the United States, we found some interesting articles, a good online directory and some very useful links.

NYFA Interactive

www.nyfa.org

This is a site put up by the New York Foundation for the Arts. It is a service specifically for cultural institutions and includes *Current*, a good online publication, as well as terrific cultural links.

OurCommunity.com.au

www.ourcommunity.com.au

This extremely complete website is a goldmine of information for community groups trying to establish and grow their capabilities.

State of the Arts

www.stateart.com.au

A good Australian-based arts site which features a fair amount of sponsorship information.

Sport Business

www.sportbusiness.com

This is an excellent, sports-oriented site. It features articles from its eponymous magazine, as well as a directory of conferences related to sports business and a good, searchable archive.

Sportcal

www.sportcal.com

Billing itself as 'the business site for sport', is not far off. This site provides good information for professionals on both sides of the equation.

Sponsorship law

North America
Sports Lawyers Association Inc.

www.sportslaw.org

Europe
British Association for Sport and Law

www.britishsportslaw.org

Australasia
Australian & New Zealand Sports Law Association Inc. (ANZSLA)

www.anzsla.com.au.

Gadens Lawyers

Lionel Hogg, a Partner at Gadens Lawyers, created the Sponsorship Agreement Pro Forma included in Appendix 3. This firm is happy to provide expert assistance or referrals to appropriate sponsorship lawyers. For more information, see www.gadens. com. You are also welcome to contact Lionel Hogg directly on lhogg@qld.gadens. com.au.

Recommended reading

The Experience Economy—Work is Theatre and Every Business is a Stage

By B Joseph Pine II and James H Gilmore, published by FIBS Press

This is a great book on the role of innovation, relationships and emotional connections in business today. It is invaluable as a sponsorship resource.

Experiential Marketing

By Bernd H Schmitt, published by Free Press

This is another book that treads a similar path to *The Experience Economy*. Slightly more marketing based, these two books work very well together.

Brand Spirit

By Hamish Pringle and Marjorie Thompson, published by John Wiley & Sons

Brand Spirit is a fantastic book for any company investing in cause sponsorship or cause-related marketing to foster connections with consumers and trade.

Unleashing the Ideavirus

By Seth Godin, published by Hyperion

If you've ever had a great event and didn't know how to spread the word in a way that works, this is a fantastic book about, as the author puts it, 'turning your ideas into marketing epidemics'. Love it.

The Clustered World: How We Live, What We Buy, and What It All Means About Who We Are

By Michael J Weiss, published by Little Brown & Company

If you are doing sponsorship marketing in the US, this is a must read. It will help you to understand that the marketplace is segmented not by age or gender, but by personal motivations and belief systems. Although most of the book is US-centric, there is a section on international segmentation, most notably Canada.

Selling the Invisible: A Field Guide to Modern Marketing

By Harry Beckwith, published by Texere Publishing Ltd

Outstanding book for sponsorship seekers, who are nearly always selling the invisible!

Sponsorship agreement pro forma

 Legal1.doc

| Warning

This document is provided as a sample only and is not a substitute for legal advice. You should seek the advice of a suitably qualified and experienced lawyer before using this document. In particular, you or your lawyer should:

➤ Check the law in your jurisdiction—make sure this agreement works there.

➤ Check for changes to the law—law and practice might have altered since this document was drafted or you last checked the situation.

➤ Modify wherever necessary—review this document critically and never use it without first amending it to suit your needs. Remember that every sponsorship is different.

➤ Beware of limits of expertise. If you are not legally qualified or are not familiar with this area of the law, do not use this document without first obtaining legal advice about it.

You should also read the guidance notes (page 151) before using this sample agreement.

Sponsorship Agreement

This Sponsorship Agreement comprises the attached Schedules, Special Conditions and Standard Conditions.

Schedules

Schedule 1

"Sponsor"

Title: ....

Address: ....

Representative: ....

Telephone: ....

Facsimile: ....

Email: ....

Schedule 2

"Owner"

(Identify the sponsee – the legal entity receiving the Sponsorship. This must be the proper name of the company or association receiving the funds and controlling the team, event or venue being Sponsored, not the name of the team, event or venue etc.)

Title: ....

Address: ....

Representative: ....

Telephone: ....

Facsimile: ....

Email: ....

Schedule 3

"Commencement Date"

(Insert when the Sponsorship starts.)

....

Schedule 4

"Term"

(Insert when the Sponsorship will end or for how long it will last, e.g. "5 years".)

....
....
....
....

Schedule 5

Option to renew

(See clause 1.5.)
Does Sponsor have an option to renew?
Yes/No
If yes:
- *for what "Period" (specify an extended finishing date or further term, e.g. 3 years)?*
- *will the sponsorship fee and other Owner Benefits be the same after renewal? If not, list the new benefits.*

Schedule 6

First right of refusal

(See clause 1.6.)
Does Sponsor have a first right of refusal?
Yes/No

Schedule 7

"Property"

(Identify the event, team, venue or other property the subject of this sponsorship.)

Schedule 8

"Sponsorship Category"

Identify the nature of the sponsorship (e.g. title/category/official supplier etc.).

Schedule 9

"Territory"

Specify the area in which the sponsorship operates (e.g. state, region, country, continent, worldwide etc.).

Schedule 10

Sponsor objectives

(See clause 2.1.)
Be specific (list bottom-line sales objectives, measurable promotional activities, business development targets etc.).

1. ....
2. ....
3. ....

Schedule 11
Owner objectives

(See clause 2.2.)
(Be specific—list expected leverage from Sponsor in developing event/sport, target participation or attendance numbers, entry fee and merchandise income, measurable business development targets etc.)

1...
2...
3...

Schedule 12
"Sponsor Benefits"

(See clause 1.4.)
List, in detail, the signage/tickets/ hospitality/advertising credits/ merchandising rights and other benefits that Owner must provide to Sponsor (be precise about amounts, timing etc.).

1...
2...
3...
4...
5...
6...
7...
8...
9...
10..

Schedule 13
"Owner Benefits"

(See clause 1.4.)
List, in detail, the sponsorship fee and contra/in-kind benefits that Sponsor must provide to Owner (be precise about amounts, timing etc. and be careful to specify whether any fees include or exclude taxes such as goods and services or value-added tax).

1...
2...
3...
4...
5...
6...
7...
8...
9...
10..

Schedule 14

| Evaluation criteria |

(See clause 8.3.)
- *Is media analysis required and, if so, by whom, at whose expense, how regularly and what details must be provided?*
- *Is a party obliged to provide reports on mutual marketing activities, demographic information, samples of printed and promotional materials and, if so, what and when?*
- *Specify, in detail, the level of performance of each party (and how it will be assessed) which is regarded by the parties as unacceptable.*
- *Specify the consequences of failing to achieve this level (e.g. right of termination, revised fees or benefits).*
- *Specify the level of performance (and how it will be assessed) above which the parties' reasonable expectations are exceeded.*
- *Specify the consequences of this level of performance (e.g. revised sponsorship fee or benefits).*
- *Specify any other relevant evaluation criteria, information or consequences.*

Schedule 15

| "Applicable law" |

(Identify the country or state the laws of which will apply to this Agreement.)

Schedule 16

| Owner Marks |

(Insert here all trade marks, names, logos etc. which Sponsor is entitled to use under this Agreement. Include artwork.)

Schedule 17

| Sponsor Marks |

(Insert here all trade marks, names, logos etc. which Owner is entitled to use under this Agreement. Include artwork.)

Schedule 18

Use of Owner Marks

(See clause 5.1.)
(List here the specific purposes for which Owner Marks can be used by Sponsor.)

1...
2...
3...

Schedule 19

Use of Sponsor Marks

(See clause 5.1.)
(List here the specific purposes for which Sponsor Marks can be used by Owner.)

1...
2...
3...

Schedule 20

Promotional and media objectives

(See clause 6.3.)
(Be specific e.g. list target media outlets, promotional events, nature of coverage etc.)

1...
2...
3...
4...
5...

Schedule 21

Competitors of Sponsor

(See clauses 7.2 and 21.3.)

1...
2...
3...

Schedule 22

Competitors of Property

(See clauses 7.3 and 21.3.)

1...
2...
3...

Schedule 23

Sponsor's termination events

(See clause 9.2.)
(Insert here the circumstances in which Sponsor can terminate this Agreement.)

1...
2...
3...
4...
5...

Schedule 24

Owner's termination events

(See clause 9.3.)
(Insert here the circumstances in which Owner can terminate this Agreement.)

1...
2...
3...
4...
5...

Schedule 25

Insurance

(See clause 16.)
Insert here the amount of public liability insurance required to be maintained by Owner and full details of any other insurance, such as product liability or event cancellation insurance, required for the purposes of this Agreement.

1. Public liability—amount.

....
....

2. Other:

....
....
....

Schedule 26

Ambush strategies

(See clause 8.1.)
Include here specific strategies designed to minimise the likelihood of ambush occurring, such as obligations on Owner to:

*   *prevent or minimise Competitor involvement;*
*   *exercise control of venue access and signage;*
*   *impose contractual obligations on bidders for commercial rights not to engage in ambushing should the bids be unsuccessful;*
*   *negotiate broadcasting agreements to provide Sponsor with a first right of refusal to take category exclusive advertising time during broadcasts of the event;*
*   *impose ticketing restrictions;*
*   *prevent the re-use of tickets or licensed products as prize giveaways;*
*   *provide sponsorship fee rebates (be very specific) if serious ambush occurs etc.*

1...
2...
3...
4...
5...

Special conditions

Insert here any changes to the Standard Conditions and any special conditions not referred to in the Standard Conditions or the Schedules.

....

....

....

Standard conditions

1 Sponsorship

1.1 EXCLUSIVITY

Sponsor shall be the exclusive sponsor of the Property, in the Sponsorship Category, in the Territory.

1.2 TERM

Subject to this Agreement, the sponsorship starts on the Commencement Date and is effective for the Term.

1.3 CONSIDERATION

The consideration for this Agreement is the mutual conferring of Benefits referred to in clause 1.4.

1.4 BENEFITS

Sponsor must confer Owner Benefits on Owner, and Owner must confer Sponsor Benefits on Sponsor, at the times outlined in, and in accordance with, Schedules 12 and 13.

1.5 OPTION TO RENEW

This clause applies if the parties specify 'Yes' in Schedule 5.

Sponsor has an option to renew this Agreement for the further Period specified in Schedule 5 if:

*   Sponsor is not in breach under this Agreement; and
*   Sponsor gives notice in writing to Owner no fewer than 3 months before the end of the Term stating it intends to exercise the option.

If Sponsor exercises the option, the provisions of this Agreement (except for this clause 1.5) shall continue in full force and effect for the further Period, subject to any differences in fees or Owner Benefits specified in Schedule 5 for the further Period.

1.6 FIRST RIGHT OF REFUSAL

This clause applies if the parties specify 'Yes' in Schedule 6.

Owner must not enter into an agreement with any other person to Sponsor the Property in the Sponsorship Category at or immediately after the end of the Term without first offering the sponsorship to Sponsor on the same terms as it proposes to offer to (or as have been offered by) other parties.

If Sponsor declines within 30 days to accept the new sponsorship terms, Owner may enter into an agreement with a third party, but only on the terms offered to, and rejected by, Sponsor.

Sponsor's first right of refusal extends to any revised terms offered to or by third parties after Sponsor declines to accept the initial terms.

1.7 NO ASSIGNMENT

Sponsor must not assign, charge or otherwise deal with Sponsor Benefits without the prior written consent of Owner.

Owner must not assign, charge or otherwise deal with Owner Benefits without the prior written consent of Sponsor.

This clause does not apply to Owner Benefits or Sponsor Benefits that the parties, on signing this Agreement, agree will be conferred on third parties.

2 Objectives

2.1 OBJECTIVES OF SPONSOR

The primary objectives of the Sponsor in entering into this Agreement are:

*   to associate Sponsor's brand with the Property;
*   to promote the products and services of Sponsor;
*   to encourage brand loyalty to Sponsor;
*   to assist in raising and maintaining Sponsor's corporate profile and image;
*   to provide to Sponsor marketing leverage opportunities related to the Property;
*   to promote community awareness of, affinity for and (if relevant) participation in the Property;
*   to continually review and evaluate the ongoing success and performance of the sponsorship for maximum commercial advantage to all parties; and
*   the objectives outlined in Schedule 10.

2.2 OBJECTIVES OF OWNER

The primary objectives of the Owner in entering into this Agreement are:

*   to secure sponsorship funds and other benefits;
*   to increase the profile, standing, brand value and (if relevant) participation in the Property;

- to promote the profile and corporate image of Sponsor and the use of Sponsor's products and services;
- to continually review and evaluate the ongoing success and performance of the sponsorship for the maximum commercial advantage to all parties; and
- the objectives outlined in Schedule 11.

2.3 FULFILMENT OF OBJECTIVES

The parties must act at all times in good faith towards each other with a view to fulfilling the objectives outlined in clauses 2.1 and 2.2. This Agreement is to be interpreted in a manner that best satisfies the fulfilment of those objectives.

3 Warranties

3.1 OWNER WARRANTIES

Owner warrants that:
- it has full right and legal authority to enter into and perform its obligations under this Agreement;
- it owns the Property (or, if the Property is not legally capable of being owned, it holds rights which effectively confer unfettered control of the Property);
- Owner Marks do not infringe the trade marks, trade names or other rights of any person;
- it has, or will at the relevant time have, all government licences, permits and other authorities relevant to the Property;
- it will comply with all applicable laws relating to the promotion and conduct of the Property; and
- throughout this Agreement, it will conduct itself so as not to cause detriment, damage, injury or embarrassment to Sponsor.

3.2 SPONSOR WARRANTIES

Sponsor warrants that:
- it has full right and legal authority to enter into and perform its obligations under this Agreement;
- Sponsor Marks do not infringe the trade marks, trade names or other rights of any other person;
- it will comply with all applicable laws in marketing and promoting its sponsorship of the Property; and
- throughout this Agreement, it will conduct itself so as not to cause detriment, damage, injury or embarrassment to the Owner.

4 Disclosure

4.1 INITIAL DISCLOSURE

Owner warrants that it has disclosed to Sponsor:
- the substance (other than financial details) of all agreements entered into or currently under negotiation with Owner for sponsorship, exclusive or preferred supplier status or other like arrangements relating to the Property; and
- all other circumstances which might have a material impact upon Sponsor's decision to enter into this Agreement.

4.2 CONTINUING DISCLOSURE

Owner must from time to time keep Sponsor informed of:
- new sponsorship, exclusive or preferred service or supplier status

or other like arrangements conferred by Owner in respect of the Property; and
- significant marketing programs and other promotional activities which might provide leverage opportunities for Sponsor.

5 Marks and title

5.1 AUTHORISED USE

Sponsor may use Owner Marks:
- for all purposes reasonably incidental to obtaining the Sponsor Benefits; and
- as permitted in Schedule 18.

Owner may use Sponsor Marks:
- for all purposes reasonably incidental to obtaining the Owner Benefits; and
- as permitted in Schedule 19.

5.2 NO UNAUTHORISED USE

Sponsor must not use or permit the use of Owner Marks (or any other trade or service marks, logos, designs, devices or intellectual property rights of Owner) and Owner must not use or permit the use of Sponsor Marks (or any other trade or service marks, logos, designs, devices or intellectual property rights of Sponsor) unless authorised by this Agreement or with the written consent of the other party.

5.3 MERCHANDISE

Unless permitted in Schedule 18, Sponsor must not manufacture, sell or license the manufacture or sale of any promotional or other merchandise bearing Owner Marks without Owner's prior written consent.

Unless permitted in Schedule 19, Owner must not manufacture, sell or license the manufacture or sale of any promotional or other merchandise bearing Sponsor Marks without Sponsor's prior written consent.

All authorised merchandise bearing Owner Marks or Sponsor Marks permitted under this Agreement must be:
- of a high standard;
- of such style, appearance and quality as to suit the best exploitation of the Sponsor, Owner and Property (as the case may be); and
- free from product defects, of merchantable quality and suited for its intended purpose.

5.4 IMAGE

The parties must ensure that any authorised use by them of the other's marks or intellectual property rights:
- is lawful;
- properly and accurately represents those rights;
- (in the case of Owner using Sponsor Marks) strictly complies with any trade mark and logo usage policies of Sponsor applicable at the relevant time;
- is consistent with the other's corporate image; and
- (if used in connection with the provision of goods or services) is associated only with goods or services of the highest quality.

5.5 ENFORCEMENT PROTECTION

The parties must provide all reasonable assistance to each other to protect against infringers of Owner Marks or Sponsor Marks in connection with the Property.

5.6 TITLE

Despite any rights to use another's marks conferred under this Agreement:

- Owner holds all legal and equitable right, title and interest in and to the Property and all Owner Marks;
- Sponsor holds all legal and equitable right, title and interest in and to the Sponsor Marks;
- naming, title and other rights conferred by this Agreement merely constitute licences to use the relevant Owner Marks or Sponsor Marks (as the case may be) for the purposes of, and in accordance with, this Agreement and do not confer any property right or interest in those marks; and
- the right to use another's marks is non-exclusive and non-assignable.

6 Media, branding, leverage etc.

6.1 MEDIA EXPOSURE

At all reasonable opportunities:

- Owner will use its best endeavours to obtain public and media exposure of the sponsorship; and
- Sponsor will use its best endeavours to obtain public and media exposure of the Property.

6.2 APPROVAL

Media releases relating to the sponsorship must:

- be issued jointly by the parties; or
- not be issued by one party without the consent of the other.

6.3 PROMOTIONAL OBJECTIVES

Owner and Sponsor must use their best endeavours to achieve their promotional and Media objectives outlined in Schedule 20. Sponsor licenses Owner to use Sponsor Marks, and Owner licenses Sponsor to use Owner Marks, for these purposes.

6.4 LEVERAGE

Sponsor has the right at its cost to:

- promote itself, its brands and its products and services in association with the Property; and
- engage in advertising and promotional activities to maximise the benefits to it of its association with the Property,

provided that it will not knowingly or recklessly engage in any advertising or promotional activities which reflect unfavourably on the Property, the parties or any other Sponsors of the Property.

7 Exclusivity

7.1 EXCLUSIVITY WITHIN TERRITORY

If the Sponsorship Category is designed for only 1 sponsor (for example, naming rights or principal sponsorship):

- Sponsor's rights under this Agreement are exclusive within the Territory; and
- Owner must not enter into any sponsorship or supply arrangements for the Property in the Sponsorship Category within the Territory with any other person.

If the Sponsorship Category is designed for multiple sponsors (for example, official suppliers or sponsors of a particular class) Owner must not, without the prior written consent of Sponsor (which must not be unreasonably withheld), enter into any sponsorship or supply arrangements for the Property in the Sponsorship Category within the Territory with any other person.

7.2 COMPETITORS

Owner must not within the Territory authorise or permit to subsist:

- the provision of any products or services to the Property, in any sponsorship category; or
- any association with the Property,

by any Competitor of Sponsor.

7.3 SPONSOR RESTRAINT

Sponsor must not enter into any sponsorship or supply arrangements with any Competitor of the Property during the Term or within a reasonable time after the end of the Term.

7.4 INJUNCTIONS

The parties acknowledge that the restraints referred to in this clause 7 cannot adequately be compensated for in damages and consent to injunctive relief for the enforcement of these restraints.

8 Marketing and service delivery

8.1 MARKETING COMMITTEE

Owner and Sponsor will establish a marketing committee to meet quarterly (or otherwise, as agreed) for the purposes of:

- reviewing the progress of the sponsorship and the mutual rights conferred under this Agreement;
- evaluating the success of the sponsorship against its objectives;
- discussing further opportunities for leverage and cross-promotional activities;
- maximising the ongoing benefits to the parties, implementing promotional strategies for the parties and identifying new, mutual opportunities; and
- maximising the Sponsor Benefits by:
  - identifying actual or potential Ambush activities;
  - using their best endeavours to prevent Ambush or minimise its potential impact on the sponsorship; and
  - directing implementation of the strategies outlined in Schedule 26.

8.2 SERVICE DELIVERY

Both Sponsor and Owner must designate a representative to be primarily responsible for the provision of the day-to-day service and support required by the other party under this Agreement. Until otherwise nominated, the representatives will be the representatives named in Schedules 1 and 2.

8.3 EVALUATION

The parties must evaluate the success of the sponsorship in accordance with the criteria outlined in Schedule 14 and with the consequences (if any) outlined in that Schedule.

9 Termination

9.1 EXPIRY

This Agreement, unless terminated earlier under this clause or extended under clause 1, will continue until the end of the Term.

9.2 EARLY TERMINATION BY SPONSOR

Sponsor may terminate this Agreement if any of the following occurs:

- Owner fails to provide a Sponsor Benefit, and failure continues for 7 days after Owner receives written notice from Sponsor to provide the Benefit;
- Owner is Insolvent;
- any event outlined in Schedule 23 occurs;
- application of the evaluation criteria in Schedule 14 permits termination;
- any major, public controversy arises in connection with the Owner, the Property or this Agreement which, in the reasonable opinion of Sponsor, reflects adversely and substantially on Sponsor's corporate image;
- any statement, representation or warranty made by Owner in connection with this Agreement proves to have been incorrect or misleading in any material respect;
- the rights conferred on Sponsor under this Agreement are directly or indirectly diminished, prejudiced or compromised in any way by the reckless acts or omissions of Owner;
- Owner has not used reasonable endeavours to ensure that the exclusive rights conferred on Sponsor under this Agreement are not directly or indirectly diminished, prejudiced or compromised in any way by the acts or omissions of third parties (for example by Ambush).

9.3 EARLY TERMINATION BY OWNER

Owner may terminate this Agreement if any of the following occurs:

- Sponsor fails to provide a material Sponsor Benefit, and failure continues for 7 days after Sponsor receives written notice from Owner to provide the benefit;
- Sponsor is Insolvent;
- any event outlined in Schedule 24 occurs;
- any major, public controversy arises in connection with the Sponsor or this Agreement which, in the reasonable opinion of Owner, revokes adversely and substantially on Owner's corporate image or upon the Property;
- any statement, representation or warranty made by Sponsor in connection with this Agreement proves to have been incorrect or misleading in any material respect when made;
- the rights conferred on Owner under this Agreement are directly or indirectly diminished, prejudiced or compromised in any way by the reckless acts or omissions of Sponsor.

9.4 IMMATERIAL BREACHES

Nothing in this clause entitles a party to terminate this Agreement for trivial or immaterial breaches which cannot be remedied, however, this does not prevent termination for regular, consistent or repeated breaches (even if they would, alone, be trivial or immaterial).

9.5 METHOD OF TERMINATION

A party entitled to terminate this Agreement may do so by notice in writing to the other at the address specified in Schedule 1 or Schedule 2, as the case may be.

9.6 EFFECT OF EARLY TERMINATION

Termination of this Agreement for any reason shall be without prejudice to the rights and obligations of each party accrued up to and including the date of termination.

10 Rebranding

10.1 CHANGE OF NAME, LOGO, PRODUCT ETC.

If at any time Sponsor changes its name or logo, or wishes to change any Sponsor's product associated with Property, Sponsor may re-brand the sponsorship of the Property provided that, in the reasonable opinion of Owner, to do so will not affect the good name and image of the Property or Owner.

10.2 COSTS

Rebranding must be at Sponsor's cost. This includes:

- direct costs to Sponsor; and
- any costs incurred by Owner directly or indirectly resulting from the rebranding.

11 Governing law

This Agreement is governed by and must be construed in accordance with the Applicable Law.

12 Relationship of parties

The parties are independent contractors. Nothing in this Agreement or in the description of the Sponsorship Category shall be construed to place the parties in, and the parties must not act in a manner which expresses or implies a legal relationship of partnership, joint venture, franchise, employment or agency.

13 Ongoing assistance

Each party must promptly:

- do all things;
- sign all documents; and
- provide all relevant assistance and information,

reasonably required by the other party to enable the performance by the parties of their obligations under this Agreement.

14 Costs

14.1 OWN COSTS

Each party must pay its own costs of and incidental to the negotiation, preparation and execution of this Agreement.

14.2 IMPLEMENTATION COSTS

Unless otherwise specified as a Sponsor Benefit or Owner Benefit, each party must pay its own signage, advertising, leverage, general overhead and incidental costs related to the performance of its obligations under this Agreement. Despite this, all signage, artwork, photography, film, video tape and similar expenses directly or indirectly incurred under this Agreement must be met by Sponsor unless otherwise provided for in the Schedule or Special Conditions.

14.3 TAXES

All amounts payable by Sponsor to Owner under this Agreement (for example, the sponsorship fee) include all government taxes (such as goods and services or value added taxes) unless specified to the contrary in Schedule 13.

However, if Australian taxation laws apply to any such amounts, the following provisions apply—

- the amounts payable include all applicable GST, unless specified to the contrary in Schedule 13;
- if Owner is registered for GST, the amounts are not payable (despite any other provision in this Agreement) unless and until Owner delivers a Tax Invoice for the relevant amount to Sponsor; and
- if Owner is not registered for GST, the amounts must be reduced (despite any other provision in this Agreement) by one-eleventh of the amount otherwise payable.

15 Notices

Notices under this Agreement may be delivered or sent by post, facsimile or email to the relevant addresses outlined in Schedules 1 and 2 (as the case may be) and will be deemed to have been received in the ordinary course of delivery of notices in that form.

16 Insurance

16.1 LIABILITY INSURANCE

Owner must effect and keep current:

- a public liability insurance policy for an amount not less than the amount specified in Schedule 25 for any single claim for liability of Owner or Sponsor or both for death, personal injury or property damage occasioned to any person in respect of the Property (including a contractual liability endorsement to cover the obligations of Owner under clause 17);
- such other insurance as is specified in Schedule 25; and
- if Property is a one-off event (or if the parties specify in Schedule 25), event cancellation insurance in an amount equalling or exceeding the value of Sponsor Benefits.

16.2 PRODUCT LIABILITY INSURANCE

If:

- Owner is authorised under this Agreement to manufacture, sell or license the sale or manufacture of any merchandise bearing Sponsor Marks; or
- Sponsor is authorised under this Agreement to manufacture, sell or license the sale or manufacture of any merchandise bearing Owner Marks;

the party so authorised must effect and keep current a product liability insurance policy for an amount not less than the amount specified in Schedule 25 for any single claim for liability of Owner or Sponsor or both for death, personal injury or property damage occasioned to any person in respect of the manufacture or sale of the merchandise (for example for claims relating to a defective product).

16.3 TERMS OF POLICIES

All insurance policies effected under this Agreement must:

- be wholly satisfactory to the Beneficiary;
- identify the Beneficiary as a named insured;
- remain enforceable for the benefit of the Beneficiary even if invalid or unenforceable against Payer; and
- include full, automatic reinstatement cover at all times during the Term.

16.4 OTHER OBLIGATIONS

The Payer must:

- not violate, or permit the violation of, any conditions of these policies; and
- provide insurance certificates and copies of the policies to the Beneficiary on its reasonable request.

17 Indemnities and liability limitation

17.1 OWNER INDEMNITIES

Owner must indemnify Sponsor and Sponsor's officers, employees and agents from and against all claims, damages, liabilities, losses and expenses related to:

- any breach by Owner of this Agreement;
- the inaccuracy of any warranty or representations made by Owner;
- any wrongful act or omission by Owner (including negligence, unlawful conduct and wilful misconduct) in its performance of this Agreement; and
- liabilities for which insurance is required under clause 16.

17.2 SPONSOR INDEMNITIES

Sponsor must indemnify Owner and Owner's officers, employees and agents from and against all claims, damages, liabilities, losses and expenses related to:

- any breach by Sponsor of this Agreement;
- the inaccuracy of any warranty or representations made by Sponsor;
- any wrongful act or omission by Sponsor (including negligence, unlawful conduct and wilful misconduct) in its performance of this Agreement; and
- all liabilities for which insurance is required under clause 16.

18 Dispute resolution

18.1 MEDIATION

Any dispute or difference about this Agreement must be resolved as follows:

- the parties must first refer the dispute to mediation by an agreed accredited mediator or, failing agreement, by a person appointed by the President or other senior officer of the Law Society or Bar Association in the jurisdiction of the Applicable Law;

- the mediator must determine the rules of the mediation if the parties do not agree;
- mediation commences when a party gives written notice to the other specifying the dispute and requiring its resolution under this clause;
- the parties must negotiate in good faith to resolve the dispute within 14 days; and
- any information or documents obtained through or as part of the mediation must not be used for any purpose other than the settlement of the dispute.

18.2 FINAL RESOLUTION

If the dispute is not resolved within 14 days of the notice of its commencement, either party may then, but not earlier, commence legal proceedings in an appropriate court.

18.3 CONTRACT PERFORMANCE

Each party must continue to perform this Agreement despite the existence of a dispute or any proceedings under this clause.

18.4 EXCEPTIONS TO MEDIATION

Nothing in this clause prevents:
- a party from seeking urgent injunctive relief in respect of an actual or apprehended breach of this Agreement;
- Sponsor from exercising its rights under the first 3 bullet points in clause 9.2; or
- Owner from exercising its rights under the first 3 bullet points in clause 9.3.

19 Confidentiality

The commercial terms of this Agreement are confidential to the parties unless they otherwise agree. However, this does not prevent:
- Sponsor or Owner disclosing the existence or the sponsorship to the general public; or
- any promotional, marketing or sponsorship activities authorised or required under this Agreement.

20 Entire agreement

This Agreement represents the entire agreement between the parties and supersedes all other agreements and conduct, express or implied, written or oral.

21 Interpretation

21.1 COMPOSITION

This Agreement comprises these Standard Conditions and the attached Schedules and Special Conditions.

21.2 PRECEDENCE

The Special Conditions and the attached Schedules have precedence over these Standard Conditions to the extent of any inconsistency.

21.3 INTERPRETATION

In this Agreement, unless the context otherwise requires:
- *Agreement* means this Agreement as amended from time to time.
- *Ambush* means the association by any person, not authorised in writing by Owner, of the person's name, brands, products or services with the Property or with a party, through marketing or promotional activities or otherwise, whether or not lawful, accurate or misleading.
- *Beneficiary* means the party for whose benefit an insurance policy must be effected under clause 16.
- *Competitor* (in connection with Sponsor) means:
  - any person who conducts any business which competes (other than incidentally), directly or indirectly, with any business conducted or services provided by Sponsor or any company related to Sponsor or whose products or services are antithetical to or incompatible with the business, products or services of Sponsor; and
  - any person listed in Schedule 21 or who conducts a business in the industry, or of the nature, described in that Schedule.
- *Competitor* (in connection with Owner) means:
  - any person who conducts any event or offers any product substantially similar to the Property anywhere in the Territory or whose operations are antithetical to or incompatible with the Property; or
  - any person or Property listed in Schedule 22 or any Property or event of the nature described in that Schedule.
- *GST* means the goods and services tax as imposed by the GST Law.
- *GST Law* has the meaning given to that term in *A New Tax System (Goods and Services Tax) Act 1999* of the Commonwealth of Australia, or, if that Act does not exist for any reason, means any Act imposing or relating to the imposition or administration of a goods and services tax in Australia and any regulation made under that Act.
- *Insolvency* in respect of a party means:
  - the filing of an application for the winding up, whether voluntary or otherwise, or the issuing of a notice summoning a meeting at which it is to be moved a resolution proposing the winding up, of the party;
  - the appointment of a receiver, receiver and manager, administrator, liquidator or provisional liquidator with respect to that party or any of its assets;
  - the assignment by that party in favour of, or composition or arrangement or entering into of a scheme of arrangement (otherwise than for the purposes solely of corporate reconstruction) with, its creditors or any class of its creditors; or
  - a party taking advantage of any insolvency laws to obtain temporary or permanent relief from the payment of its debts or from creditors generally.
- *Media* means any of communication to the public at large, whether by radio, television, newspaper, electronic media (such as the Internet) or otherwise.
- *Owner Benefits* include additional fees or benefits that accrue to Owner by application of the evaluation criteria in Schedule 14.
- *Owner Marks* means the name of the Property and the marks and other symbols outlined in Schedule 16.
- *Payer* means the party obliged to effect an insurance policy under clause 16.

- *Sponsor Benefits* may be reduced by application of the evaluation criteria in Schedule 14, and if reduced must be construed accordingly.
- *Sponsor Marks* means Sponsor's name and the marks and other symbols outlined in Schedule 17.
- *Tax Invoice* has the meaning given to that term by the GST Law.
- *Term* includes the period of any option to renew this Agreement if clause 1.5 applies and the option is exercised.

21.4 CURRENCY

References to currency are to the lawful currency of the country or region of the applicable Law, unless otherwise stated.

21.5 EXAMPLES

Examples given in this Agreement do not limit or qualify the general words to which they relate.

SIGNATURES

By signing, you indicate acceptance of this Agreement (including the Standard Conditions and the Special Conditions) on behalf of the entity you represent and you declare your ability to sign this Agreement on behalf of the Sponsor/Owner (as the case may be).

Signed for and on behalf of Sponsor by:)
)
)
                                            (signature)

Full name
Title
Witness
Date

SIGNED for and on behalf of Owner by:)
)
)
                                          (signature)

Full name
Title
Witness
Date

Index

For more information

Kim Skildum-Reid

Kim Skildum-Reid runs Power Sponsorship, providing top-level consulting, workshops, in-house training, keynote speaking, books, and extensive online resources to sponsorship professionals worldwide. For more on Power Sponsorship, contact Kim at:

Kim Skildum-Reid

Power Sponsorship

admin@powersponsorship.com

www.powersponsorship.com

Anne-Marie Grey

Anne-Marie Grey is a world-leading expert in cause, arts, and community sponsorship, strategic philanthropy, and corporate and social responsibility. She is available for speaking, training, and other advice. She can be contacted at:

Anne-Marie Grey

greyokeefe@aol.com